MW00930641

I MIGHT BE NOTHING

journal writing

I MIGHT BE NOTHING

journal writing
Lara Gilbert

abridged and edited by Carole Itter

introduction by Carole Itter

© Copyright 2004 Estate of Lara Gilbert. All rights reserved.

No part of this publication may be reproduced, stored in a retrieval system, or transmitted, in any form or by any means, electronic, mechanical, photocopying, recording, or otherwise, without the written prior permission of the author.

Printed in Victoria, Canada

Cover photograph of the author by Sarah Itter
Cover design by Megan Hunt

A cataloguing record for this book that includes the U.S. Library of Congress Classification number, the Library of Congress Call number and the Dewey Decimal cataloguing code is available from the National Library of Canada. The complete cataloguing record can be obtained from the National Library's online database at: www.nlc-bnc.ca/amicus/index-e.html
ISBN: 1-4120-1804-8

TRAFFORD

This book was published *on-demand* **in cooperation with Trafford Publishing.** On-demand publishing is a unique process and service of making a book available for retail sale to the public taking advantage of on-demand manufacturing and Internet marketing. **On-demand publishing** includes promotions, retail sales, manufacturing, order fulfilment, accounting and collecting royalties on behalf of the author.

Suite 6E, 2333 Government St., Victoria, B.C. V8T 4P4, CANADA

Phone	250-383-6864	Toll-free	1-888-232-4444 (Canada & US)
Fax	250-383-6804	E-mail	sales@trafford.com
Web site	www.trafford.com	TRAFFORD PUBLISHING IS A DIVISION OF TRAFFORD HOLDINGS LTD.	
Trafford Catalogue #03-2181		www.trafford.com/robots/03-2181.html	

10   9   8   7   6   5   4   3

INTRODUCTION

Twenty journals were filled during Lara Gilbert's brief lifetime, which she began writing at age seven; one hundred pages per booklet, handwritten on both sides of the page. That makes about 3,200 pages of journal writing in fifteen years, an astounding chronicle of a young girl's life. One early notebook is missing; all the rest are intact. The original diaries are remarkably consistent in shape – hard cover, lined notebooks, varying a little in style but most are a standard 7"x9" in size. Her handwriting is easy to read and she rarely alters a word or crosses out a phrase. Each entry is dated meticulously with a) the day of the week, b) the month, c) the day of the month, d) her age and, often, even the time of the day. Such a conscious effort to detail the entry so precisely allows us to see her concern to be as accurate as possible.

These journals have been entrusted to me, her mother, with instructions that nothing should be done with them until the year 2000. There is an awareness that these diaries will some day be published and although she sees them as exceedingly private at the time of writing, she writes that they are meant to be read at a later date. As well as her journals, there are many poems, a few short stories and some essays. In one journal there is a list of the books she had read during that time, many from the public library; even so her own collection held possibly 1,000 titles, including the best from her early childhood.

How did I choose what to include in this manuscript? A Utopian dream would be to include all 3,000-plus handwritten pages. It is well known that the suppression of women's journals has been notorious. In my selections here, her writing is intact with very minimal editing. In her early writing I was searching for clues – clues to why a brilliant scholar, a "perfect" teenager, a considerate and caring person, an award-winning high achiever, could go through so many horrible changes in just a few years. She was a genuine person of great honesty; she was without pretension in her words and actions; her credibility was never in question.

I found something excruciating as I read through the journals, and this seemed to be confirmed with the reading of each successive journal, and it was not that her journal was written for an audience, but that the journal was her best friend. Here she turned for solace, for a way of trying to sort out her feelings, and as a place for laying out confusions and resolutions.

Critical to the onset of her serious depression were years of alleged sexual exploitation, first by her paternal grandfather who died when she was 4½, and then subsequently or maybe overlapping, by her natural father with whom she lived part time. The alleged sexual encounters were so seductive and so frequent that she "thought it was normal for fathers and daughters to do these things" (quoted to a close friend in 1992). She never liked it; she listed anal penetration ("the finger game"); oral fellatio and playing with testicles; cunnilingus ("a whiskery face, going down between my legs, and I am 8 or 9"); frequent genital playing and eventually one full encounter of vaginal penetration. She writes in a short story of a day in Grade 3 when she hurt so much it was hard to sit down at school. Alleged broad sexual gestures continued to plague her throughout her teen years even though she saw far less of him, having moved in permanently with me when she was 12.

So little was known, until the mid-1980s, about the long term effects of sexual abuse on children. I did not suspect any abuse, and had I known, I would have moved mountains to stop it. And yet she had all the major symptoms throughout childhood – symptoms now well delineated yet not known to me then: sleeping problems, eating problems, a pervasive sense of hopelessness and helplessness, very low self-esteem, uncomfortable in her body, and constantly needing to be reassured.

Part of her wanted to be a writer; she grew up with artists and was not discouraged. Some of her psychological symptoms, such as dissociative disorder, are not uncommon to writers; if it was in her, I did not see it as a disorder. As I went through the volumes of her writings, I heard her clear concise voice. It is a gift. My initial selections were, of course, far too lengthy. What I was searching for were two separate factors: First, the obvious – to establish her health, motivations, abilities, hopes for her future, plus her times of unease (whether social or academic) throughout her teenage years as a somewhat typical teenager. Second, and so important that it was almost an investigation, I looked in her earlier writings for signs of serious mental disorder, even the smallest indicators that I, her mother, must have missed in our day-to-day relating – which I had always thought was pretty good, even excellent.

Her mental deterioration was almost classical by clinical definition. The onset of depression was in her teen years and then the subsequent, very worrisome complications of depression followed later. She wrote of her terrible struggle to manage her self-destructive demons over which she could find no control. As well as her highly literate background, she brought through five years of university science a scientist's rationale and analytical reasoning to her own behaviour. Still the destructive actions would continue, sporadically but always with life-threatening consequences. Her pre-medical training in genetics, biochemistry, physiology, biophysiology, immunology, linguistics, microbiology, enzymology, recombinant DNA technology, plus her astounding scholastic achievements seem to almost perversely complicate her insight into her mental disorders.

Her willingness to try therapy and numerous types of anti-depressants, plus other pharmaceutical "uppers" and "downers" and even extended treatments of electro-shock therapy, in a real belief that these things would change her around – all contrasted with her impulsive and reckless use of street drugs and over-the-counter drugs. Self-medicating, desperately.

Again and again, she turned to her journal in repeated efforts to stabilize herself, to reaffirm her raison d'etre.

Carole Itter
2003

"... many women wrote their diaries by keeping up a pretence that they were private, while intending them to be published at a later date. In this way, they could communicate to an audience thoughts and feelings that were too personal or controversial to be revealed through their fiction, but which they wanted, and needed to convey."

Elizabeth Podnieks

Chapter One

Age Fifteen

December 2, 1987
Age 15

Uncle Bobby's dead! I use the exclamation mark because I am sincerely surprised. He's the last person I would expect to die. He had a heart attack in his home, and no one knew for a few days. I guess it would have been around my birthday. I'm not in utter grief. Bobby was always the loner of the family; very private about his life. The only times I would see him were at family gatherings on holidays. He would sometimes talk to me, telling me about early civilization or politics, and I'd listen, not understanding much but realizing that this man was to be respected. He was warm, though private, and if he were sitting in a room with cats, the cats would be on him. I always had a notion that cats know it if a human is kind-hearted and good.

Bobby gave me some of my most prized books. Among these are "Jane Eyre," "Emma," "A Woman in White," "Translations from the Chinese" (a book of beautiful poems and illustrations), and "The Tale of Two Bad Mice" which has been one of my favourite stories for as long as I can remember.

Well I don't know what else to say.

Goodbye, Uncle Bob. I hope that wherever, whatever, whenever you are now, that you are at peace. p.s. I love you.

December 9, 1987

It hurts so much! I can't believe it. I thought I was over it. But it didn't start hurting till today, after the funeral. My dad gave the "sermon." [Great Uncle] Bob didn't want a minister. It was a beautiful speech.

My aunt was sobbing even before the funeral service got underway.

To end it, they played Bob's favourite music. I recognized it immediately: a prelude of Bach's. That very piece is on a tape he gave me years ago. He introduced me to Bach. I used to listen to it over and over, that tape. I'm listening to it right now.

It hurts so much. I just want to sink into the music... forever.

When I heard it at the funeral, it felt like knives slicing through me. It totally overwhelmed me.

I had so much to learn from you, Uncle Bobby. You were too young to die. After the service, in my room I cried and cried, listening to the music. He introduced me to music and literature. He loved me.

His ashes are all that now remain. NO, no, no. He still lives in the music I'm hearing, and the poems and the stories he's given me. He will, forever. Like the end of this prelude, he softly fades from existence. But the memory of the poignant, yet joyous, notes still linger inside of me.

* * * * *

But still I've been very depressed for the past few days. More than I've ever been in my life, I think. It's because of school. I've endured school for ten years without giving up ever but I feel close to it now.

It's so stifling!! I feel absolutely stifled there: my creativity, curiousity, etc. are so restrained that I feel like screaming. I hate being held back, restricted. Also, we don't get any freedom in some classes, especially social studies. Throughout the whole hour you can't say one word to your neighbour or get up off your chair (unless you are going to the bathroom). It feels like a prison. What makes it most unbearable is that what we're learning in social studies is SO dull and presented in such an uninviting manner.

You can't yawn in social studies or the teacher comes over to you and tells you that you have to stay after school. She's so strict, it's incredible. I don't know how I make it through the morning with all of them. The afternoon is always a bit better. The other teachers at least give you freedom to speak and move around and one of them can even be interesting.

I have only eleven more days of this semester to go, then I change over to whole new subjects and teachers. Thank God. This has been by far the worst semester of my life.

Today in guidance we were shown a film about suicide and a woman from the Crisis Intervention and Suicide Prevention Centre came to talk to us. (Good timing for me, eh!) I found myself listening closely to what she was saying to us and at times I thought I wanted to run out of the room because it was scaring me that I was actually on the verge of contemplating suicide this past week. Believe me, I no longer am. This helped to bring me to my senses.

My counsellor caught my eye during the talk a couple of times. She seemed to be giving me an encouraging look, as if she understood the depression I've been going through. I know she's someone I can always turn to. Just noticing her in the halls gives me encouragement to get through the next class. She's an amazingly understanding person.

A couple of days ago I saw her while on my way to math class. She said, "Have you seen the photo of you?" (meaning the one of me and Mike kissing, across from the office with the other dance photos). "You look quite nice together," she said, "almost like it's from a magazine. I like it!" That's about the first encouraging thing anyone said to me about my relationship with Mike. No one I know at school approves of it. If he were a bit older, say, then it would be fine, of course. But ohhh nooo, not if he's younger. This kind of thing adds to the frustration building up in me.

I don't know how to get out of this pit of incomprehensible depression. I don't know what to do. I don't know what's worth living for. What do I enjoy in life these days?

Listening to music, playing the piano, writing on the word processor and in here... oh yeah, and watching "Family Ties" on TV.

Everything else I hate.

Bobby dies, school drives me insane, I lose Mike, I lose myself...

What does anything matter anyway? We're all going to end up in self-destruction; we're heading that way. Pollution, diseases, poverty, war, nuclear war – nothing left.

What a world we teenagers have been left with. And those who have made it this way depend on us to bring it out of the pit of despair.

First we must bring ourselves out.

* * * * *

I just feel empty and bored and lonely. Not to mention depressed. I have a social studies essay to do on Crowfoot, and English questions to finish.

I don't want to do any of it. What will I gain from it? How many hundreds of hours have I spent working on school work: essays, studying for tests, Qs, etc. I'm sure some of it was worthwhile, but most of it was a waste of time. And yet I do it. I do my two hours or more of homework every night, only occasionally leaving it for lunch time the next day. Why do I do it when it's so obvious it's a total waste of time? I'm not saying school is a waste of time; certainly not. But I'm sick and tired of it, of being held back because 99% of the class hasn't understood the work, and being forced to do hours of math problems, English questions, etc. that I already completely understand. It's like I've been punished all through school because my learning rate is different from other students. I can remember from Grade 1 onwards, coming home every day to the question, "How was school?" and answering (ALWAYS) "boring."

And this is called an education. I know, I know, why don't I just go to a different school, a "special" school. Well there aren't that many, if any, in Vancouver, and definitely none in my area. It would probably take three buses, an hour-and-a-half of travelling, each way every day. I wouldn't see my school friends anymore; wouldn't see any friends out of school time at all since they would all live miles away. Then there are the costs. That would be the worst part for me – not really the worst I guess (missing my friends would be the worst) but definitely the key factor.

So a different school is out of the question. Anyhow, the students at Britannia are mostly Oriental and are very diligent workers and academically inclined. There's plenty of competition (sort of) but that's not what I'm looking for. I guess it comes right down to the teachers.

Thank God for my counsellor. Maybe she'll have a way out for me.

One other thing I'm sick of: being known as the class brain. Lara always know the answer; Lara always gets the top scores on the essays and on the tests; Lara always gets the top term percentage; Lara always gets the scholarship end-of-year award.

I'm sick of being singled out; respected by some, laughed at by others, but never just considered one of them. Never "good old Lara." Always "Lara, the genius." Admittedly it's nice for a while. It does feel good to ace a tough test, amaze the teachers with my essays. But it starts to get burdensome. Everyone counts on me being the top. And when I'm not, they eye me suspiciously, scornfully. In English it's got to the point where I rarely put up my hand to answer, because I'm tired of doing what everyone expects. Anyhow, when I do answer, I get these looks which seem to say, "Ooh, Lara, aren't we smart today," or "Of course, you would know the answer."

All these reasons that I've explained over the past few days – teachers, boredom, homework, etc. – are why I can't stand school anymore. I hope university will be better. It had better be, for all the money it'll cost.

I guess I might as well do some homework. After all, if I don't do my homework, my marks will drop. If my marks drop, my chances of scholarships drop, my post-secondary education decreases, my career options decrease, my income decreases. That's why I do my homework. Not to learn about Crowfoot (I already know about Crowfoot; why do an essay on him?) but to ensure my future. What a life.

January 19, 1988

My moods have been changing so abruptly that I've not written in here for a few days. I guess because I usually write in the evenings and that's when my mood swings downward.

I haven't felt really happy in a long time. There have been moments when I'm quite contented, such as now. But I don't get that elated feeling anymore. And I miss it. Oh, I'm not complaining; I do have good times…

I still have this very melancholy feeling inside me. It shows up mainly in the evenings. I get listless and depressed and just plain unhappy.

Is this what every teenager goes through? I thought I made it through my puberty stages.

Around the age of 10 or 11, I first started to become aware of the world around me: I realized I wasn't the only individual; I realized that life isn't all play and no work, and it struck me hard at first.

It seems like that awareness has just hit me again, but it's a deeper awareness this time, not the kind of thing one can put into words.

I know that I'm going to need the will (and a lot of optimism) to survive in this world. I try to hang on to my good moods but I'm finding it hard. What is there to be optimistic about in this world?

I know – that's a very bad outlook.

I'm working on changing it, but it's not too difficult to view the world as rather bleak and uninviting when you're 15…

Oh, just let me be, depression. Let me be, world.

February 1, 1988

There are some people in my life who really affect me. My dad is one. I called him, on an order from my mother and invited myself over there for next weekend. Not that I wanted to. What do I do at his place? Help a bit around the house, do my homework, read, go to a dreaded poetry reading or two, maybe a movie. My room is about the size of three closets (small closets) put together. It looks out into a smelly drunk-ridden alley. I stay in that room most of the day. It's a real thrill.

I feel so guilty at times about not spending time with my dad. If his living conditions were different, I probably would. I know, I know, I should want to spend time with him no matter where he lives. But that's not true. Do you know what it's like to live in a tiny house crammed with stuff, that has a thick layer of dust and grime on it, a house whose floors haven't been washed in the five or ten years he's lived there, with the rooms smelling of burned dinner, cat food, cat spray, cat barf (which I am always discovering in the most outlandish places – for instance, on my desk), with a closet-size bathroom that smells so bad you have to hold your breath or puke – I could go on forever.

Besides all this, I never have a moment to myself. The house is always full of people; either kids from next door, or friends of his. You see I can't just slink off and enjoy myself in my room when company arrives; my room is in the middle of everything on the first floor. Someone's always going through it to get to the kitchen. As a female 15-year-old, I need a lot of privacy.

This is what gives me guilt. All the things that disgust me about his lifestyle. I know he just can't afford anything else, but I still am disgusted, therefore guilty, because I know I should accept my father for who he is, a very poor poet – no he's an excellent poet – I mean a poet with not much income.

We get along pretty well, actually. I think my personality (my hot-temperedness and argumentativeness and the way I put off everything to the last minute, as well as my wit and occasional optimism and will power) comes more from him than from my mom.

I wish I could accept his living standards, but it's so hard when you're used to a big, comfy room and four floors and eating out and TV and privacy and better sanitation.

I'm freezing up here in my room, so I'll sign off and go downstairs for a while.

February 15, 1988

In ten minutes I turn my lights off and face the darkness and loneliness of night – trying, struggling to get out of my mind the haunting images that torment me: the disfigured faces of anxiety, of hate and selfishness and guilt, taking their form in my mind in various ways: as my stepfather saying "Fuck you" to my mother, as my dad saying "You don't spend much time with me these days…" as Mike saying "Oh, I don't care," as myself saying "I can do anything, I can be better than anyone, I'll always be on the top, I'll always be the smartest and the best."

I can't stand this! I need to forget it all and remember everything positive about my life. I mean, from the outside, my life seems perfect. But the deeper you go, the scarier and lonelier it gets.

Sometimes I feel like I'm all alone and I'm just drifting through life and shit, what does it matter anyway? We're all going to die. We're all living the same meaningless lives. Then why do I feel alone? Maybe because I want to find out the meaning; but how do I think I'll discover it? Through studying biochemistry eight years and winning a Nobel Prize? Will that make everything clear? Will writing a novel that becomes a well-loved classic answer all my questions?

Then what are my goals in life, if these are worthless?

What is my fate, my future, what am I? Well, it's two minutes past 10:30 so I'm late for my engagement with sleep. For now, I'm just a 15-year-old girl.

March 20, 1988

Sooner or later you are expected to shake off innocence and face reality, and if you don't, you're called emotionally disturbed or insane.

I guess reality doesn't have to be all bad. It can be as good as you want to make it. Often I don't know whether I could feel all warm and joyful at the least thing... I loved that feeling of elation that you could slide into and stay wrapped up in. I don't know how long it's been since I've felt it around me, encouraging me. Generally I either feel bored, lonely, depressed, bitter, humourous, content, or occasionally even thrilled – which is rare. I can't complain too much; I realize I should be even grateful for what I have. It's my own fault I'm such a pathetic being. But I can't help but wish myself away from all this...

You know, I had imaginary friends and fantasies and a language of my own and even an imaginary world: Kawiakee*. Now I don't believe in any of them – except maybe Kawiakee. It will always be very special to me. My paradise, my escape. But other than that, I've abandoned all of my make-believe. I've abandoned it for reality, and I can't turn back; I'm trapped, at the bottom of a dark pit closed off from sunlight and happiness, and I want to get out but I don't know how. And the floating notes of Bach run through my head – they have the answer, the solution – but I don't understand them. They speak a different language and I don't know how to interpret them; all I can do is let them run through me over and over again until they lift me into the deep darkness of sleep. Does anyone know how to get out? How to see sunlight again?

---

* She refers to this land in her final suicide note as the place she was returning to. - Ed.

April 2, 1988

I was slowly, reluctantly getting ready for bed, trying to ignore my familiar friend, Mr. Hopelessness, who was creeping up on me again. "What is there worth living for?" he whispers and gives a melancholy laugh which really gets on my nerves. I look in the mirror while flossing my teeth and I see him staring back at me with large, sympathetic eyes. I turn around and continue flossing.

Funny, I consider myself a happy person, not happy in the sense that I skip and dance at every joyous moment in life, but in the sense that I do make an effort at enjoying what there is in life to enjoy. If I'm enjoying myself, I call myself an optimist and congratulate myself on my success in enjoying what there is to enjoy in life. If I feel like shit, which seems to be most of the time these days, I forget the optimism and I indulge in self-pity and my Mr. Hopelessness. Good old Mr. H. He's always there for me.

* * * * *

I'm sure this will sound corny and self-pitying (I guess everything I've written so far sounds that way), but I have to say it. I don't find facing reality a very healthy thing to do. In fact, I think I can get along fine without ever letting myself become totally aware of what's happening in the world. Because I don't like much that's going on around this old planet of ours. I'd much rather just ignore it and proceed with my naïve methods of obtaining little bits of happiness here and there than be brave and say to the world, "Hey, I realize you're in quite a mess but that doesn't scare me because that's what I'm here for. I'm here to save you, to stop all the wars and poverty and government rulers. I'm here to turn you away from self-destruction." Shit, at this point in my life I'm more worried about avoiding my own self-destruction. God, I'm a selfish, self-pitying creature. But I can't help being a coward right now. I'm just too confused about everything to even try to face up to reality and distinguish between good and evil. Hell, I can't even face up to Mr. Hopelessness.

There should be some word that can take the place of all negative emotions, so that you can forget about trying to sort out your worries from your angers from your frustrations; there would be only one word to deal with. So instead of it being you against hate, depression, humiliation, guilt, etc., it's just you against that one word. It would certainly make it a lot easier to try and conquer these emotions. It would at least give one a half-decent chance, with a one-to-one fight.

Then again, I'm not supposed to be fighting my negative emotions. I should be accepting them as only natural, and learning from them, not adding to them by wishing they would go haunt someone else. I should try to – oh, hell, I'm sick of what I should be doing. The trouble is I know what I am supposed to do, but I also know that knowing is not going to automatically change me and make me do what I should. It just frustrates me more because I don't feel I have the ability to act on what I know, to do what I fully realize is what I should do. Is any of this making sense? I am having a hard time figuring out what I know from what I think I know today.

Getting to sleep is becoming more and more difficult. I often lie in bed for hours, waiting for sleep to take over me. Whether impatiently or patiently, I lie there and toss and turn, and wish the state of unconsciousness would not be so hard for me to reach.

I don't think this is caused by a fear of sleep: I tend to look forward to sleep and rest from a hectic and sometimes unsatisfying day. Sleep provides a temporary break from my need to be constantly doing something.

A couple of nights ago, I had a particularly hard time of it. A part of me was fretfully awaiting sleep and a different part of me was enjoying the silence and solitude. That part of me was drifting through thought without really doing any thinking. It was as if I were observing thoughts but not participating in them, like when you're watching a not very interesting program on television.

I slept for six hours that night, but strangely enough, I was in a good mood the next morning.

What I do a lot of in bed when it's dark and quiet is to go over the day's events and relive certain ones that weren't satisfying to me from some fault of my own. I act out again in my mind, this time doing or saying what I should have done before or what I had meant to do but couldn't find the courage to. I don't really like this habit of mine. Frankly I find it very annoying. I don't know why I can't just accept the fact that I can't always act in the way I would like to; things can't always turn out the way I want them to. But once I start going back to a scene, I can't stop. My ability to turn off this annoying retrospection is taken away from me. I am forced to sit back and watch. It can get to be very agonizing to see yourself in the same frustrating situation over and over again.

In bed I also sometimes relive particularly troubling scenes that happened months or even years ago. They keep coming back though I would very much like to shove them deep into my subconscious where they belong. Lately an interview that took place about three weeks ago has been haunting me in such a way. As I go through it the first time, I shudder at my stuttering and muddle-mindedness, and the next few times round, I say what I meant to say, and totally astound the interviewers with my incredible articulation and intellect. I've always had difficulty expressing myself verbally the way I would like to.

Most of my reliving sessions involve going back and changing what I said. I guess I have trouble facing my weak verbal skills so I make up for it at night, when it's dark and quiet and no one is around to laugh at me.

June 4, 1988

I don't really know what someone else would think of the thousands of words I've poured out year after year, without restraints or restrictions. Why is it so different to write about The Origin of Comets than to write completely with your own free will? And so much harder to judge "free" writing than "essay" writing? So I just don't know the worth of all these pages, to someone else, that is. Their worth to me is impossible to describe, it is so immense. I'm feeling pensive and almost dreamy. The murmur of the night-world outside is there, and it always gives me a lonely but still pleasant feeling. I can pick out certain specific sounds, like the blowing of a train whistle, and a passing car, but the rest, further out towards the waterfront, is a gentle blend of hums of traffic and wind through the trees, and some mechanical construction taking place near the water. People's voices become distinct now and then, like ghostly reminders that there is life out there. I love the sounds of night, wherever I am.

Now I can hear a plane overhead, but the sound fades fast. I've always felt a shudder of sadness sweep through me whenever I've heard a plane fly by overhead, in the city or up the coast. I don't know why, but it just overwhelms me with a melancholy not unlike the one I am experiencing now.

Time to sleep before I get carried away. Goodnight.

June 9, 1988

I don't know how to start. I don't know anything. I'm changing. I can feel it. I can feel myself going through a major personality transition – deep inside me two forces have been struggling and one has finally won. But I feel lost and I wish things hadn't shifted so suddenly.

I guess it isn't really sudden. This whole year has been different. I spend many of my classes wandering the halls with, sometimes without, my best friend, Jan, as if searching aimlessly for something I know I can't find in these old familiar hallways. But I have to wander them; something in me lures me to them and I let myself forget everything, and just walk, trying not to let the cold truth sink in too deep. This is your last week within these halls. Forever. I don't think I can cope outside the security of these walls, yet I know this freedom awaiting me will be the beginning of a new chapter of my life. It's an agony that has changed and mixed up everything inside of me – torn myself apart. It's something I have to go through alone, but at times I feel close to drawing Jan into the deep murky waters with me, so we can drown together – but I come to my senses quickly and look away from her inquisitive and concerned eyes, and instead gaze silently out the window to the familiar scene of children playing in the courtyard.

It's so vague right now – life, love, and the meaning of it. I'm not accustomed to accepting vague answers. I want a concrete reality to deal with. But in this case, I have no choice. So I guess I'm changing myself to adapt to these hazy images of the future, to make an effort at accepting them.

But how do I know what matters and what doesn't?

July 31, 1988

I don't want to be a doctor working in a hospital; I'll study to become a paramedic and work in that field for a couple of years or until I burn out, whichever comes first. I made a mistake – I don't plan to study medicine right away: I want to attend university for a couple of years and study biochemistry as well as physics, literature, Latin, philosophy, and maybe genetics.

After working as a paramedic for a while, I'd like to go back to school and take some courses in a specialized medical-related science field. I would like to do research in that area, plus experimentation (may to do with genetics and disease?) and hopefully my work will help the world in some way – not just the people living in it, but the world itself.

How I'll fit travelling (and romance!) in with all that, I don't know. Maybe my research will take me all over the world. Maybe I'll provide medical aid in a third world country. Somehow I'll explore the world and meet new people.

Then, of course, there's another direction I could and might take. That's to become a screen playwright (is that the right word?) and write a classic which will be remembered for ages. Or maybe I would write a novel or two which would be adapted for the screen and I could get involved in the movie and meet and consult with the director, etc., chat with the stars, etc. I can just see it: "'Pain and Glory,' starring Kevin Costner, Michael J. Fox and Jessica Lange, based on the book by Lara Gilbert" – but that's just a fantasy, some way of imagining my name with the stars. You have to realize, Lara, that they're just plain, real people, often egocentric and demanding. They pretend to be other people. Doctors heal and cure and console. It's not too hard to pick which profession I'd respect more. But why then, are movie stars so idolized and worshipped, and doctors are just doctors?

Fame is something I ain't looking for in life, thank goodness. I hate being the centre of attention. I'm too shy and modest and introverted for that.

September 9, 1988

All through the day, especially during physics, I feel this heavy longing, like the feeling of being utterly exhausted. You want to lie down so badly and go to sleep, but you can't. This is different, though; I'm not sleepy. I couldn't figure it out at first. It's a heavy burden I can't shake off; it's the loneliness enveloping me. No matter how hard I concentrate on the subject material, it's always there – the knowledge that all this might never have had to happen; I can see the other might-have-beens and they pull me towards them and I want to let go and just forget I ever made this decision. The International Baccalaureate program doesn't leave time for emotion or reflection. It doesn't leave time for fantasizing about ambulances or movie stars. The fact that I am going to be an E.M.A. (Emergency Medical Assistant) is just plain accepted in my mind; it's basic knowledge. It's always there, that assurance, but it doesn't change the thirty-word problems I have to do in math or the fifteen-page review in French or the 250 pages of "1984" or the ten pages of philosophy or the essays in biology or the eleven textbooks I have to cover with paper, with many more coming. That's my weekend I've described. Oh, boy. But it's registration day with St. John Ambulance tomorrow morning, then out to my cousin's barn to see the horse, Cajun, so I don't know when there'll be time for the estimated eleven hours of homework.

September 15, 1988

I hate to sound pessimistic, but school really is bleak. Classes are unusual and interesting, but school is pretty grim. Do you realize that I will be leading a discussion (with four others) for fifty minutes one day? A seminar??!? That's in English. In history there's the twenty-minute presentation of a book review. I have four novels to read as quickly as humanly possible, by Monday or Tuesday.

At times the overwhelming dread comes out from within my dark deep thoughts, and the images, or rather, the nightmares, of myself talking to a class for an hour, writing an essay on some topic I have no knowledge of, studying for seven International Baccalaureate final exams, seven provincial finals, plus the scholarship exams, all in the spring of 1990. How am I to do all this that I've never done before? It twists me around and I writhe in the horror and panic of the nightmare. I groan and cry and always, the torture ends with an image of my wrists being slit by a rectangular blade. I feel the sharp quick pain as an incredible pleasure that burns wonderfully, like the sensation felt when you wrap burning-hot hands around a glass of ice. With the blood that pours out, all the worries and tensions and freakish nightmares flow from my body and mind, empty out, leave me behind in peace, deathly peace. The pleasure of being able to commit suicide – I wish I had that luxury.

Often I'm able to push back the dark feelings and concentrate naively on one tiny aspect, or one goal glimmering in the future as senselessly luring as a nugget of gold.

September 20, 1988

What do you do when life is not working out, when you can't seem to fit in to the stream of things? When you can't work up the courage to run into a busy street on a rainy, dark day and just get things over with. But you can't work up the courage to look forward to anything either. And you can't stand the way things have turned out, but you know you couldn't stand the way things were, either. If only I weren't me.

October 4, 1988

I can hear fireworks in the distance, but I can't remember why there would be any. I can also hear firecrackers down the street. Those must have something to do with the approach of Hallowe'en.

I'm babbling because I can't seem to express in words the agony I'm going through. It's not the agony I thought I would be going through at this moment: physical pain, perhaps of a broken arm or twisted ankle or bruise on the head. Instead, it's mental pain – no, it's anguish.

I am such a fucking coward, coward, coward. I can't face up to enjoying or looking forward to school (in fact, I hate it) and I can't face up to getting out of school – either by admitting I hate it and transferring out, or by doing something to myself that would require me to miss a lot of school and ride in an ambulance, such as throwing myself in front of a moving car.

I had the perfect opportunity – absolutely perfect: it was nearly dark out; I was walking down a side street, and a car turned the corner and drove towards me, I knelt down on the sidewalk, as if to tie my shoes, planning, as I'd done hundreds of times in my mind, to suddenly run onto the street from between parked cars just at the right moment, just when I would be hit. But I couldn't. I couldn't run. I realized that it was now or never; if I couldn't bring myself to do it now, when everything was just right, then I would never be able to. But still I didn't. I walked home feeling worse inside than ever before. Feeling worn out and empty, without hope, without any feelings. Just barely there. I feel worse now. No, I feel better I guess. There's always tomorrow morning. I can always try again then. That's what I tell myself. But I'm too fucking afraid to do it. Yet I managed to convince some part of me that it will happen. I've lived these past couple days on just that fantasy. On my fantasy. Nothing else real matters. What I think is really scaring me is that this hints to me that I don't have any trust in my own dreams. I can't make them come true.

I've so much homework to do which I haven't even looked at, simply because I thought I would be in an emergency room right now. Well I'm not. Maybe I never will be.

Why isn't life fair?

I'm so nothing. Not even depressed. Worse than the worst depression. No use saying I'll write tomorrow. I probably will, but what difference will it make? I'll be writing these same words for two years. That's a long time when you've only lived sixteen so far.

16

October 23, 1988

Why am I so intent on somehow getting out of the International Baccalaureate program? Mainly because I'm not the type of person who enjoys, or is even willing to do, five hours of homework a day. I want to be able to do what means a lot to me, as well. And not to mention the difficulty of it all. I can't seem to get into the mode of thinking critically. Maybe it's because my thoughts are always preoccupied with first aid and ambulances and paramedics. My main frustration is that I've finally put together what I want to do with my life, but I don't have the chance to do it until I get this damn International Baccalaureate program out of the way. Fucking stupid decision I made. Shit, shit, shit. I just can't cope with lecturing thirty minutes about William James' "Pragmatism in Theory of Knowledge," or writing 750 words on the psychological effects of imprisonment on individuals.

I simply don't want to cope with cramming in Grade 11 and first year university chemistry this year, and higher level physics – here you have to be at genius level to get an A, and three hours of discussion per week in history about topics on which I have been uninformed and ignorant up till now.

My personality has changed: I'm no longer a meticulous, stressed-out over-achiever, which is basically what most of the I.B. students are. I was when I applied, But everything has changed. I've discovered more about what makes me tick and want to live. And it isn't getting up at 6:30 every morning and racking my brain until I go to bed at 10:30. I need more freedom with my time. Oh, God. I need to get out of this.

Someone realize this. Let me get hit by a car and spend a month in the hospital. Let me have the courage to drop out. Fuck. I can't ignore my pride, you know. What do I do?

There is no one I can say this to so I had to write it out. I don't want to die – I still love life, just not this kind of life. I want to change it so badly, but I don't know how. How? What should I do? What's the easiest way out?

I DON'T KNOW HOW I AM GOING TO SURVIVE.

October 26, 1988

I can truthfully say that I am experiencing the worst times of my life (so far). I feel like crying most of the time, but I'm afraid I won't be able to stop. I did cry last night; Mike called and said he found someone else. I told him I understood, that it's not fair to him that I can only see him once a month. When I hung up I said to myself, it's not fair to me either. Funny, all this time I've thought I'm an academically inclined person. A "student." I just assumed that I'd spend the next eight years at university after graduation, study science or medicine or something. But now, when I imagine myself doing that, I feel no excitement whatsoever. I feel only indifference and sometimes even disgust. I want to have time in my life to exercise, get enough sleep, spend time with friends, play the piano, write, read, research topics of my interest, and relax. Do you realize how utterly impossible that is in the International Baccalaureate program? In any school program? I feel like I should have school over with; I should be graduating. Ten years is surely enough. During those ten years I've gained knowledge, sensibility, an open and critical mind, and love for learning. Now I'm ready to move on and focus these skills on my specific interests. But I'm not allowed to. I think the reason I applied to I.B. was not for more intellectual stimulus, but for a change. I knew I needed a change. But it didn't dawn on me until I'd actually undergone the "I.B. experience" that this is not the change I was thinking about.

October 30, 1988

I finally was able to do it! For some reason there was no problem – my feet moved, my brain cooperated, everything was perfect! Except the timing, which is a shame. I mean, everything really was perfect. It was dark, the ground and air damp from an earlier rain. A car approaches; I see its headlight and hear its engine from where I am pretending to fumble with my shoe behind a parked van, and I try to estimate when I should venture across the street, considering the different factors of its speed, how far down the street it is, and how fast I want to break out from behind the van. And I notice a door open a few houses down across the street, which is good, just in case I am hurt but the driver keeps on going. And so the time has come, I am ready. I am too satisfied to feel any nervousness, and – NOW – I run out into the street, the headlights suddenly in my eyes, and I realize with frustration (and, I admit, a bit of relief) that unless I stay still in the dead centre of the street like a fool for another moment, there is no chance the car will hit me. So I wave my hand to the driver in apology (though I hear no brakes squeal anyway) and just ran to the other side of the street and proceed home. But I was prepared, I really was ready, mentally and physically, for the moment. Now I have confidence that I can, and will do it.

November 5, 1988

I can hardy believe it: it's really over. I am no longer going to Churchill*. Well, I still have to give back my 300 text books (okay, okay, I'm exaggerating a bit) but that, hopefully, can be done later in the week, at the end of the school day, so I don't have to face all the students.

My being sick actually came at a good time. Now I don't have to simply refuse to go Monday morning; I have an excuse. My mom understands, though, I'm pretty sure. But it all depends on her meeting with the Superintendent of High Schools. I'm sure it will go fine.

November 12, 1988

I could stay up tonight and write and think and dream and cry and smile but I probably won't because all it will do is make me tired tomorrow. Is all we do only done to achieve results we want, or think we want?

Does any action actually come from inside; is anything done just because it was meant to be done? Our whole life is spent trying to achieve results. We do what we do in order to somehow influence the future, our future and the future of others. We always have tomorrow in our minds before tomorrow's even here; we live in not just the present but countless times beyond and behind us as well. If we didn't live in a kind of time that goes one way, forward as we like to put it, would we think the same way? Do the same things? Be the same people?

What I am getting at is this: Who you are depends on how you perceive time. When you are young you don't really perceive it at all. Then you start to ponder it, after accepting it or maybe before. You change as your perception of time changes.

Then, to find out who we are, as individuals, we need only to penetrate time – to explore our perception of it, explore and discover.

Shit, I'm tired. Goodnight.

---

* Sir Winston Churchill Secondary School, site of the International Baccalaureate program in Vancouver - Ed.

"We go to extreme lengths – we devoted daughters, we women, we children, we slaves of the men we love – we go to extreme lengths in our efforts to justify our unacceptable loyalties."

Joy Kogawa

Chapter Two

Age Sixteen

December 24, 1988
Age 16

Something happened which triggered a memory of mine, one which I've kept totally secret for so many years. It's a haunting, nightmarish memory, even more so since it is one of my first memories. It shaped my character, my personality, my future too. What I have chosen as a career I know now to have come from that incident. I thought on the drive home that I might finally write it all out, pull all the secrets and memories that incident years ago resulted in, but I just can't. Simply can't.

December 29, 1988

To be a writer or artist or poet, and not just to be one but to make a living as one, you have to be either terribly good or terribly stupid. My father fits into the "good" category, and not just because he's definitely not stupid. He IS good. He is GOOD. A large portion of the time I am baffled at what he writes. I read the poem again, positive there have been a few typos or something, and then again, and the words gradually begin to move towards a pattern, a dance, the music of poetry. In that sense my father is a great musician, to whom one never tires of listening, although perhaps succumbs to exhaustion as a result of the intense and constant concentration his poems gently but firmly demand.

But who am I to judge his writing? I am his young (in the sense that I am the youngest) daughter. I must have a bias when it comes to criticizing his work. In fact, I find it hard to judge anyone's creative works because I feel I am judging the person in the process. What is created does not stand alone, but is connected inseparably from its creator, in my opinion. Then to praise one's creations is to praise the creator. To criticize a creation is to criticize the creator.

An instance years ago demonstrates how this is tied into my inner beliefs and always has been: I was angry at my father for some reason or another, I'm sure a very reasonable one it seemed at the time. I must have come to my wit's end in trying to express this anger and obtain satisfying results, because I remember stomping over to the book shelf, my book shelf I believe it was, and grabbing a copy of a book of his poems that he had given me, and screaming, "And I hate your book!", throwing it to the ground. I have no idea if this incident remained in his mind for long or if he would recall it now, but it has stayed in my memory ever since, and I remember having nightmares full of rage and guilt and shame. I had done something unforgivable in my mind, dealt the worst and cruelest blow one could possibly deal to someone one loves. So no, I don't think I am capable of viewing his work objectively.

When I say that his writing is good, I am saying that HE is good. To stretch it further, or really just to restate it, by describing his writing, "the fruits of creativity," I am describing him. One can see that by saying I intend to describe my father's writing, I judge his writing above himself. His art, his music, his creations, whatever one wishes to feebly describe them using the fragile tools of language, they are larger and more evident, more conspicuous than the man himself. To have the ability, and yes, the courage, to create something larger than oneself, is the mark of a truly remarkable person. This I believe my father to be.

To know whatever is written down on a piece of paper, every little line and circle and squiggle has meaning and exists and will continue to have and do so forever, is the joy of writing. To know that every little mark written down has a meaning that ties into the meanings of the marks around it, forming the patterns and passages of words and sentences that are unique as snowflakes, is the joy of a great writer.

To hope to achieve this joy is simply joy, period.

* * * * *

I can't believe I'm actually going to write this. It's awfully strange, and an awfully long time to be keeping it in. But the strange thing is that it hasn't been something on my mind a lot. It's just been something that is part of me, like the fact that I have a mole on one of my toes, and I don't go around talking about it or do I think about it.

It happened again, just recently. I guess it was time. What it is, is dreams. Dreams that "foretell the future." I don't realize they ARE going to until that future event happens. Not all my dreams are like that. In fact, I haven't had many at all since the clump back when I was 10 or 11. But I've always thought secretly that all dreams come true, or were once true. We dream the past and the future. They imitate life, or perhaps life imitates them. But they're not always the actual image of what happens. For instance, one dream was of books of all sizes and colours floating in through my window to me, and I remember feeling so excited and in love with them. About a week later, I found out that my childhood companion was moving and he had a huge box of books for me that he didn't want to pack along.

But some dreams are very straight forward. Years ago, I dreamed that it snowed one day and I forgot my "galoshes." (I don't know why, but that was the word in my dream.) And I went to school and we had to walk outside and my feet got soaked. A few days later the class went skating at Britannia ice rink and it snowed and I hadn't brought my boots.

And one night at my dad's, I slept-walked down the stairs and said very clearly (my dad told me this later, I have no memory of it): "Where is my bird?" We don't, and never did, have birds. The next morning my dad found a dead little bird outside the door to the alley.

Damn it – there are so many more but I've blanked them out from my memory. I wrote a few briefly down in an old little journal of mine that must be somewhere at my dad's house. I must find it. Trying to remember them, I get glimpses of objects or moods; a candle, a turkey, darkness streaked with silver. But I can't remember.

January 5, 1989

I got to wondering, on the toilet (an ideal place to wonder), whether I would ever write the book(s) I've always imagined would mean so much to me and those who read them. I very well might; I very well might not. If I do, it will probably be once I've retired. In fact, spending my last decade or two writing is a very nice thought. One has gained a certain amount of wisdom by then, I would imagine. What I would find very meaningful would be to collect together all my pieces of writing, from my first entries in a diary and the little poems and stories I used to love to make up at the typewriter, to whatever will be written during the many years to come; in short, my life's writings. To collect it all together is something very important to me. Maybe I'd even try to get it published, but the main thing is to have it there, existing, for myself to enjoy, and then for the next generations after me. To keep a part of me living even after the physical part dies – something that writing can accomplish beautifully. For a piece of writing is alive forever.

* * * * *

Here's my description and analysis of one of my dreams:

Suddenly a man comes through the door, holding a spear of some sort with a wooden or bone handle. I grab a poker-type spear next to me and jump to my feet. He is pointing the spear at me, threatening me it

25

seems. The others stand to our right and left, uncertain what is going on. He moves towards me, and I panic and start jabbing him. He isn't wearing a shirt but when I jab him I see no blood, though I feel the spear penetrate. I am finding it hard to get him; the spear is hard to manipulate, but I manage to stab him in a few places around his chest and arms and once near his testicles. Suddenly the joust stops, and he is seriously hurt I realize. The others tend to his wounds and I realize with horror that he is my brother/my father (I am not sure which) and he was only intending it as a game, never thinking to hurt me. I am overwhelmed with guilt and grief. I realize that I hurt him terribly, and he had kept on "playing along" because he thought I was simply playing around too, and wasn't meaning to hurt him, whereas I had actually thought he was a burglar or a crazy murderer and I had to protect myself from him.

* * * * *

My anxieties about the correspondence school work stem mainly from the fact that I'm not seeming to keep up; I set an amount of time per day to work on each course and a date I must have one paper done by, but I let my time slip by, and large amounts of work pile up, becoming a "huge weight" and it can't even be accomplished by spending hours of struggling over it; the "running start" doesn't help. Maybe I should simply set out and do what I planned to get done, with the attitude that "I'd better hurry" and get it done, rather than getting behind one day and having loads of stuff to catch up on the next day, so that I can get extremely frustrated and then depressed resulting in physical pain. (I've got into the horrible habit of lightly cutting the inside of my arm with a very sharp blade so as to concentrate on the physical pain and let go of the mental anguish, just like the fight that breaks out in the dream and someone gets hurt.)

I have had thoughts, late at night when I am in the kitchen getting a snack and the house is dark and quiet, about using the knife-sharpener as a sort of weapon if someone tried to break and enter; the man "playing" with me that I don't realize doesn't mean any harm is more likely my father than my (half) brother.

I always have had a deep sense of guilt when it comes to my father because ever since I was 12 or 13, I've spent nearly all my time with my mother.

I usually don't realize I've hurt him until thinking about it later; for instance, if I decline going over to his house for the evening because I'm simply tired, he is always pleasant with me ("shows no blood") even though I stab him in the dream.

I try to hold myself back from him perhaps (the poker-spear in the dream) and this ends up hurting him when he had no intention of ever hurting me.

This dream is not yet fully explained I think. It may take more pondering over, perhaps an eternal correspondence to surface, before it can be analyzed completely.

* * * * *

I mentioned the obsession I've taken up of scratching the inside of my arm with a razor. Today on the news there was a report that over the weekend, there had been six attempted suicides at the Willingdon Youth Detention Centre. Slashing the wrists and forearms was involved in several.

January 22, 1989

I'm so restless. Even my "visit" to Vancouver General Hospital Emergency parking lot today was anti-climactic. I guess everything will be for a while. But it was kind of funny at the V.G.H. I propped myself against a concrete pillar in the covered parking area, three ambulances to my left. I got cold after a while so I decided to put away my book and go to the bus stop. Not much was happening. So I left but as I walked down Laurel Street, I saw an ambulance going into the parking lot. So I nonchalantly wandered back into the parking area with its lit up red EMERGENCY sign greeting me, and tried to casually watch the emergency medical attendants unloading the gurney. Then I started walking back to the bus stop but another ambulance with lights and sirens going whizzed by and so I went back to watch from a distance. Then again, and this time it was an Advanced Life Support Unit with the real paramedics inside so I just had to catch a glimpse. This kept happening and I began to feel stupid and a little overwhelmed not to mention freezing cold so I managed to pull myself away from Emergency which now had several ambulances parked every which way, and actually go to the bus stop and wait. And wait. The bus took ages and I got colder. But it was still a nice journey. A siren screaming in the distance – closer, closer, then further away. Back and forth between the two sirens.

Fantasizing in bed last night for an hour I tried to imagine I was lying on one of the beds at the station during a night shift. My partner was watching television in the big room down the hall. I incorporated the radio my mom was listening to downstairs into the fantasy this way. I let the wonderful feelings soak in. I can't begin to explain why this fantasy appeals to me so much, but it does.

January 25, 1989

Something I've learned more fully than anything else in the past few months is that there is a whole lot more to education than school. I'd say school comprises a mere fraction of our education. Does a child learn more sitting at a desk and listening to a teacher explain politics at the provincial level or actually visiting the provincial parliament buildings when the politicians are in session? We stay cooped up in a stuffy, overcrowded room artificially lit with perpetually flickering lights for a third of our day for twelve or more years of our life, to learn about the world we live in.

The world is out there, outside, not inside the vomit-green hallways and classrooms of our so-called institutions of education.

I've managed to penetrate the real outside world in the last few months more than I've ever had the chance to before. I'm involved in community work, in athletic programs; I have a sort-of part-time job, I have time to probe the depths of classical (and, I admit, popular) music on the piano, and investigate the shelves of emergency medicine literature at the Justice Institute library. I have begun driving; I have explored parts of Vancouver by bus and on foot (namely areas around hospitals and other medical institutions) that I've never known existed, and I have unveiled abilities of mine that are frighteningly exciting.

I just have to remember that if it weren't for the fact that correspondence courses take up only three hours or less a day, I wouldn't be doing all this. My school work is a blessing and a curse. There have got to be some changes at least tried in the school system. Either decrease its intensity and phony importance or expand it to include the many other aspects of education, the process of learning about ourselves and our world.

Come to think of it, there are a lot of changes that need to be made in this world we like to call ours. This planet is destined for doom and

I'm not meaning to be melodramatic here. One in five people is functionally illiterate. Millions are dying of diseases that were likely triggered by man himself. Millions are starving while millions of others feast at banquets, laughing and planning the future of their countries. Millions are discriminated against, tortured, jailed, executed – and I'm not just speaking of situations like apartheid and South Africa. I mean right next door to us as well, in the friendly U.S.A., where people who have chemical imbalances in their brains or chromosome abnormalities in their cells are sent to the electric chair. That's our way of dealing with problems. That's fucking like locking the barn door after the horse is stolen. To cope efficiently and humanely with "criminals" we need to go to the roots of the problem – childhood abuse, genetic disorders, psychological cruelty, ineffectively-tested chemicals dumped into foods to preserve them; the list goes on and on. But no, we wait until the problem has climaxed before we notice and we let ourselves feel proud, society-protecting, just as we lock up those who trouble us, and throw away the key. Here in North America we are shocked at the idea of hundreds of black activists jailed by a government that seeks power, not peace, yet we breathe a sigh of relief when the maniac down the street is finally put away or Ted Bundy is finally electrocuted. We are dealing with humans here, with people. We are all people! We realize, or many of us do, that whether our skin colour is white or black or in-between that we're all the same underneath, but we're so far away from accepting other differences.

I'm not saying child killers should be let alone to do what they choose; I'm not that naïve. But if more time and money were put into, say, psychiatric help for those who have already committed an offense and financial and emotional support for the young ones who have had nothing but violence and unhappiness in their homes, maybe we wouldn't have to revert to locking up or killing those who act against society's rules. What really gets me is this: society (or government, whatever) punishes someone who has killed another person, by execution, but itself is totally absolved from this rule; for some reason some kind of murder is perfectly acceptable but another isn't. We are all murderers ourselves if we believe in capital punishment, but we don't apply capital punishment to ourselves; we don't go by our own rules. The logic is very weak; in fact, I think it's nonexistent, and trying to explain what the problem is often just takes one in circles. But something's wrong here.

29

And, of course, there's the depletion of the ozone layer, the greenhouse effect, nuclear weapons aimed at every area in the world except for New Zealand, supposedly, and there is ongoing war in nearly twenty countries. If one thing doesn't get us, another will. While medical researchers struggle with the last touches on a cure for AIDS, two power-hungry superpowers push a little red button and send huge ugly weapons at each other for the last time. They are the murderers. And I don't want to die under their hands, over their squabbles. But we will all come to a point, the world, everything, when we must start over again. Einstein said that he didn't know how the third world war would be fought, but he knew how the fourth would be: with sticks and stones.

What a strange, beautiful, and cruel thing life is. No one can prove it exists, we exist. There is no way of knowing if what we experience is part of a complex scheme or plan that involves hundreds of civilizations in hundreds of galaxies, or if it is all just a figment of one's imagination. But there, you see, if I really thought that I dreamed the whole thing up, I wouldn't have written "one's imagination," I would have written "my imagination." I cling to the apparent materiality of reality (Yuck, that sounds terrible.) How else can I justify my wish to devote my life to medically helping individuals? I want to reduce or relieve the immediate suffering of a very few when the next day none of us may be around, maybe because we blew ourselves up, maybe because someone decided to quit imagining. One can't live from day to day wondering "what is the point?" or one will soon succumb to the intentional ending of one's own life.

Did you know that suicide attempts were once classified in the courts as murder attempts and treated thus?

What a peculiar state we live in.

February 26, 1989

Why the fuck do I write about boring things like grades? Why do things like that, abstract things that we pretend exist and allow to rule our lives, things like money and fame, fashion, religion, grades, what this planet thrives on, why do they matter so much? Maybe we consider them vital because we see on television a family in Africa living in poverty, disease, the little children crying with snot and flies and tears crusted on their faces, bellies bulging so that they cannot stand up, legs and arms just dark sticks, and we think: look what happens when we don't have money, fame, religion, etc.

Every day I bring myself to believe that nothing matters, that there is no meaning to the outcomes of our lives and the world and beyond. Maybe there was a reason in the beginning, a cause, a plan, but it has ceased to function, or has been overwhelmed by the goings-on that can only be described as simply disgusting. I guess I need to escape from the responsibility of accepting the world of chaos we live in.

Sometimes I experience something interesting and hopeful: I may be glancing at the hairs on my arm or walking down a sunlit alley and I feel myself switching back to "reality" from something else. That something else is a distant view, part of this reality, but so far away, not necessarily by time or distance, maybe by levels of being or thought. I realize that I have been looking at the world for a brief moment from an entirely different perspective. I am amazed at what I see, like when I read a story that is funny but sad, too. I feel like crying but I don't really at all; I feel like laughing. I feel like I could feel anything. Looking at myself from far away. Knowing nothing and not caring. "Let it be, let it be." Let it end itself.

So I guess I believe that the only outcome possible is for us to end ourselves. It is inevitable. Now I know what the ad on the bus meant that read "World Peace is Inevitable." The world will be at peace when we have extinguished ourselves. Peace means nothing existing. It means believing that nothing can exist and still be something. I realize that statement has two interpretations, so I'll clarify it: I don't mean that it isn't possible for anything to exist without being something; I mean that nothing is actually a something because there is no such thing as nothing, and it can exist, and it is peace.

March 8, 1989

Things I am ashamed of: (not all listed here)

Moving to my mom's at 12 or 13 years old and never going back to my dad's to stay. I've deserted him. I haven't allowed him back in my life. I don't want to be back in his.

Wanting to get hit by a car so that I can ride in an ambulance but not even considering the agony it would put my parents through.

Not being able to believe that anything like the future of this planet means anything, matters. All that seems to govern fate is whether we believe the outcome will be happy or sad. If it's happy, we try for it, although happy to one person isn't happy to another necessarily. Without humans, everything can exist in equilibrium, because emotions are not brought into the matter. I am ashamed of being human and being part of the downfall of a species and likely all species. I am ashamed of not even caring if we destroy everything in the process of destroying ourselves.

I am ashamed of wanting to work in the field of medicine, of wanting to bring immediate relief when nothing matters if tomorrow we're all gone. Emergency medicine – I could become so absorbed in saving a couple of lives now and then that I don't even look at existence in perspective again. Emergency medicine is short-term aid to the suffering. How can I want to help people in accidents and medical emergencies without caring about the outcome or future of Earth. This is our only home. Why don't I care?

I am ashamed of letting the little things get to me just as much as the big things, of being just as much ashamed of being cruel to my cats as not wanting a happy future for my descendants.

Why can't I put immediate, everyday life into perspective with the millions of years this planet has existed? And vice versa?

Why do I always have to be so caught up in the immediate that I feel like screaming at the long-term.

Damn it, why does my wrist have to ache and my light have to cast a shadow over just where I'm writing.

I have billions of minutes left to live and wonder and feel ashamed and I may never feel any more satisfied or know any more answers than I do now know. What's the purpose?

March 20, 1989

So I live still with my dreams and presentiments, my hours of imagining and gazing and wandering and planning; but how can I plan when I don't know yet? When I don't have all the pieces of the puzzle yet, let alone the knowledge of how to fit them together to form the complete picture of my life. I wish right now I had some bit of reality to cling to that would show me things straight as they are instead of having to speak and think metaphorically. It all sounds nice and flowery to write that way but it's like liquid flowing from container to container, changing its shape and colour so that it isn't what it was a minute ago. (There I go again with my metaphors.) I need something solid, unchanging, tangible to fasten my ideas and hopes. A person, or an event, or a fact, or even a dream. A real dream, a "knowing" dream. My "knowing" dreams lately have been about such trivial matters it's almost ridiculous. I have no idea how to grasp hold of my ability, channel it to where I want to go, no idea at all.

March 23, 1989

I'm tired of being naïve, okay? I'm sick of it all. All this sweet sad mushy bullshit that means nothing, all the lovely metaphors and clichés that would be nauseating if it weren't for the fact that they're "normal," what every teen reads in trashy romance novels. "Their voices had been the song of angels." Now what do you think of that? It's referring to William Golding's "Lord of the Flies" choir of young boys who become savage hunters, murdering their fellow peers. I don't know if I really agree with the inference that inside all of us, to some extent, is an evil, savage instinct that is kept in check to some extent by civilization, laws and morals; that we can only achieve a certain amount of justice/democracy before we fall once again to our natural level of being, the animal level. We have defects: We humans have one major defect which, to Golding, is this inner savagery. But to me it is the ability to be aware of this defect, the ability to seek a better, kinder life superior to what our natural animal level allows. (You see?) I'm terrible. I think of it as: "If we just don't realize we're not happy, or we're murdering others, then we don't need to feel discontent." Why is this how I feel? Why don't I want to struggle with my peers for a happier, more peaceful world, for a world, period, even? Because I know that it will never be achieved. "You'll get back all right – I just know," Simon says. And I know too, that thought may try to attain a higher level of being – and must try, that's the pattern of it all, it must be tried for – it will never be achieved for the world as a whole.

I want to work in emergency medicine. I don't understand why, but maybe it's because I want to help others and see that I have helped them, rather than reach and strive for goals that are not within our grasp. I also believe that if we could get rid of just a bit of intelligence, hopefulness and ambition, we could be happy as we are, because we wouldn't be aware of any other way of being. We'd have nothing to relate our emotions to, so they would be neither happy nor sad, good nor treacherous. Everything's relative. I like that Einstein, but I don't know if I really agree with his statement.

I dream often of giving in to insanity. Throwing things everywhere, screaming, cursing. I can't do it in real life though. I think of it often, but fondly, not with any conviction.

Happy Easter, old friend. And here's to you in the future. To me, after I've grown up and found this notebook in an old box of stuff in the basement, I hope life is all right. I hope I haven't yet given in to insanity. Maybe I'm a paramedic, maybe a university student, maybe a mother. Maybe I killed myself years ago.

April 24, 1989

My head must be the size of a beach ball, I'm so proud of myself at the moment. I felt like I was going to burst; I was sure I was dreaming, I wanted to scream with joy and pride.

No, I didn't save a drowning victim from death or an auto accident victim from paralysis. What happened was this: My English instructor (a new one for me; there was a change of instructors for some reason) gave me a 95% and a 100% on the two papers I got in the mail today. She wrote the nicest comments – so many "excellent"s and "brilliant"s – that it made all the hours of struggling with my thoughts to get them on paper worthwhile. On the 100% paper she wrote that was the only time she'd ever given 100% for that paper. I am so glad I got a change of instructors. I want to celebrate – I think I'll sit down and put all my energy into the 1200-word essay I have to send in with the next paper. I'm writing about how Ralph in "Lord of the Flies" contributes to the collapse of society on the island because of his weaknesses as a leader, weaknesses which are in everyone (the human defect which I talked about in an earlier entry and which is a major part of Golding's theme).

May 10, 1989

Today, despite my decision to turn over a new leaf and face life with optimism, I've been more grumpy and depressed than I have since I left Churchill High School. Nothing went right today. NOTHING.

In general, I feel swamped in all these things I must get done and pressured by everyone including myself to do them. My piano teacher told me to practice two hours a day or don't bother at all. My mother is kind enough to remind me frequently that if I don't get these correspondence courses done by September, I won't enter Grade 12.

* * * * *

My father got back from a three-month trip and I've barely talked to him at all. I haven't called my half-sister or dropped in on grandma in ages. Carolyn asks me to play cards, go to a movie, my mother asks me to mow the lawn, Lin asks me to babysit, Ria asks me to babysit, Michael asks me to give him piano lessons, Huey asks me to help him with his election speech, Rene gives me free tickets to a dance performance, Julie states that we'll go to a movie tomorrow, Jan refuses to do anything with me and I don't blame her. That is all in the last three days. How do I fit in weight lifting, walks to the library, shopping for a bathing suit and a Mother's Day present, etc., etc., which must be done before next week starts. How many hours of anxious anticipation and angry frustration did I waste today?

Oh if only I could push it all away. If only a siren could save me from myself.

May 15, 1989

I want to mention something peculiar – it's a strange, unpleasant sensation in my chest I've had a few times today and once in a while in the past few months. It's sort of like what it might feel like if your heart swelled up really big and went sort of berserk for a couple of seconds, then quieted down again. It's not just a speeding up of heart rate, it's more like skipping a few beats. And it hurts afterwards, sort of tight and achy for a minute or so. And it's very real, not like the fantasies I imagine where I'm drowning or dying from overdose or have broken limbs (and paramedics come to my rescue – barfo). I know this because I don't enjoy it, and I enjoy(ed) those fantasies. However, I do look forward to having another of the "beat-skips" because I made a deal with myself: if I have it two more times tonight, I'll tell my mom. I had it while watching television before coming to bed, so just one more time. Maybe it'll wake me up. Wouldn't mind a trip to the emergency room in the middle of the night. But it is scary, I guess. I mean, I don't know if it's something like a heart condition, or just the effects of anxiety (which isn't likely 'cause it happens at the most unexpected times).

Just in case:

> Now I lay me down to sleep,
> I pray the Lord my soul to keep
> If I should die before I wake
> I pray the Lord my soul to take.

35

May 16, 1989

Well it didn't happen in the night, or if it did, it didn't wake me up. I was beginning to think it was all in my imagination until about twenty minutes ago, when it started again. They're like twinges, or gulps, and they're unpleasant. I almost feel like my heart is going to stop beating. It's happened five times in the past twenty minutes. I don't have any energy. But I'm in a good mood, beside feeling shaky and weak before and after each twinge. Well, I guess it really is something. But the question is should I tell my mom now, or wait until evening? If I tell her now, she'll call the doctor's office, and get advice from him. He would probably either tell her to bring me into him today or tomorrow, or tell me to go to the hospital, depending on how serious it may be. If I wait till evening, after our doctor's hours, she would probably take me directly to emergency. And it would be at night – exciting. So I guess I'll wait another couple hours – till after dinner?

I had to tell my mom; it was getting worse and more frequent. She called the doctor, and he said (I talked to him) that what it is was palpitations, and they are not dangerous. But to be on the safe side I have an appointment with him tomorrow morning. He said he'll hook me up to a heart-line, or electrocardiograph machine. Wow, that'll be neat. Meanwhile I'm stuck with the hiccupping of the heart. Actually it's a lot better than it was an hour ago when I told her. It was happening three in a row every twenty seconds or so. Now I get light ones, about one every two minutes. My heart rate is 110 a minute, a bit high but nothing terribly abnormal. I bet that once I'm in his office and hooked up to the machine, I'll be absolutely fine.

May 17, 1989

I've only had five light flutters in my chest today. And I probably won't have any tomorrow. So it really is unlikely that it's serious. But it's strange – I feel like something's wrong. I don't feel right. All I want to do is lie on my bed with my sleeping bag over me, like I'm doing now, and keep my hand over my heart, sort of protectively I guess. I feel very peaceful and calm and unflustered, but not particularly cheerful. Not gloomy or anything but unexcited by anything.

* * * * *

36

Tomorrow I face the person I love. And it will be without passion or affection, fervent ardour or warmth. But there's no alternative in this situation; concealment of my fierce longing is my only option. So what is the purpose in going tomorrow? To etch his face and body into my memory so that he will always be there for me in body as well as in spirit? Or to postpone the agony, the inevitable anguish I'm so afraid of becoming a slave to. What this love for him has done to me has as yet been only beautiful and exciting, tranquilly impelling, so that everything positive inside of me is aroused and wanting total rule over my innate pessimism.

But in the background of this virgin wilderness of emotion lurks the knowledge that pain must replace this joy, as night displaces day, and this haunts me with unrelenting persistence, and I wonder how much longer I can withstand the power of reality.

Last night I cried as I watched a man and woman on television make love in a dark room, the light from the fireplace playing over their naked bodies. There is something unexplainably incomprehensible about love, that same something that accounts for love's simultaneous powerful presence and elusive tangibility.

Before I drain myself of passion I must complete an exercise in cadences for my music composition course.

October 11, 1989

Reading through some entries in my old diaries I realize that I came to accept, years ago, the tragic aspects of life. In my songs and poems, there was the presence of a yearning for something besides what we are given and must face, but also a resignation to live with reality, however cold it may be. I wonder now if realizing these kinds of "unpleasant things" about the reality of the situation on this planet rather early altered my outlook from what it would have been if I was an optimistic child. Specifically, did my tendency to view romance as being naturally and inevitably tragic have anything to do with the people I "chose" to fall in love with? When I look back on all the boys I liked, I realize that either I wasn't really friends with any of them (but was boy-girl friend) or nothing ever happened between us. They all resulted in me not really wanting to be around the guy at all after a certain point, or never having the chance to be around him and get to know him at all. In other words, once I get what I dreamed for, it isn't satisfying the way I expected it to be. I no longer want it.

November 3, 1989

The rain is coming down in torrents. I sit in this old wicker chair, facing the window and watching it fall. It's chilly inside, and more bitter outside. I look at the reflection of the grey sky in the wet street and feel like anything is possible, everything so right. Once again I can feel that sweet, shivery joy that reminds one of the possibilities in life. A grey-blue tint to everything, yet a warm glow from inside makes the outside view not harsh at all. It's taken me nearly a year to re-realize this. While old passions and loves are still with me, and will not likely ever leave, something more is here now that can remove the hurt of unfulfilled dreams – something that is more than even love itself, something at the root of everything – the reason for it all. I'm closer to understanding the search. "This is the end of innocence" (from a song on the radio) and the beginning of a different kind. The sky is still grey-blue and rain falls, falls, falls.

November 16, 1989

I had an appointment with the counsellor for a routine grad credit check. Here was my chance to get to know the new counsellor. You know what I did? I spoke in a voice barely above a whisper and answered in monosyllables. He asked me to tell him about myself and all I could say was, "I'm an only child. I live with my mom and stepdad." There were long pauses of silence during our "conversation" which disturbed both of us. We didn't hit it off. He asked me about leaving the International Baccalaureate Program and taking correspondence, and I said what I said to everyone who asks me. Four people asked me today why I dropped out of International Baccalaureate: My chemistry teacher, the principal, and the vice. The last two I met with today to find out if I could get my Grade 11 passport stamp (worth about $175.00 towards university). Neither was sure, so I have to meet with the vice principal again on Monday after he's called the former high school and the Ministry of Education.

Shit, I so wanted to get off on a good start with the counsellor. I wanted to get to the point where I felt comfortable telling him personal things. After all, that's what counsellors are for. And he's definitely a genuinely nice, concerned person, even if this is his first year counselling teens. I thought that maybe, just maybe, I could at some point tell him about the knowing dreams and flashes. Who else could I tell? I need to get someone's assurances that I'm not weird or crazy. I want to ask someone what I should do with what I have. It feels like I've been dumped with a neat toy but no instruction manual, and the game is rapidly turning into a nightmare. When I wake up I force all memories of my dreams out of my mind, and I no longer try to "un-concentrate" to pass messages or impulses to people. But things still manage to happen, like last weekend at Carolyn's for dinner. Her stepdad told me he had a dream about me being pregnant, Friday night. That was the night I babysat my baby niece, and did a lot of thinking about motherhood and aunthood. And during a Japanese dinner with my mom a couple of weeks ago, I was thinking about this guy that I love and suddenly out of the blue, she tells me about her mad crush on an older guy in university, and how it never worked out. If only I could find someone who knew about this sort of thing and could talk to me about it and sympathize with me; above all, point me in the right direction. So this unproductive session with the counsellor resulted in me letting myself down.

"Writing a diary and saving it was an act of faith and an act of optimism, for it implies that Virginia (Woolf) believed that it had worth and it might serve some future purpose. ... Keeping the diaries which she has written was her way of shaping how she or someone else would write her life."

Louise DeSalvo

Chapter Three

Age Seventeen

December 23, 1989
Age 17

A few days ago, on the bus, I watched a man die. He was very old, and just keeled over. The bus driver left to call an ambulance. Most of the passengers got off to find another bus. The only person left was a man holding up the head of this old, dying man in the back of the bus, keeping his head from touching the slimy floor or cold metal armrest. I went over to them and knelt in front of the old man. The younger guy was taking his pulse. I asked him if there was a pulse, and he shook his head. The old man's eyes were open only a bit and his mouth was open a crack, his tongue wanting to slide out. I then felt the man's wrist, dead, lifeless, what?! I shook his shoulder and said, "Can you hear me?" Dead? I got up and sat in the seat facing them. I know CPR but no, this isn't right. Not on this old man. Then one last goodbye: a long gasp, flutter of eyelids, shudder of body, and he was very dead. I could hear the sirens now. I quickly stood up and got off the bus as fast as I could. It affected me so much I cried the rest of the way downtown. I felt wrong and peculiar for a couple of days until I mentioned it to Vicky and discovered that nearly the same thing had happened to her just recently, and it had affected her similarly.

* * * * *

I'm so depressed. I feel like moving out of the house – moving to Australia. As far away as possible. Start all over again. Forget him. But I can't, and I can hear God laughing at me for getting myself into a mess I can't get out of; I fell in love with him. It was my doing. If I'd tried hard I could have ignored the feelings, but I chose to nurture them with all the naïve, headstrong passion a teenage can muster. Now I'm paying for it with another feeling that's new to me: desolation. Night after night. I no longer want to go to bed. Sleep is death in disguise and the "knowing" dreams come then. Nothing of him, ever. I only dreamed of him once or twice in all (about him at my dad's and me taking a photograph, once). I never saw him after our "chance" meeting at Nanaimo and 1st Avenue, and I never spoke to him after that night I took the first aid exam. So the last time I saw him he smiled at me, and the last words I said to him were "I'm sorry."

I realized while brushing my teeth that it would be kind of a strange situation for he and I to get to know each other. I can imagine going to dinner and talking, but I can't say that we'd find a whole lot to talk about. We might hit it off great; we might not. This is not to say that this love is physical attraction; what I love about him is what I see when I look inside him through his eyes, and how it makes me feel. I know I'd love to spend time around him, with him. But friendship has to be two-ways, and he might not have found me interesting or his type. We still could have tried it out, tried a friendship. It might not have worked out. Even if he agreed to try, agreed to meet me at Grandview Park, it wouldn't necessarily be "happily ever after."

I don't know why I never thought about this before. I guess I've been concerned with it on a different, more emotional, spiritual level. God, Lara, you're simply never practical, are you. And of course this would have been what he would have been thinking after reading the letter. "How do we know we have anything in common? How can we be sure we'd become friends? Wouldn't it likely be a failure?" My answer to this is simply, "I know it would work somehow because, somehow, I know you and I know I love you." This is really not adequate of course. If I'd looked at it from his point of view I would have written the letter rather differently, maybe suggesting we meet for lunch at a café on Commercial Drive and talk for a bit to see if we could strike up a friendship. How aggressive and intimidating a come-on my letter must have seemed to him, me merely presuming that if he would come to Grandview Park we would get to know each other and fall instantly in love and want to spend the rest of our lives together. Although I didn't say exactly that, the way I worded much of the letter I'm afraid it sounded like that. I regret, now, coming on so strong and so sure of myself, of us. I didn't ask him if he'd like to try building a friendship, I asked him if he'd agree to having a friendship. There is more than a fine line between the two. There is a big difference.

But all this doesn't mean it would have turned out differently if I had written the letter differently. Even if I had made it clear that it was a friendship I wanted to try for and nothing more (I should have realized that if he already has a girlfriend I wouldn't have a hope in hell) he would still, naturally, have been hesitant at doing something so impulsive and potentially risky. Now that I've thought of it realistically, I actually feel better. It's not so much feeling that I've been rejected personally, as feeling that my approach was not quite right for someone rational and down-to-earth. I still have to deal with the fact that I can never have him. (I hate that possessive "have" in there, but how else do I put it?) That letter was a good thing for me to do (for myself) because it substantiated his refusal so that it was something definite, nearly concrete. Otherwise I wouldn't ever have been able to accept the fact that HE doesn't want ME, because I would never let myself fully believe it. And it allowed me to accept the rejection on a less personal level, by putting some of the blame on the letter and not me. (After all, if I could write like Shakespeare I could attract anyone.) So now it's just unfulfilled desire – only a desire – one that is more powerful than any other I've ever experienced.

December 29, 1989

Just the physical act of writing makes it enjoyable and meaningful to me. Little squiggles, scratching pen on paper, across the page then back, and another line, circles and half circles and crosses and strokes. I remember when I couldn't yet print and I wanted so much to be able to because there was something magical and powerful about written language, I knew. I would fake it with little figures and symbols, showing my mom sentences.

Once I learned to write, I tried inventing my own alphabet and language. Kawiakee (or Mush as I called it earlier but everyone laughed so I changed the name) was more than a secret code for me. From twenty-six letter symbols and a number system and a few basic words, an entire world came into being. I could write in here for hours about Kawiakee, there was so much to it. I fantasized and dreamt about it, wrote stories (and an attempted novel) set in it, gave myself a Kawiakee name, put together a life-story of myself (never wrote it down) about actually being born there before Goshiba (the Being, or God I guess you'd say in English) transferred me to this world. So my search for "Why am I here?" came to be "Why was I put here?" Kawiakee culture was as real to me as my own world's, and so much more acceptable to me because it included the good points of this planet's cultures and excluded the bad or destructive points. It was perfection at its most believable, a delicate balance between reality and Utopia with innocence as the scales. Needless to say it doesn't work for me anymore. But that's just it: things now have to "work," and only concrete things work. I've lost so much as I've progressed through my first seventeen years of life, and even if I could, I wouldn't want it back which is nice and also a damn fucking shame.*

January 8, 1990

... I've subconsciously ignored the "knowing" dreams and flashes for years; as a science student I am very aware of the difficulty, practical impossibility of reconciling something like clairvoyance with logic and science. How can I, at my studies, think scientifically, but with regard to myself think in a different, more open, less rationalized way? I can't separate my working self from feeling self. I'll have to find some common ground where each self is acceptable to the other, but I don't know how yet. Silly of me to think I could find direction from the counsellor. And I doubt I would have felt comfortable talking with the other counsellor, either. What I need for advice is someone I know already, who has experienced the kinds of things I have. But what does one do? Advertise? Walk around saying "Hi, have you had clairvoyant experiences recently? If so, let's talk." People keep things to themselves, because I guess they think others don't experience it and so wouldn't understand. I'd have to get lucky and get a hint from someone in a conversation, that I could follow up with some questions. But how ridiculous of me – if we have ESP or whatever, why not communicate that way? I've tried and have been successful sending feelings or requests (simple things) to people, so why not try something a little more complex? But it goes in circles. I'm so unsure of myself in this because I have no advice on what to do, how to do it. How do I do it?

January 21, 1990

To be able to see the structure of it all, the web of seemingly tangled strands – people's lives, spirituality, morality – is like nothing else because it is a glimpse of the "Understanding."

But still it seems as if human happiness was not meant to fit in with the structure of things (an idea put into words in a recent Woody Allen movie, "Crimes and Misdemeanors"). Yet happiness is what we live for, strive for. Single-celled organisms have been doing fine for millions of years, without needing to experience happiness or presumably any other emotion and they "fit in." But we have only existed for the last couple

---

* At this point in the journal are some sentences written in her special code, signed Ayesha Cema-cusha, which is the name she gave herself. - Ed.

46

seconds of the geological hours (or days, or whatever) and what a mess we've made. And we live for happiness and think we're so superior because of our ability to experience emotion, and of course because of our so-called intelligence. We're not really a lucky quirk of fate, are we. We're more like an unsuccessful experiment, or a mistake of chance.

And yet, in my human selfishness, I would not give up my chance to live and experience and feel, for anything.

January 27, 1990

Yesterday, my best friend, Jan, and I spent hours at the University of British Columbia (UBC), going from building to building and sitting in on some classes, at the back of the lecture hall. We checked out the Student Union Building, ate lunch in the cafeteria there, tried to look inconspicuous and failed dismally (we carried no bags), enjoyed every little moment of it. What a place! I can't wait! I'm glad we got a preview yesterday, not only because it excited me about next year but because that may be the longest time Jan and I will ever get to spend together there (chances are we won't have any classes together).

It'll be so different, and I know that once I'm there high school will seem like only a dream, a distant, insignificant event. It's real! I actually WILL be going to university in a few months; taking biology, chemistry, physics, calculus, and English. I still haven't decided whether to enter the honours program or not. I don't really have to decide until my second year, but if I think I might try it, I should take enriched biology and calculus classes. I don't know if I want to heap even more stress on myself during my first year there, but if I plan to go for my Master's it's best that I enter the honours program. Specialization, and early, is important to me. I know what I'm interested in and I don't want to waste time.

February 2, 1990

Less than a week? It feels like I've been putting off writing in here for longer than that. I kept waiting until I was in an emotional enough state to make what was happening in my life seem dramatic. But it's all melodrama – I'm doomed to lead a life of melodrama.

Rain, snow, rain constantly without an hour of peace from wetness. How can one help but be disappointed with life much of the time? If human life was so wonderful, why has it done so much wrong to other life? How come we have so much at our fingertips but can't seem to put it to good use? Why are we so self-centered and selfish, why is that human nature? School is a disappointment because more of the answers are within the grasp of the very ordinary people called teachers; we are our own teachers, we learn from what we experience, and school does its best to prevent meaningful experience from ever finding us; that's why they confine us in plain rooms, within dark hallways, inside dead buildings with their stale air. The only reason I like Grade 12 is this: it's relatively so much more relaxed and interesting than the previous years. It's far from meaningful, though. University will be a real change, because with specialization comes a sense that it is worthwhile, things are being accomplished, concepts learned and understood. No time for trivial matters unrelated to one's studies. My Castalia awaits me, and it unnerves me to think of how much it appeals to me even though I doubt I'm the kind of person who could study for eight years (EIGHT MORE YEARS?!) at an institution. And my goal? To learn how to play my own glass bead game, I guess: reach a level of understanding and acceptance that everything begins to fall into place, together; to come to the realization that everything is really one thing, somehow, some way.

February 8, 1990

Another week stretches into a lifetime. Why then is the year going by so fast anyway?

Someone asked me how old I am today. I was at a loss for a moment before I remembered and answered 17. Sometimes I feel as if I'm as old as I can get. This week and especially today I've felt so heavy and listless, so lacking in energy I wonder if I actually sleep at night; this kind of tiredness doesn't usually accompany nights of decent sleeping. I'm not alone, however: many of my friends say they feel a similar kind of exhaustion. In the last couple of weeks we have taken the usual number of tests and had the usual amount of homework, but (suddenly, it seems) so much else is being heaped on us – copies of old scholarship exams given to us for study, math and chemistry and essay-writing contests to sign up for and take; university and college applications submitted; time approaches to start worrying about scholarships to UBC, Simon Fraser University, University of Victoria., etc.; tours of campuses; the January provincials being talked about. (We didn't take them; they're for semester-run schools. But they are a reminder of the fast-approaching exams in June which are so incredibly important.)

* * * * *

I keep the radio on all the time, to let the music drown out my discomfort and my painful thoughts. I hate being around people at home (at school I don't mind) so I stay in my room as much as possible, even declining invitations to join the adults downstairs. I eat my meals separately from my mom and her partner, or at least in front of the television, away from them. I'm not an adult, I'm not a teen anymore and I just don't belong. I don't have time just now to find a place where I belong; there's too much to prepare for in my mind, the future is nearly tangible and I have to get what there is together so that I am ready when it happens. Deciding takes so much time and energy. Who will I be four years from now? The way the school system and society in general are set up, I have to decide this now, or at least before June.

February 24, 1990

I brought my soup upstairs with the excuse that I had to keep working on literature homework, but really I just don't want to sit with my mom and her partner and eat lunch. I'm back in that low, bitter, listless mood. It's my own fault, I let myself sink deeper and deeper into agonizing depression by refusing to concentrate on homework and household tasks that have to get done. Those things usually keep my mind occupied, so I don't keep going back over things that mean so much, that changed me and made me want more.

But here I am puttering about without really doing anything, staring into the murky green depths of my pea soup and not even being able to feel angry, only despairing and frustrated. It might help if I could pinpoint the reason for this mood, but all I can figure out is that it has something to do with unrequited love and something to do with the grey misty rain and calling seagulls. I wish I had an older sister to talk to on rainy Saturdays when I can't stop the memories from cruelly flooding back.

March 5, 1990

I think I'm more sensitive to love in all its forms – from my cat's intermittent adoration of me to Jan's infatuation with a Grade 11 "fob" to the long-lasting, unconditional love between my mom and her partner. Each must be treated with equal respect and each can lead to a new understanding.

49

I am more aware of a longing to be "grown-up," an adult, and I find myself trying to achieve that on the outside by the way I dress and behave, but I still know that accomplishes nothing. Maturity can't be bought or imitated.

I'm not perfect; I can't excel in everything. But there are areas in which I have ability and, more importantly, a very strong desire to pursue meaning and truth – to understand the gene and the human, to find a solution to some problems, ONE problem even, that we vulnerable beings face. But another responsibility accompanies this: if I help the human race it must be to let us help the rest of the world, and not to allow us to continue to exploit what we mistakenly view as ours, as if all other living things are inferior to us.

I seek some sort of enlightenment and believe it will come with gaining of maturity. I study day after day and dream of winning scholarships; I worry and agonize over all the possibilities of failure that exist in all of one's life.

Sometimes I wonder if any answers lie in my "knowing" dreams, but still am unsure how to begin to search. Basically happy, very interested in the world expanding (in my eyes) to encompass me, and awed by what one can see when one looks with open eyes and an open mind.

April 26, 1990

What bugs me all day and night, every day, is the fact that I cannot (am not able to and must not) express my feelings to these people I admire and love so much. I end up feeling sorry for myself, which is just another form of selfishness. Am I doomed to fall in love or feel devotion for people whom I can't communicate with because of age differences, circumstances, or my shyness?

What I'm trying to say is that what I really, really would like is a friendship with a guy – not a physical sort of thing, but a close friendship – and I'm no good at making friends. It's this that makes me so depressed at times, not bombing exams or worrying about schoolwork.

What to do?

May 12, 1990

I've reached my limit. I am absolutely sick of studying hard every single night, I'm tired of this obsession with letter grades and percentages, I don't care about scholarships. I want to give up on English and biology because the teachers are impossible. I wish this could happen a month from now. This is the most important month of all, and I just had to give up caring about school now. The year was going so great, I was enjoying school, I took pride in keeping up with homework, correspondence work, the Environment Club, band, and even a social life. And then, pretty suddenly actually, that motivation and drive were gone. It began with bombing a biology test – I got 40/50 while I usually get 47 or 48. And it was a subject that interests me: the nervous system. WHY have I lost whatever it was I had? Most of my close friends lost it before Grade 12; I think a year by correspondence helped to extend it to now for me.

Who gives a shit if I get 80% instead of 95% on the finals? I think the only thing that can keep me caring about my courses is my love of my teachers. It feels unbelievable good to get an interim report in the mail from my chemistry teacher, with a handwritten comment ("Well done, Lara. Keep up the excellent effort!") from a man I respect tremendously and whose opinion I value greatly. A "Wow" (also handwritten) by the vice principal on the same interim was nice, too, although a bit ironic. It wasn't too long ago that I received a phone call (two, actually) from him about missing an algebra class or two. Does he know who I am? Has he made the connection? Or does it matter to him that he makes a comment like, "Super results from a fine young lady" about the same person he checked up on last month because she skipped class? But the praise for my hard work that I get from other teachers IS genuine, and so it means a lot to me. Heck, even my French teacher congratulated me on an interim for being the top student in French 11, and I spend about an hour a week on French homework. But the course I truly try in, algebra, is the one that I'm least good at, naturally. I've worked so hard to excel in that course, and it's paid off: I have a really good grasp of the material, and I know I'm well prepared for math next year, plus I've tied for top place in algebra with a future engineer, who verges on genius. I've got 98% in algebra, 96% in biology, 93% in chemistry, 96% in French, about 91% in physics (by correspondence), 87% in literature, and 88% in English. I've reached my peak; I have the top percentages in all my school courses. The only way I can go now is down.

And I'm sick and tired of this obsession with marks and being the best. It's ridiculous, self-centered, narrow-minded, and dangerously competitive. I've given it up, except maybe in algebra. I still haven't got any recognition from my algebra teacher, not even a "good effort" which is all I want. I mean, you can't count the hardworking, conscientious, responsible, outstanding student – blah blah crap that's straight off a list of computerized comments. That's a matter of picking a number or two that corresponds to the student's letter grades and filling in a computer sheet for the report card. He may do that in his sleep for all I know. I would simply LOVE a little genuine attention from a man I think is wonderful in every respect – and yet mysterious, enigmatic in an exciting way. He's a regular Mr. Rochester. It's funny, Jan likes him very much, too, and she goes about getting his attention in a totally different method: she listens to a Walkman and eats during class, she doesn't do her algebra or geometry homework until the night before the test, she is totally open around him, she leaves class in the middle of the hour to go to the washroom and doesn't come back until the end of class (but then we all do that), she regularly skips his classes, and she admits, unabashedly, to doing all this – right to his face. Is she successful with her method? Yes.

But I don't want him to notice me as a wild and unconcerned student. Maybe dedication and hard work is just too boring to be noticed. I'm not bitter at all, I just want his attention very much. I admit it's for selfish reasons.

Something else much more significant than all this happened Friday at school when I left literature class to go to the washroom. I passed by the first aid room on my way to meet Jan (she was going to get out of accounting so we could bum around before lunch) and like I always do, I peeked in. You never know what may be going in the nurse's room; it's one of my favourite places. Well what do you know, there's a man sitting where Nurse-What's-Her-Name usually is, and he looked like someone I had a crush on, very tall, not a heavy build, light brown hair, fine bone structure and facial features, and lovely eyes. Of course it should have come as no surprise since before I went to sleep the night before, I had an anticipatory flash of seeing a man instead of a woman in the first-aid room. But I was stunned nonetheless, and had to walk by the room several more times in the next ten minutes. Then, in the afternoon I left class to go to the washroom, this time missing English (my teacher must think I have chronic diarrhea). Passing by the first-aid room, I tried to look in nonchalantly but of course utterly failed and ended up in eye-contact with the mysterious man in the chair. It didn't last long, but I felt something. He wasn't nonchalant about it either, I could tell from his eyes. Maybe he just wondered who the heck this girl was who kept strolling by with neck craned towards him. But maybe not. I beckoned to Jan to leave geometry and come talk to me, but she was totally involved with someone on her Walkman so I ended up going into the classroom from the back entrance and yakking with her inside – the teacher had finished the lesson and he's used to me doing that.

*****

Newsflash: a police stakeout is occurring a few houses down the street which I can see outside my window. Just heard my mom whisper it to her partner, then lock our door. Just another evening in the Downtown Eastside.

May 19, 1990

I think the letter-grade system should be abolished. It wouldn't work at first, I guess, because all those students conditioned to study in order to get good grades will have suddenly lost their motivation and their reason for trying hard in school. It would have to be done gradually, making sure that the other reasons for trying hard are made apparent, and also that the courses are interesting and the teachers are good. An interesting and enjoyable course that seems worthwhile and relevant will give a student all the motivation he needs. Forget exams, grades, competition; forget who's top of the class, who's class dunce, forget the Bell curve. Forget the reward system of high marks and praise for high achievers and the punishment system of low marks and lectures for low achievers. It should be obvious that we all learn at different rates and in different ways; the grade system discourages the slow learners and gives meaningless rewards to the quick ones. Any teacher will admit that the system is not all that fair, but more importantly, it's useless and harmful. People who love numbers and love excelling may be tricked into accepting the system and even making it the guiding force in their academic lives (as I have) and people who don't like numbers and who are creative and not "textbook people" may be turned off by it so much that they fail, rebel, or drop out. Whichever type of person it is, he or she loses out on a real education.

May 24, 1990

Who gives a sh_ _ about the attendant/nurse. It seems like that silly fiasco happened an eternity ago, in a dream, and now I've woken up. After 17 years. I'm not sure I want to write about the last two days, but I don't want to go to sleep and face nightmares so I'll give it a shot. Sorry if it's jumbled and in fragments.

It began yesterday evening. This is the part I least want to put onto paper, but if I don't the rest won't make sense. I have to write something. This guy, actually a man in his thirties (I think) and I went out for dinner last night. I don't want to mention his name or anything just yet, but he is a close (and long-time) friend of the family so going to dinner with him was like going to dinner with an uncle. I always thought of him as a really nice person, just one of the warmest and most pleasant people I know. Well, my mom and her partner were both out yesterday and all of last night too, so after the dinner which was pleasant and uneventful, we returned to the house. I need to sleep now, so I'll finish later.

May 28, 1990

Couldn't bring myself to write about the rest. I've made my mind up to just do it.

Back at home, I told him I had a lot of homework to do, and I went to my room. After a while he came into the room, I guess because he was on his way to the guest room (in my mom's studio) where he would be sleeping that night. He walked over to me, and I thought he was looking at the homework I was working on. But he wasn't. He asked, "Would it be rude if I kissed you goodnight?" I thought he meant a little kiss on the forehead or cheek, a fatherly sort of gesture. But he didn't; he pushed his lips so hard against mine that my neck hurt trying to keep my head steady. The awful feeling, the rude force of his lips, just disgusted me. It seemed to last forever; it was no peck on the cheek. It was a long, forceful, demanding kiss that said, "I want you." After he pulled himself away, he made some gross satisfied sound like a heavy sigh and went to his room. I was so surprised that I couldn't do the next algebra problem, an easy one. Anyhow I couldn't see through my tears.

In the morning (after a fitful sleep, worried the whole time about being alone in the house with him) before I left for school and he left, he said goodbye to me with a hug. He moved his hands down my sides, keeping one hand just above my hip with gentle pressure as he spoke to me.

That day at school was the craziest I've ever had. First block I had to write a chemistry test, a major one and quite difficult. I lasted for ten minutes, then the awfulness of what had happened to me (Christ, he's a married man and a close friend of my mom) struck me and I got this sick feeling in my stomach which spread all over, to my chest and head and arms and legs. Couldn't think properly, couldn't stand it. I left the room. My seat is next to the door so no one, not even the teacher, noticed I'd gone. I took a drink from the fountain in the hall, and paced back and forth hoping the feeling would go away. I stopped and leaned against a locker, and everything seemed to be slipping away, my grades, my family, my body, my life; nothing was important. This feeling overpowered everything else and I saw for the time how brutal reality can be. I didn't know how to face it, stand up to it. Another teacher happened to walk by then, and he stopped to chat. I tried my best to hide my horrible state and appear normal, but soon I slipped to the floor and he was asking me what was wrong and what had I eaten for breakfast and if it was cramps. Like a real baby, I just moaned quietly and whispered, "I don't know, I don't know." I'd lost total control.

June 23, 1990

I didn't receive a major entrance scholarship from UBC. For the past month, every day I get home from school I hope and pray for a letter from UBC – I wanted a scholarship so badly, one that would cover the first four years so I wouldn't have to worry myself or my mom about money these next few years. But even with my "A" average and top academic standing and excellent letters of support from teachers, I guess I just didn't qualify. Fuck, I even scored high on all the prize exams I wrote. WHY??!? Why don't I get a scholarship??? Okay, I'm selfish and greedy and demanding and immodest, but I THINK I DESERVED ONE.

I still have a chance at the smaller scholarships (winners will be announced in August I think). But God I've been depressed about it. They said winners will be notified by June 15th, and when that day came and there was no mail for me, I felt like such a failure.

It's nice to know that my family and teachers don't think I'm a failure; they're proud of my small achievements and haven't even mentioned the fact that I didn't win anything big. They're probably more realistic.

June 28, 1990

Here I am, lying on my bed and unable to sleep because I'm so tired (?!?!?) and simultaneously bubbling with emotion just the way I hoped my family wouldn't be at the ceremony. Now I'm crying, for the second time since grad. My family was very proud of me – grandma gave me such a long, fierce hug and they all kept congratulating me. (For what? I forgot I haven't mentioned the ceremony.)

I received an achievement pin for being on the honour roll every year, a $2000 scholarship from the Overseas Chinese Voice newspaper, the gold medal (not real gold of course) for being the top student (academically) and along with that the Governor General's Bronze Medal. It still hasn't sunk in yet that I graduated at the top of my class. I'm so happy! But the fact that UBC didn't give me a four year scholarship puts a cloud over my awards, in my opinion.

I often wish I could trade my natural intelligence for natural friendliness; I wish I could be truly "sympa" as the French say because people are so much more important than letter-grades and academic awards. I admire all the winners of service awards so much.

You know, for that $2000 award, they mentioned I was the top student in all my courses but they said nothing about my being on the badminton team, in the band every year I've been at high school, and in the Environment Club. For practically everyone else they mentioned extracurricular stuff ("so and so is not just an excellent student but a good citizen as well...") and I'm kind of ticked off they overlooked that in my case. I guess because the extracurricular stuff took a lot of effort since it's academics I'm good at.

July 13, 1990

Maybe I can somehow locate a psychiatrist who deals especially with the paranormal. But I want to talk to someone who knows me, and will believe me. That of course is vital. I can't get anywhere if the person doesn't believe me, except an insane asylum. Anyhow, I can't afford a psychiatrist. Better to find someone who was once in the same situation I'm in, so he or she can relate to my situation and help me understand all this and make use of this potential.

I won't be able to put my own self aside in order to help others until I understand myself. How can I possibly get anywhere near the "Understanding" until I have a clearer picture of my role in it all? They're definitely connected somehow. At least that's what I'm hoping.

July 19, 1990

I've been purposefully depriving myself of sleep these past few days (up until last night when I indulged in ten hours) simply because it brings back the way it felt to be in Grade 12. To hear the alarm go off and feel so sleepy yet be able to smile because I know the day will be worth the effort. Studying (or, in this case, reading) until dawn and realizing another day has begun and I've been there, watching it begin. I get a strange, masochistic pleasure from sleep deprivation. Ironic, considering how much I complained all my school life about insomnia. Now, if I don't sleep, it's my own choice and that makes all the difference.

I borrowed some books from the library on the paranormal and clairvoyance. One is actually the diary of a very clairvoyant boy living in Victorian England, and another is about a man who, after much inner struggle, finally came to accept his psychic abilities and make use of them. The others are discussions about clairvoyance and case histories. I didn't borrow anything that was arguing for or against psychic powers, since I already know they exist. Funny that I know SOMETHING that hundreds, even thousands of scientists are currently trying to prove or disprove. How ridiculous; what a waste of time. Clairvoyance exists. Period. Anyhow, this reading has been super for me. I had an interesting experience yesterday night, which I'll have to describe later since my mom needs help in her studio now.

August 21, 1990

I am very seriously considering medicine for a profession. I keep wavering back and forth, but the last while at work* has boosted my confidence regarding "people skills" and stress endurance. I'm coping with the sudden change in hours, the exhaustion upon getting home at 6:30 p.m. after having been up and going strong since 6:30 a.m., the interaction, constant interaction with co-workers and others on campus, and the challenge of new tasks that require new skills, which must be learned quickly and on the spot. It's not like school. I think I've had my mind set on research because that would resemble school. But medicine is a totally different world. I'm so eager to explore it.

Here's a possible plan: three or four years of undergraduate studies in biochemistry (specializing in genetics and/or immunology); apply to medical school; assuming I get in, four years of theory and clinical education, a year of whatever it is of internship, as soon as possible working in emergency; a residency in emergency; finally working there as a doctor; either staying in that specialty, changing areas (e.g. into

---

* The summer work was in the Supplies Department, Chemistry Building at the University of British Columbia. - Ed.

family practice), or going into research. I know that ultimately I will do research. But I've read that the vast majority of medical researchers are doctors working in either a hospital or at a university and conducting research IN ADDITION to practicing medicine or teaching. So becoming a doctor would be a very appropriate route to enter the field of research.

The thing is, emergency medicine is my real love, and I don't know how many medical schools and hospitals consider that a specialty yet. From its calendar it doesn't appear UBC trains emergency physicians. Another thing, I've heard that emergency physicians are surgeons. Whether or not I want to go into surgery is something I have not considered at all. But maybe not all hospitals operate that way. If I can find a medical school well-known for its emergency aspects of training, I'll consider all this further. I'm going to write to McGill and ask for information on their medical school.

September 1, 1990

I have moderate-sized ovarian cysts. The strange thing is, it's halfway through your cycle that cysts can rupture and cause pain. I rarely have much pain during ovulation. But these cysts are all we can blame for now. If medical research weren't dominated by men, you can bet we'd know more about dysmenorrhea and what causes it. The one good thing that has come from this monthly experience is that I don't take health for granted. That's probably spurred my interest in medicine. I understand the fear of pain; not what is assumed to be a cowardly, unfounded fear, but the desperation associated with pain that worsens and worsens.

There has to be a limit to the amount of pain that is bearable; can a human stay alive through pain that is extremely intense? I've felt like I'm dying; not like I WANT to die, but like I am past the point where I can survive such agony. It's a feeling of barely being conscious, feeling like a prisoner to the pain, trapped inside it, inside your body. Wishing it were possible to separate yourself from your body, to leave your physical self which at the moment is synonymous with pain.

From whatever illness, pain is something that can and should be alleviated if at all possible. Even if doctors can't cure a person, providing comfort through medicine and compassion is, in my mind, a noble profession.

Someday I'm going to be a doctor. I know that medical school and residency will be the toughest experience of my life, but I'm not afraid as

58

I used to be. I've ALWAYS wanted to be a doctor, but I never let myself believe it would ever happen, because I was afraid of failing, of burning out, of regretting my decision, and scariest of all, realizing after seven years of university that I didn't really want to practice medicine after all. Well now I know I do want to, and I'm no weakling; I may burn out, but I have as good a chance as the next guy.

October 9, 1990

That's it. Life stinks. I can't believe how cruel it is. There really is no reason to anything.

I had an awful "knowing" dream last night. It left an awful impression on my mind throughout the day of imminent disaster. Finally, two minutes ago, the disaster struck. The studio where my mom stores all her art burnt down tonight. It's all gone. My mom's art, her life, her self. I can't stand it.

I feel nice and sick. My mom must feel so bad. But it's hard to tell, because it's like she's a different person after the fire. Part of herself as a person was lost along with her art, I think.

The word "unfair" keeps leaving my lips as I mumble to myself. But of course the word "fair" doesn't exist in the real world. They shouldn't allow it to be in the dictionary. I'm so mad about the fire. By the way, it made the front page of the newspaper because it was a really big fire; it started in a rooming house next to the studio.

November 17, 1990

I inadvertently insulted my two favorite professors on Friday (to their faces). I was being careless and selfish. While walking to chemistry I told a friend all about how utterly boring chemistry has been. The professor was right behind me when I said it.

In English, our instructor was handing back our essays on poetry and when I picked up mine she said to me, "That was a really great paper, here," and was going to continue, but I cut her off, saying "thank you" and leaving the room. She had given me an A+. She was complimenting me. She was being friendly – we would often chat before class started. She's so nice. Why in hell did I do that? Did it give me some perverse pleasure to be cold to her? I wanted to be friends with her, and she was giving me a chance. We could have talked. I blew the opportunity and I can't figure out why I was so stupid and mean.

You know, I really doubt I'll get accepted into medical school. I'll blow the interview. I'm an obvious failure face to face with others – what makes me think I'd be a good doctor for Christ's sake??! I've been reading my previous diaries and I'm up to Feb. 1988. What a joke my life has been. Absolutely meaningless – I never did anything worthwhile. I was always so self-centered. My concerns were so insignificant and still are. Boyfriends and grades, is that all I've been living for these past eighteen years? Shit.

My life has been one big escape from reality. What would you think if I told you this diary, all of my diaries, are one big lie? Maybe they are. I don't know who I am, if I have any right to think the way I do. Do I even exist? I used to think my diaries were my most valuable possessions, but now I'd like to burn them. Maybe this is their end. Stories are supposed to have a beginning and an ending. I began ten years ago. This can't go on forever.

"The voices of exiled survivors are frequently not heard. Many of them point to ways in which limited definitions of incest and shifting public policy work to exclude – in fact, to exile – what women experience as a continuum of intimacy and abuse."

Mary Lynn Broe

Chapter Four

Age Eighteen

December 8, 1990
Age 18

I couldn't live without my night world – in the past week I've dreamed about practicing medicine, meeting a couple of guys I had a crush on, but only vaguely. Also had the most frightening dream of my life – it wasn't what happened that was scary, though. For some reason, I was absolutely terrified; I don't remember ever feeling so afraid before, awake or asleep. Part of the dream was a car chase, and the other part was me and my mom trying to get away from a man in a large crowd. I was pulling her along by the arm, trying to get her to go faster, but there were so many people around us that I couldn't move fast myself. The man was getting closer to us and suddenly I realized that he had hold of my mom's other arm so that I was, in effect, pulling him along after us. He locked. my gaze and I couldn't look away; he was smiling and repeating over and over, "We don't talk too much, we don't talk too much." Just saying that to myself now scares me, and it doesn't make a bit of sense! He had a pretty nondescript face but I think I would recognize the expression and the look in his eyes if I saw him again. His hair was wavy and greyish, and he was just unshaven enough to look shaggy, or rather, shabby. When I woke up from the dream (in the middle of the night), I lay in bed for some time totally freaked out.

December 20, 1990

What an incredible day it's been. Wow! I never thought it would be possible to have such a relaxing, comfortable day. I didn't go outside because of this flu coming on; I spent most of the day on my bed or my chair, wrapped in blankets. What bliss, after three-and-a-half months of chaos. This time has given me a chance to think over my future plans objectively (if that's possible) and without my mind cluttered with copious amounts of semi-useful information. I've decided that at the present time, I DO still want to be a doctor. The problem is in how to combined medical practice and research; what kind of education would be best for a researcher/practitioner? The M.D.-Ph.D. program would be ideal except that I think it's especially for those who plan to eventually teach as well. I hate teaching, and I think I'll be busy enough with research and practice. Also, the schedule of interrupting your medical school education to get your Ph.D., then returning to medicine, doesn't appeal to me. Anyhow, you have to graduate with an Honours B.Sc. with high marks to be accepted into a Ph.D. program without an M.Sc. I'm not sure if I'll be ready to write a thesis in three years. But if I don't get a Ph.D. and just a B.Sc., and not an Honours B.Sc. either, I won't have enough basic science background for research. So maybe the thing to do is to get a M.Sc. before applying to medical school. That would also increase my chances of getting accepted into medicine. But it means waiting six or seven years instead of four before entering medical school. What if I get so preoccupied with biochemistry studies that I lose interest in my distant goal of going into medicine? Maybe that extra time will actually be good, though, in giving me a chance to mature and make a more thought-out decision. But will I get a chance to work in research between the time I earn an M.Sc. and the time I enter medical school? It seems really stupid to spend six years in biochemistry and then go right on to medicine without applying what I learned in biochemistry. But the longer I wait before starting medical school, the older I'll be and I'm afraid I won't be as good at studying or as able to handle the stresses of 100-hour work weeks during internship while I'm older. A 26-year-old is full of energy and has stamina and optimism; a 30-year-old is probably less energetic. Then again, spending your prime years suffering in internship and residency is kind of sad; you miss out on all the normal things adults do at that age. Socializing is almost impossible. Waiting a bit longer before starting medical school would give me a chance to live a bit, and perhaps marry and even start a family, while working as a biochemist. The main problem I have with that is how to deal with my impatience – I WANT TO STUDY MEDICINE RIGHT NOW. And if I want to settle down after medical school, I'll be nearly too old to safely have children, and my social skills will be so lacking that I may not even find a man I want to live with. So I'm screwed either way when it comes to having a family. Women doctors have it really hard in that respect.

December 26, 1990

My mood swings are damn annoying. I'll probably discover, halfway through medical school, that I'm manic-depressive or something. In the last twenty minutes my mood has soared or sunk several times, and I have no idea why. I've been puttering around, doing not much at all, and I was reading earlier. Nothing to make me particularly content or depressed. But here I am, depressed at this particular moment. I felt quite happy when I picked up my diary to write, and seconds later for no apparent reason, I felt grumpy. Life sucks.

No, it doesn't, of course. Things really couldn't get much better, I don't think. There are no sarcastic overtones here, either. I mean it. For one thing I'm on holiday. For another, I'm at the age when you're old enough to be fully trusted by family to stay out late when you want with whomever you want and basically to have control over your life, but you're still provided with food, shelter, and support. I do contribute a little bit financially to the household and I help with some meals and cleaning, but a lot is done for me and given to me for free. It's an ideal situation, but it can't last for too long. Eventually I'll feel guilty about this freeloading and, hopefully, independent enough to live on my own. That will probably happen in two years or so. For now, I'll enjoy it.

School is ideal too. Well, close to ideal. I feel really confident about how I did on my exams, and in fact I checked out my calculus mark (the only subject for which marks are posted yet) and it appears I got 100% on the exam, but that seems crazy so there must have been some scaling done.

December 31, 1990
Last day of 1990 and of this decade

I woke up at noon today, had breakfast and a bath, and did some chores, and now I have the rest of the day to myself – ah, bliss. Another week of this leisure. I wouldn't want it to last much longer than that since it's too easy to take it for granted and become permanently lazy, and also since I want to get back to UBC. I just remembered that I handed in an essay on Atwood's "The Handmaid's Tale" the last day of Term 1, and the instructor said she'd have these essays marked by the first day of Term 2. I'm very curious as to what she thinks of this essay I wrote. In my opinion, it's too long (well over the 600-word limit, and that's after deleting large portions of it), some ideas are a bit radical, and I tend to go off topic. But I go off topic in such an interesting manner that I can't believe she'd disapprove. The topic, by the way, is the link between power and language in Gilead. I loved the topic and could have written twenty pages on it. I mentioned Orwell's "1984" and the present state of affairs regarding power and language, and how it was evident that Atwood had drawn from these two things (and, of course, others) in writing her novel. But the topic of the essay wasn't really supposed to be about the novel's relationship to "1984" or how the novel mirrors today's situation more than one might think. I just couldn't resist including these ideas and others which fascinate me. I had a good time writing that essay, a rare thing for an essay-hater.

February 16, 1991

I'm reading "Hamlet" and shit, is it ever amazing. Such full and interesting characters, a hundred times rounder than today's movie characters. Except for the women (Ophelia and Gertrude) whom I find a bit fickle and dull. (I take that back, at least about Ophelia. Her flower scene is one of the most touching and hypocrisy-exposing scenes I've ever read or watched.) With the other plays of Shakespeare I've read, I never became too engrossed in the plot or characters' problems. The conflicts in "Hamlet," however, I find easy to relate to for some reason and I feel so much for him that I sometimes want to burst while reading.

One line particularly touched me: "You cannot take from me anything that I will more willingly part withal; except my life, except my life, except my life." There is such poignancy in those words of Hamlet's as he simultaneously feigns madness and tries to convince himself his life has value, his life which now must be focused on setting right the "disjointed times," and which he suspects he will tragically or deliberately lose in the process anyway. "To die, to sleep; To sleep: perchance to dream: ... in that sleep of death what dreams may come..."

Inspired by my reading and by an in-class essay in English on Friday on the topic of sonnets, I wrote a sonnet yesterday evening. It was so much fun to write, I think I'll write some more if/when I have the time. It's not a good sonnet, of course (I'm no poet) but maybe it's a good imitation of a good sonnet. I wrote it with the intent of trying to make it sound 16th or 17th century, mainly because I want to show it to a couple of friends, pretending that I'm studying it in English, and ask them for advice in interpreting and for their general opinion. It would be interesting to have a discussion about a sonnet which, unbeknownst to the other person, was written by me. I think this is the only way to hear an unbiased opinion on a piece of my own writing. I'd love it if Jan said, "Oh God, not another impossible sonnet – why couldn't those poets write in English? This thing doesn't make a bit of sense." But I might cry if she called it stupid.

Anyway, here it is:

Sonnet #27 (ha ha)

Oh God I have committed crimes far worse
Than have been played by villains on the stage;
Know not how to express my soul's outrage
Except to trouble paper with this verse.
Confined to false illusions and adventures
Created by the mind, I built a cage
To hold compassion, leaving Vice to manage,
So that I cannot feel for those he hurts.
My sin is this: Because from grace we fell,
I loathe all earth, our warring race the more,
For evil comes from even honest merit
And never can peace reign without fierce war.
We men travail to build an earthly hell
Which, though we die, our children shall inherit.

* * * * *

I'm so depressed. I don't let myself admit it; I hide it from everyone because I feel guilty about it, about feeling this way when everything is supposedly so perfect for me. I have everything. More than I want, and that's the problem! I don't want to be insane. Watching the "Twin Peaks" television series gives me a chance to express my pent-up crazed feelings by sharing them with Lynch's strange characters. That's why I always wish I could watch the show alone, without my mom there too. I'm afraid I might do something, like scream or laugh; I can't let out this secret. This diary is going to be, has always been, my place to set down everything I can put into words, and as time goes by I am more and more unable to keep that happy face on and write lovey-dovey, corny stuff. I can't hold it in now so there's going to be more hate in this writing. I hate myself so much. Everything I do, I do because I hate myself and I'm trying to make up for what I've done or not done, trying to redeem myself.

The sonnet says more than I could admit before. It's not just a bunch of poorly-rhymed lines – it existed before I wrote it down; it was always there in my head, ringing in my ears but I don't think anyone would care to interpret it. Donne titled his sonnets "Holy Sonnet 14" etc; mine will be "Insane Sonnet 1" etc. So what. What wonderful difference does it make to the world. I'm so sorry for everything, but how can I ever make up for it all? I feign sanity to simplify life. Hamlet feigned madness to simplify his; so that any outbursts from him when he could no longer hold in his grief and revulsion over his father's murder and mother's betrayal would not be taken as unusual; he would thus not have to hide anything. He so hated the world of "seems."

* * * * *

I have no substance, I'm nothing but this feeling. I'm being dragged down into it. This is what I've been waiting for all this time: the time has come to probe the meaning of the "knowings" and I must leave my physical being to do so. Before I go insane. I dreamed last night that Sally tried to lure me into bed with her, so that we could have intercourse. And also a building was burning. I can't remember the rest. What's going to happen when I go to sleep tonight? Am I going to lose myself? I DO want to. I'm less noble than Hamlet. A ghost informed him of horrors; for me it is a part of myself. I torture myself. I hate myself. Not to be is the only answer in this case. Let it stand. The imagination, the collective imagination has had enough.

I have created such a nice perfect world of "seems" for myself. I just haven't faced anything. The "Understanding" is just a bewildered drabness of no substance or feeling. I've waited so long for this.

When will I get rid of all this?

Why is this happening?

February 18, 1991

I think I'm going to have to study "Hamlet" inside and out: it's going to become my next obsession. Since "Twin Peaks" took many quotes from Shakespeare, especially "Hamlet," it should be a fairly easy transition. And it might even do me good in English 100, as well as in my family's eyes. My aunt is a "Hamlet" expert and my mom abhors my devotion to television shows, whether they're high quality like "Twin Peaks" or mediocre like "Family Ties." Shall I write about how "Hamlet" fascinates me?

He has a goal which he knows must be accomplished for the good of his country, as well as to avenge his father's murder. But the gravity of the situation, and of the result if he carries out his act (i.e. he will have killed a man and he [Hamlet] may go to Hell if his deed is not a righteous one – i.e. if the Ghost is really an evil spirit), prevent him from acting immediately. Well, good; rash acts are rarely fruitful, but Hamlet finds that the longer he waits while weighing the pros and cons and investigating the truth of the Ghost's words, the more conflicting ideas disturb him. His intellect is too cautious and pure (i.e. untainted) to allow his body to carry out such an act as murder. The two women in his life, his mother and his former sweetheart, have in his eyes betrayed him.

As his family structure breaks down and he sees through his relatives' and friends' false exteriors into their seemingly rotten or simply foolish interiors, he also understands the state of political affairs in the country he may one day be responsible for. He feels he is the only one who can admit to the corruption – or maybe it's safer to call it outlandish extravagance and hideous incest – being rooted in Denmark as a result of Claudius' accession to the throne. His mother is not only oblivious to it, she is apparently in love with Claudius and for all Hamlet knows (at least near the beginning of the play), she may have been an accomplice in her former husband's murder. Ophelia is forced into rebuking Hamlet's affection in order for her father and the King and Queen to probe and disrupt Hamlet's personal life in a stupid attempt to prove him mad. The rest of them are sycophants or idiots. It is Hamlet's personal responsibility, burden, to take care of the matter through direct revenge, but the ramifications of his revenge (i.e. the exposure of Denmark's rottenness) are of much broader relevance. But then one comes to the question: what choices does Hamlet really have? Could anything he does wholly solve the broader problem? Will it even cure his inward conflict and disillusionment? Is he the type of person who will never make a situation better but only worse because of his keen perceptive abilities which inevitably bring him so much gloom and indecision? Or would anyone put in his position also have the difficulties he does with focusing energy on action rather than melancholic contemplation? I think he is unique; after all, Shakespeare's characters are rarely anything but.

If that is the case, i.e. if his problems stem from his own character as well as his surroundings, then who are we to judge him? I see no point in criticizing his every action or even trying to sway the interpretation of his character to seem more bold and masculine.

He is who he is. The combination of circumstances of character is tragic, but either one alone is not. And such a situation is bound to end in misfortune. Fortune, or fate, governs the outcome in the end. Hamlet's recognition of this as the end of the play approaches (e.g. "If it be now, 'tis not to come; if it be not to come, it will be now," etc.) is what, I think, gives him the dignity and resolution to finally accomplish what he had intended to do. This might be because the role of fate takes some of the burden off his shoulders and the less pressure helps him to make up his mind; or because he has come to accept the idea of his own death and come to terms with the fact that any former plans he had for personal greatness have dissolved – his death is an inevitable part of the resolution of the conflict. It is necessary: he is necessary. It is his intervention which must restore order, and he MUST intervene. It is not his decision to make (as to whether he acts or not) because the greater design of things is, in actuality, in charge. When he accepts this, he regains his peace of mind, and only then do his thoughts materialize into deeds.

This is my shabby interpretation and is completely open to debate, of course. I may not agree with what I've written in a couple of days, but it's pleasurable to focus my tangled thoughts on someone else's problems. That sounds so heartless.

March 21, 1991

I think I had a "knowing" experience of some sort that was really a connection; connecting me to some broad, all-encompassing force or body of knowledge – like a collective unconscious. I was in bed and was thinking about the movie I'd just watched on television ("Altered States") when I started thinking things, or rather feeling things that had never occurred to me before. They were marvelous ideas about the essence of life on earth, the motives that drive human behaviour, the very origin of life itself and the connections we all have to the first living being, the original cell that was alive but all alone because of this miracle of life that made it different from all else. Ideas came to me about loneliness and fear of death and how everything we do is based on escaping or dealing with these particular emotions: death IS loneliness, and through something that could be termed the collective unconscious we fear both, because we remember the original, precarious state of life on this planet. We realize the hand that chance played in creating this living cell and we sense the miraculous and transitory inanimate world, each of us. We have no way of proving to ourselves that someone beside ourself exists: no wonder we are born self-centered and believing the world revolves around us, exists for us. Alone, separate from everything else which is non-living, we create other life in our minds and have it lay before us because we cannot face the truth: we are alone. The rest of the living world is our own invention, a dream from which we will wake up

70

one day in order to die. But if we die, then nothing else can go on existing! Death must then be feared and avoided to all extent.

There are two contradictory theories, of course: that all life does exist, and evolved from the first single-celled organism with which we share much of our DNA and memories or consciousness; secondly, that no other life exists, just the self, and all else is an invention, and the profound loneliness we feel because of this fact is behind every aspect of our behaviour. So it is everything, or nothing but the one self, the original being that is still the only being? It is both, though words can't express the idea in the way it came to me that night: nothing exists, and everything exists within that nothing. We simultaneously share the original being's state of mind (i.e. self-centeredness) and also the realization that life is a mere stroke of luck. Life is not truth; the world can and will continue without us as all life, or us as a species, or us as the self.

We are alive and we care about ourselves and hopefully about others, too; therefore, we conclude that there must be a meaning to life. The "Understanding," this meaning, has been something I've longed to know for so long. Now I've been given, somehow, a different interpretation, suggesting that this meaning of life only exists because we exist to search for it: the "Understanding" is an inherent part of our self and not a separate, independent truth. There is no independent truth; life is not truth. It creates truth for itself that can only be applied to itself. A meaning or a truth cannot exist separately from the consciousness of living things.

This sounds rambling and a little incoherent written down, but it came to me as I lay in bed on the verge of sleep, in a matter of seconds, and not in words but in some other kind of communication which I translated into words (or tried to) during the experience and afterwards. It was such a profound, meaningful communication of ideas that it changed my mood and outlook from then on.

It's not associated with a person or anything tangible because it came from something outside our perceived reality; I guess you can't even call it a "thing." This is the connection I've been waiting for, trying to achieve for so long. It's in the process of happening. Every day I sense things and non-things more clearly than the day before. My mood is totally tied in with this sensing, I'm realizing now. I'm elated all the time. It's like having an incredible beautiful piece of music being played for you, and the notes are keys to the mysteries to all existence. By sensing the "music," all your senses are sharpened so that you feel emotions and perceive things you never have before. The music is the medium through which you experience everything; it is what connects you to the "outside," the reality not normally perceived by us.

There are certain things I can do better, or differently, than ever before: understanding people's behaviour and caring about their experiences and feelings without mixing up my feelings into it (i.e. an objectiveness that is still capable of emotion). Also, I can write things I didn't think I could. I got an A+ on the "Hamlet" essay I earlier described as dreading to write. I can relate to, identify with, what my biology prof is teaching us about evolution, population dynamics, ecology. I share in others' experiences; I often know what others will say or do or write before they do so; I even get flickers of recognition when I attempt to communicate the "knowing" way – suggesting people are actually understanding and responding! But I'm not responding terribly differently to this keener perception; I still have to learn how to translate what my senses pick up into action that is meaningful. I mean I can write in here about all this, but I can't yet react the way I'd like to in other respects: I want to DO things, make things better, help people and plants and things.

The crux of all this, on a personal level, is that I too have these feelings of fear of loneliness and death and before, being psychic intensified the loneliness because I felt more separated from other people and their reality than I ever thought possible. Unable to escape the universal, primal state of mind, I felt trapped and verging on insanity. But now, through being psychic, I am aware of being part of a larger existence, something bigger than me, the self, or all life. I'm not alone any more – in this respect, my search is over. I still have much to learn, however, and experience, and most importantly, to do.

I will live a finite number of years and what exists apart from me will also, but everything connected together will live forever: each part of reality will come and go but always replace then give way to another part – these connections, over-lappings, create the infinity that is so important because it defies an end, a nothing.

During my lifetime I will be able to do something – somewhere, someone is doing something – I look forward to EVERYTHING! Even my calculus midterm, which I should review for a little while now.

April 16, 1991

I have a ten-week summer job in a research lab in the Biochemistry Department at UBC, working for a doctor who is investigating bacterial genetics as it can be applied to the evolution of sexual reproduction. I'll be washing glassware and pouring petri plates, keeping track of the number of colonies at any given time and doing odd jobs. It pays $7/hr., $1.75 more than my chemistry job last summer. I'll be working along with another student which helps lessen my anxiety about goofing up in the lab; the hours are flexible (but generally nine to five, five days a week), and the ten weeks don't have to be in a row.

I couldn't have asked for more. WOW! I left my resume and a letter of reference at the biochemistry office and filled out a rinky-dinky application form, and thought that I'd never hear from them, because, firstly, the proper way to apply is to contact a faculty member directly, and secondly, I'm a first year student and haven't taken any biochem courses yet. But someone wants me! Incredible luck.

The doctor/researcher is a warm, talkative woman, and has that rare friendliness that's given to anyone, unconditionally. She'll be wonderful to work for; the job will be fascinating; her project interests me very much.

Another great thing about this job is that it starts May 6 which means my mom and I can take the trip to Vancouver Island that we planned.

May 26, 1991

Who knows what happens when we sleep – what world exists for us, what state our mind is in. Reality is only relative, totally dependent on what state of consciousness we're in. I can't take anything concrete at face value anymore. The more obvious something is, the more I feel I should mistrust it. I only believe what's in the dreams. Maybe someday they'll lock me up. Then I can sleep all the time!

Up at 7:00 a.m. tomorrow to go to work. Blech. It's so hard to deal with the so-called real world. Normal, nice people. Predictable schedules. Ordinary occurrences. It's so mundane it scares me; it's too weird. Or I'm too weird in it. I'm not a good actor. I'm not covering up my weirdness very well. I at least don't blab things to people, because I'm shy. So people just think I'm introverted. When really I'm fighting to relate to all this mess surrounding me, trying so damn hard to fit in and feeling empty, stupid, guilty. Fear is more real than the world around us.

I don't know if it comes from inside us or from some other world. Sometimes it comes and I don't know why. It's so strong it's reeking, stinking, writhing and I grapple with it as if with a slippery, horrible snake. For no reason! There's no reason to panic, but I freak!

June 1, 1991

I'm going to volunteer at a hospital in August, hopefully St. Paul's since it's closest and has real character. I really look forward to being in a hospital environment. Being at work is also exciting because it's a biochemistry research lab in the basic medical sciences building, and the university hospital is across the courtyard. On Thursday I worked thirteen hours on a long, complicated experiment, not taking more than twenty minutes to eat lunch. At 9:30 p.m. I was finally finished and the last one in the lab. I closed up the two labs, the freezer room, and the lounge-computer room then walked out into the bristling moist night, the massive concrete windowed building shielding me from some unknown, the hospital hanging over me as I walked alone, exhilarated. I could have walked around forever. I've never in my life felt so glad about what I was doing, and how much effort I was putting into my work. I felt so good and confident about continuing in this field and eventually going into medicine. For the first time I knew definitely that I want to be a doctor.

I think it would be a great experience to spend time helping out in a hospital, doing anything really. I need to become familiar with the environment. Actually, I already feel familiar with medical environments, much more than even a year ago. It's not like on television hospital shows or in ambulance novels. It's a real feeling, the drama is not sensational but a part of yourself. It's what I'm going to do – that finally hit me. It's like my life was – has been – a dream of living parent-less in a frightening place, no food or friends or safety, just a yearning to live in a house with a loving family and enough to eat. Then I wake up and realize it's been like that all along; what I used to think was a fantastic impossible hope is really a familiar reality. The reality is not mundane, though: it is exhilarating. Like being in love. Perfectly ordinary, perfectly special. Talking to a patient, comforting him, deciding on treatment, going back to my cot for thirty minutes of sleep before my next twenty-four-hour shift. I never get depressed when I'm busy doing interesting, worthwhile things. I know this is what I want to do. Research too, of course. Research is familiar to me now too. Not that I know anything about it! I just feel acquainted with it, whereas I used to be mystified by the "R" word. And I'm not disillusioned – the reality IS satisfying, after all.

June 29/30, 1991

I just read the last few entries, starting with when I began my job at the lab. I have only two more weeks at work. Where has all the time gone??? I'm trying to characterize a mutant strain of the bacteria Halomophilus influenza, one which has elevated spontaneous competence (a greater than normal tendency to take up extracellular DNA and recombine it into its own genome). I started with a strain called RR 531 (RR stands for the initials of the doctor/researcher) but I got very unusual results with my initial experiments – just basic time courses where you measure the bacteria's competence (i.e. transformation frequency) at various stages of culture density.

There was very little difference between the two strains, and often the curves weren't smooth. I spent the first few weeks trying to pinpoint the problem – was it my poor lab technique or was something unusual happening with the bacteria that we didn't anticipate? The doctor's (and my) first guess was my technique – after all, I was doing some complicated stuff for a first year student. This job has involved way more than washing glassware and pouring plates and counting colonies. But finally we were able to eliminate technique as the major factor. From tests I did with 531 which involved screening for cells that were sensitive to the antibiotics kenamycin and novobiocin, she has hypothesized that 531's mutation giving it enhanced competence is not a point mutation resulting in what she calls the "sxy" (sexy) phenotype, but actually a duplication of the portion of its chromosome containing the sxy wt (wild type) gene. The reasoning behind this I find just fascinating but I can't go into it now. (I'm getting sleepy and what I meant to write about was my transcript of grades; my cousin's visit; my upcoming visit to the Queen Charlotte Islands with my mom; and of course, my English teacher.)

All this has made me certain I want to pursue genetics. Probably not bacterial genetics, though.

Anyhow, I stopped trying to work with 531 and instead tried another mutant strain which has been more predictable. I did a "big" experiment last week in which I tried to prove that 529's (the new strain) mutation is linked to the gene for streptomycin resistance, because if it is, it may be another allele of the sxy 1 gene which she's already studied in detail. I'm hoping it's an entirely different mutation because that would give her more information in the long run. But it would be impossible for me to actually disprove linkage to strep with the method I'm using, so I'd be at a dead end. If it is linked, I'll get a chance at doing a backcross: I'll prepare DNA from 529 and use it to transform KW20 (wild type) to StrR. Some KW20 cells should also pick up the sxy 529 gene which I can test for. This backcross will get rid of any extra, deleterious mutations 529 may have, since I'll be creating a new strain of good, pure wild type with a single mutation. Then any peculiarities in its behaviour compared to regular KW20 can be attributed to its sxy mutation. If the backcross is successful this also suggests that the mutation is a point mutation, i.e. a single amino acid substitution in a protein. Then I can go ahead and have a detailed look at this strain, trying to gain insight into just WHY it's so eager to recombine foreign DNA and if this could have something to do with the evolution of sexual reproduction. That's the big question: Why sexual reproduction? Why genetic diversity? Contrary to Grade 8 biology textbooks, it is NOT a widely held belief among evolutionists that sexual reproduction evolved because genetic diversity is an advantage. Rather, a change in an organism's chromosome(s) is much more likely to do it harm or plain kill it than to let it survive better. Perhaps the organism, probably bacteria as they were the first on earth, took up DNA for extra food and some DNA, by chance, got incorporated into the chromosome.

Sexual reproduction an accident?! We humans have such a biased view because we think of intelligent life reproducing sexually and brainless life asexually. Naturally, then, there's a logical, meaningful explanation for our method of reproduction having ever come about. It would seem that sex does allow for more complexity in a species, but maybe this is a random, chance happening. There's no special reason for us to be here, except that a little wee primitive bacterium many years ago was starving and somehow acquired the ability to use DNA for food.

Interesting stuff and shocking too! I didn't mean to talk about this. Next time I'll get back to what's happening in my life outside the lab, which isn't much of a life considering it consists of only about four hours a day. I work ten hours and ride the bus for two and sleep for eight.

August 2, 1991

I feel more and more uncomfortable getting along with people – I dislike being around relatives, and I only get together with my friends these days. Family is my biggest problem – or rather, I am the problem. I feel like an outsider, like I don't fit in, but it's really because I don't try to fit in. I'm so incredibly lazy these days with regard to responsibilities. I haven't kept up with my weight-lifting program, haven't learned to drive, haven't babysat my niece, haven't volunteered at a hospital. My month-and-a-half of holiday (did I mention my ten-week UBC job ended mid-July?) is slipping by and I don't care. I did have a good time in the Queen Charlotte Islands with my mom a couple of weeks ago, and I'll write more about it some other time. Spent three days up the coast, again with my mom, and loved that. Interesting that just before I began my summer job, my mom and I drove to Long Beach on Vancouver Island, and just after I finished working at UBC we took at trip to the Charlottes. My incredibly intensive ten-week training/work period in a research lab was flanked by several days in B.C. wilderness and beaches. Somehow it was appropriate.

* * * * *

Still think of my English teacher, although much less often. I haven't continued reading the "Alexandria Quartet." I saw a guy I dated once a couple times this summer but couldn't bring myself to get physically involved with him. I don't want to touch him, or anybody. Never felt so apprehensive about touching and kissing. Men, I mean. Still, I haven't gone back to that gay club he took me to a couple of times. I don't want that kind of a one-night relationship either, even if it's with a woman. In general, I feel like I've taken several steps backwards in working on interpersonal relationships, on my "knowing" experiences, and on involving myself in the real outer world instead of being so introverted.

I may go on the birth control pill to control my dysmenorrhea but that would mean getting a pelvic exam. I've had nightmares in the past about being touched deep inside me with metal objects. This is not something I'm looking forward to doing but I know it's for the best because my periods are just hell. The Advil is having less and less effect each month and I'm on the verge of having monthly hellish experiences again. A couple months ago I had to leave work because of cramps (two Advil and one Gravol didn't help, then I ran out of painkillers) and I couldn't make it all the way by bus because I knew I'd throw up. I had to call my mom from a store downtown, to drive me the rest of the way home. I threw up during the drive and then spent two agonizing hours in bed before the pain, nausea, weakness, sweats, and chills, and the terror of feeling this way forever finally subsided. I was then able to keep down a couple of Advil.

* * * * *

I want to be a shaman of an Indian tribe 300 years in the past. That was medicine – it was an art, a spiritual process, to heal a person. Now it is many numbers, and tubes in and out of a person, and beeps and clicks and lines on machine faces. Depersonalization is the worst malady of today's medical system. I don't think I could make it through med school and internship and residency without learning to forget to care about the person as well as the disease.

I'm so tired now.

Sometimes I get self-pitying and I want to stop doing all the hard things in life like getting along with my family and being responsible and getting good grades in school, and I just want to do something silly and outrageous, something totally against my family's beliefs, such as take up modeling as a career. Wouldn't that just change my life around. Of course, the ethics of getting paid for your face and figure trouble me but according to the magazines and television and movies (and friends) it is cool and glamorous to be a model, to be hot and sexy and rich and fashionable. People say I could be a model. It's times like this I think I actually could be one, morally as well as physically. I've never been so disgusted with myself.

October 2, 1991

Things are up, for the moment. Phoned my grandma and my aunt yesterday and had a nice chat. I'll visit them on Saturday, maybe my dad too. Just talked to him on the phone, probably the longest phone conversation I've ever had with him. Forget homework: To spend time with family IS more important even though I've been avoiding it for years. It feels so good to have chatted with my dad for thirty minutes about anything and everything; it's wonderful to know I feel good about something I should feel good about. I'm normal, maybe. Usually I feel like a real shit for being a stranger to my dad (and grandma, but especially my dad). This is the first time in ages I've felt happy about how I've acted towards him. I love him. Sometimes I'm intimidated by having such intelligent, wholesome people as parents (having two fathers who are both geniuses isn't always easy, and having the perfect mother is a little scary because I'm not perfect at all). But that timidness can be overcome. I just have to be myself and be satisfied with that.

November 3, 1991

In my Friday, August 2nd entry, I mentioned feeling "apprehensive about touching and kissing." Disgusted, nauseated, depressed was more like it. I went through a period where I despised physical contact. I can guess why – this period had its beginning in late May 1990 (when a friend of the family made an improper sexual advance to me*). But it's over now. I've met a guy I trust, respect, admire, and care about. I think I'm falling in love. "It's in the winter that I am inspired to write; to hope, dream, and fantasize; to fall in love; to believe in myself. A snow-covered world feels so secure, wrapped-up, quiet, soft. There is nothing to fear. Instead of dread or depression, I have a growing, unsuccessfully restrained anticipation of something unknown as yet but definitely exciting. Like the fizz of a firecracker before it goes off: there's an energy in the air."

Sorry, I'm too tired to write anything original. The above is from my Sept. 27, 1991 entry.

I've never known a guy like him. He's unselfish and compassionate, intelligent and witty, bright and energetic, and still a normal, fallible second year university student not too sure about what the future will bring. I can relate to him, understand his apprehensions, because I share them. So often with people I feel the channel connecting us is closed. There is a barrier to communication and understanding, and to a feeling of kinship that is possible without words. One can still make friends in situations like that – I guess most casual friendships and acquaintances are like that. When the channel is open, however, there is total openness and understanding, no inhibitions at all. We trust each other through our eyes. It's what I've hoped could happen (i.e. was capable of happening in this world) and now it has.

We work closely together in labs seven to ten hours each week and over the past two months we've built a foundation of sorts. The possibilities are now infinite. There is so much complexity to him – I love that. Yet he is one of those naturally good people. Sounds corny, but you know what I mean. I don't have time to write – I mean I don't want to dissolve the magic by putting all my feelings and all our experiences to

---

* Described in Chapter 3, May 28, 1990 entry. - Ed.

date in plain words. We're going to a play together this coming Thursday night, "Romeo and Juliet" at the Freddy Wood Theatre on campus. I'd been trying to think of something we could do together that wouldn't be mundane or clichéd like going to a movie or going dancing. Then I remembered the Freddy Wood Theatre and I checked their programme. What luck: A Shakespearean romance. This will be our first outing together. I hope to discover if he's feeling the same way I am. It's hard to be sure right now if the reason he's being so friendly and considerate (he even walks me to the bus stop after labs, in the opposite direction to his dorm) is because he's interested in me or because he's that way with everyone he knows. I hope it's a combination. He'll make a truly good doctor one day.

Anyhow, let it be known that I asked him to the play: yes, Lara has finally done something meaningful to further her interpersonal relationships. And I should mention his response: "I think it's important, since we're so busy in the sciences, to get out to cultural events as much as possible." Before hearing this, I had no idea if he had any interest in the arts. It turns out he went to every production at the Freddy Wood Theatre last year! I'm in love.

"... in the case of a child who has been sexually abused by a parent from early childhood, and in such a way that the abuse grew gradually from apparently loving behaviour, the abuse may be neither unusual nor extraordinary."

Jennifer Freyd

Chapter Five

Age Nineteen

November 26, 1991
Birthday, Age 19

I'm so out of it, I can't even remember what day of the week it is. NO, it's not because I've had a few drinks – even though I could legally have done that, being 19 today – it's because of these damn fucking cramps. The birth control pills I've been diligently taking for the past three months have not helped nearly as much as I was told they would, by my mom and my doctor. What left is there to try? This sucks. One day I swear I'm going to do research on what causes and what can alleviate menstrual pain. It's absurd that so many women must go through such excruciating pain monthly, and keep quiet about it, as if this torture is their burden, what they deserve, and they must bear it quietly and without complaining.

November 29, 1991

I used to think I was pretty clever. Always on top of things: a fanatic for organization, time management, and completion of homework. I really actually studied hard and conscientiously for exams. It was as if I truly cared about grades. Well, the game is over, I can't pretend this bullshit any longer. Over the past three months I've let the fact that grades are irrelevant sink in deeper and deeper. I been depressed more than usual, especially in September and October which is when I started on the birth control pill. I've also come to the verge of falling in love. I've felt more and more alienated from family (not their fault in the least) and I've become less confident about myself; I feel more uncomfortable than ever around people I don't know very well, I guess because I'm insecure. I want so badly to be friendly and get to know people – fit in – but I seem to be lacking some important asset – maybe I have a mutant gene for a sociability trait. Or perhaps I'm the saddest kind of introvert there is: the introvert who desperately wants to be an extrovert.

Anyhow, I don't want or need high marks anymore. What satisfaction is there in ranking in the top ten in the first year science student body of 1,440 students, when I didn't make a friend last year close enough that I could feel comfortable calling her/him up over the summer? So what if I'm going to be a research scientist one day – I'll never have gone to a dorm party or dated a guy seriously, or spent Friday night at a nightclub with lots of friends. I've never had time to develop a genuine social life, and now that I want to, I find I'm lacking the necessary skills to even begin. I don't know how one goes about being sociable. I want to get together with people for lunch but I don't know how to ask them or if they would want to, so I eat in an empty lecture hall every day. The damn cafeterias are always full at 12:30 so I don't bother going there; anyway it's depressing seeing so many people around who are in groups of four, five, six, or ten, and everyone's so incredibly talkative and normal and happy. They talk about normal things. I failed dismally at being normal around J.G.

I've accepted the probability that he doesn't want a romantic relationship, but at least we should be able to be friends. But this is exam time. I have to study, cram, if I want decent marks, but I don't care. Not in the least. I care about J.G. and I would like to get a phone call from him. Maybe I'll get the nerve up to call him some time. But it really is up to him now to initiate something. I asked him to "Romeo and Juliet" (during which, by the way, nothing happened – I'd say we took a step backward in our friendship). I suggested we go out for dinner sometime – I offered to take him to a restaurant in Chinatown. He lives in Tsawwassen (but right now, on campus) and has been to Chinatown only once before. But he didn't respond to my suggestion. I forget now, I think he just changed the topic of conversation. If I phoned him, would that seem too aggressive? He's called me before, just about homework though.

He's so wonderfully normal. And at the same time, very intelligent and compassionate and dedicated to his studies. How does he stay so normal? How does he have the time and energy to play hockey and go skiing and party and spend so many evenings at the Pit Pub on campus? He has so many friends. He's rolling in money. And he's extremely handsome and well-dressed. The perfect 19-year-old. I mean the typical 19-year-old. I think he's so special though; I can see his unique kindness and gentleness so clearly. He's just so sweet, in the best sense of the word.

December 2, 1991

J.G. and I don't talk or laugh together, or be affectionate with one another nearly as much as that first month-and-a-half we knew each other. For some reason it's all gone downhill – that's how it really feels, like I'm slipping because the ground is moving beneath me, I'm falling and I have no idea why. I can't pinpoint why we're not making any progress. Well of course it's something to do with how he feels about me or about another girl perhaps, but why this change? It was all going so

84

well, I was almost going to let myself free to truly love him; we have so much we could give to one another.

My self-esteem has plummeted as a result; I feel inadequate and more unsociable and introverted than ever. As well as confused – about why am I like this, what the hell is wrong with me, how can I change to make him like me more. I know you're supposed to be yourself around others, especially special others, but I haven't a clue what my self is right now, so I don't know how to behave; I don't have a foundation to build on as I become more comfortable expressing myself around him.

This whole thing is like a gigantic puzzle – maybe a jigsaw puzzle – and we've each been putting in pieces to build the picture, and now it's so close to complete, I get excited imagining what the picture as a whole will be like, and I look forward to sharing it with him – but something's wrong, nothing's happening, I gradually realize; I've put in all the pieces I am able to, I have no more to add, but J.G. isn't playing anymore. He won't add his final pieces, or maybe the pieces are lost. Suddenly there is a communication barrier between us – I don't want to question him or pressure him, he is quiet and distant (maybe he thinks I'm hiding the missing pieces) and everything comes to an awful, disappointing standstill...

I just wish I knew how he felt. That's probably the only solution, the only hope left: confront him about how he feels for me and try to understand his behaviour from his answer to me. "I really liked you, but I met someone and – well – we're thinking of dating. Sorry." Or maybe "No, that's not what I had in mind, ever! How could you think that? I'm sorry to have been leading you on, but I thought we were just friends. I think it would be best if we kept some distance between us now... "

That would break the spell, all right. But I would risk losing his friendship.

One of the reasons I had such high hopes about going to see "Romeo and Juliet" together was just that: it would provide the perfect context in which to open up to each other about our feelings. What more could I ask for – we saw one of the most romantic and poignant love stories of all time. Think of the conversations we could easily have gotten into afterward. Well, it just so happened that afterward (and before the play) we ran into a zillion of his friends, all nice people but not an easy environment in which to discuss romance, so I never brought the topic up. I just let myself be introduced to buddy after buddy, an equal portion of them females, and I began to get that sinking feeling you get when you realize you don't know someone as well as you thought you did. He shared so much with these other people – I had   no idea what they were talking about. Something about hockey, and also car insurance, and an anthropology course, etc. etc. I kept wondering why J.G. and I haven't had these conversations yet, and that perhaps if I just talked more like his other friends, we'd be an instant couple.

I would have brought the romance topic up later another day, except that a rather awkward situation befell us just before we said goodbye after the play, and I don't think he wants to remember it so I haven't mentioned the play again. Neither has he.

December 13, 1991

Chemistry has nothing to do with emotion and so I resent it and even hate myself for my devotion to this science that is just a science, a collection of facts that are human-less; it will exist when we do not, independent of our passions and loves. And then to remember that chemical neurotransmitters in the brain create our emotions – a brutal blow – this brings me back to that state of mind where meaningless reigns with absolute power. But of course, the chemistry and physics in my brain are responsible for this state of mind as well. And drugs could change that state of mind. Pheromones – that's why certain people are so overwhelmingly attractive?

There is nothing organic about organic chemistry. But then we are not organic either, because chemistry controls everything going on inside our bodies. The very basis for our existence, the "information" making us who we are and allowing us to produce more of our race – basically the true foundation or meaning of life – is a chemical molecule. I guess this is why I'm fascinated by biochemistry and why I want to do research involving DNA. But this interest comes from my own DNA since that's what makes me, me. So I'm a slave of my DNA; it is the reason for my existence – I exist for it to replicate itself. I am not the reason it exists. I really do believe in the selfish gene theory, that life exists for the sole purpose to replicate DNA. There is nothing magical or spiritual behind the secret of life; the secret is readily explained by physical principles that govern the non-living world as well. No, of course, I don't believe this!!! Didn't I learn in Grade 12 that one of the thermodynamic laws, the Law of Increasing Entropy, is defined by living organisms, at least in the sense that our cells struggle against it but do not ever really win. This struggle for order, sense, and continuity pervades every aspect of our lives, in fact, from the workings of our cells to our day-to-day existence.

And doesn't religious faith defy all chemical laws? Chemistry and physics just can't be all that governs our existence...

February 9, 1992

I haven't been writing in here because I don't feel like a whole person these days. But it could be that not writing in my diary only contributes to these bad feelings.

I'm trying to keep up with the Honours Biochemistry program, with the social scene (I'm failing at that, of course), with J.G. (also bleak), with family events, with planning for the summer, and especially with old nightmares which have been haunting me forever, it seems. When something happens to you as a child which scares you more than anything else up to that point or since has, the memory of the incident doesn't fade with time. Instead it works its way into practically every aspect of your life, from day-to-day habits, social relationships (especially with guys), and family relationships, to academic goals and career plans. It even invades your sleep. It causes panic attacks when something occurs to remind you of the incident; it creates a need in you to act out similar incidents in your mind, again and again, thousands of times, in an absurd attempt to change what happened. It even lets sadism and especially masochism creep into your behaviour occasionally. Sometimes you feel like you're going insane. But you may have "forgotten" this awful incident even occurred in your childhood!

I think now that if I hadn't blocked the memory for so long, I could have dealt with it earlier. I have post-traumatic stress disorder. Some chance reading I was doing made me aware of this. Interestingly, PTSD also tends to make a person feel "detached or estranged from others." So maybe my difficulty with people is not innate. I would like to unlearn it. Somehow, I have to get counselling. I can't go to a psychiatrist and have the cost covered on my medical plan, because the forms describing the treatment have to be signed by my mom (I am on the plan as her dependent). I can't talk to her about all this yet because she was involved in the incident. I don't think I could afford a psychiatrist's fees, so I have to look for other available counselling. I'm so tired these days. No motivation to study. I'm sick of biochemistry. I want to be an English or psychology major instead. I'm just being childish, though.

February 10, 1992

Life's peculiar. I don't know what I want to do – I don't like my courses; I'm unsure about going into research or medicine; I can't find any goals to strive for or dreams to guide me. The reason behind the drive I used to have for achieving is now plain to me, and I'm left blank. No meaning. I don't know what I – that is, me, as I was born – want to do. I have to decide what I want to do with my life, but to do this I have to understand myself completely. This "thing"* has been obscuring the real me since I was a little kid, 5 or 6 years old. This thing scared me so damn fucking much that it makes me angry at my mom for doing that to me, even though I know it wasn't her fault. I thought she was going to leave me. What if she died? And my father was doing nothing to help. But I understand now how the incident influenced me and still does. I'm working on shaking off that influence. The peculiar thing is I don't know if there will be any other influence left once I rid myself of this one. Was this the only reason behind my wanting to go on? There must be some other meaning behind my drive.

February 21, 1992

It's been a shitty year, really. Since September, nothing's gone super and school isn't making up for that – it's even contributing to the dreariness. I would like to imagine that these few months are an in-between phase, that I'm going to emerge as a more whole person with more of a drive than ever before. But I don't feel it coming.

What to blame this on? The birth control pills which I started in September? Second-year-blues which apparently are not that uncommon among science students at the university who have chosen their major and have to live with it (arts students don't have to declare a major until third year)? My shitty chemistry homework assignments and labs? This disappointment that nothing has really happened between J.G. and me? The unearthing in my mind of an old nightmare that took up perhaps fifteen minutes of my life many years ago and has taken hold of me more than any other event in my life, a hold that's grown stronger and stronger as I've wanted more and more to enter medicine, a grip I'm finally able to loosen a little by consciously remembering the incident and trying to interpret my depressions, obsessions, and phobias based on the effects it had on me. But I ain't no psychologist. And I ain't rich

---

* The incident is eventually detailed. - Ed.

enough to go to one, either. So really understanding this problem that underlies some of my other day-to-day problems, in a psychological way, is not possible at the moment.

February 22, 1992

In general, things aren't awful. I hope I don't make them sound that way. This is just such a fruitless mood I've been in, that I can't help complaining about it. To tell the truth, the real tough days were a while back, in January and early February. I'm now out of that depression, but into stagnation unfortunately. But I'm working on it. And keeping in mind, always, the psychology involved. I keep asking why? why? in here: why am I so unmotivated, uninspired? But I know the reason; it's a matter of understanding it better. Reading on child psychology and stress disorders has been useful. I'm aiming to understand my problem at a deep level, deep enough that I can change my behaviour that's so unproductive (including obsessions with first aid, emergency medicine, etc.) and hopefully to an extent, that will let me write freely about the incident. A year ago, just thinking about it freaked me out, which is why I've avoided probing and delving too deeply into the issue all these years. I must be making some progress now, however, because I can at least think clearly and objectively about the details of what occurred, and try to understand why I was so scared.

May 10, 1992

Looks like I'll be writing on Sundays this summer. This is the time of the week when I'm especially low since another work week looms ahead.

Actually, today I was less depressed than usual. Yesterday night I phoned Vancouver's Emotional Crisis Line because I was feeling so closed-in and withdrawn, unable to help myself to cheer up with the usual methods. I couldn't get out of this hole and I felt guiltier than ever because I was supposed to see my father and grandmother this weekend, but I couldn't let them see me like this. I couldn't face them, and this made me more depressed. I was absolutely sick of feeling like this, and wasting myself and my time.

I asked the man on the phone if he could recommend a good counselling centre. He gave me a phone number, but first he coaxed me into talking about the situation, and I couldn't believe it, I actually did, and it was a relief to finally tell someone that I think there is something wrong with me. I want to change. It feels so encouraging to know someone's listened to you and been supportive to your decision to get help.

Whether or not the birth control pill is largely to blame is still hard for me to say. I can't deny that I've tended to get depressed a lot all of my life. There have also been terrific times, but the depression never fails to return. I know that if I stopped taking the Pill, I would still feel similar, even if not as bad. The problem was with me to begin with.

Now I'm going to talk to someone face to face. For me, that's a challenge! I feel more like avoiding people these days. But I must have made the right decision because today I managed to visit grandma for two hours and feel like myself, and comfortable. It has literally been years since I could feel natural while visiting her. I hope that seeing a counsellor will help my relationship with family members, my motivation for work and school, my self-esteem, my appetite and sleep and general mood. I might have to try anti-depressants.

Time to go to sleep. I've had weird dreams lately: a hand chopped off from an arm; a man chasing me in a picture-perfect paradise resembling our land up the coast (this is a recurring dream which changes slightly each time); and, of course, nightmares about failing exams, although exams are over. I almost depend on these dreams. I hate them but they do affirm my state of mind. Something is wrong. I keep seeing that severed hand, perfectly life-like. These dreams are like signals of what's going on in my deep mind, and so when these dreams improve, I will know I am changing for the better.

May 15, 1992

I'll have to wait until August to get any sort of in-person counselling, I think. I can't find a place that counsels evenings or weekends, and I couldn't take time off work (they're really busy). At first, this devastated me. Then I realized what a baby I was being. I'm not a weakling. In fact, my mood has improved over the last couple of days. I feel better than I have in months – I think just because I finally got the courage up to think about and try to work out my problems with the help of another person.

At the bottom of every neurosis of mine is the conflict of that incident from when I was little and I thought my mom was going to die, and my dad was doing nothing to help her. At the root of this is, I believe, the relationship between my parents. My dad's aggressive, hot-tempered nature, my pity for my mother (I always took her side in the arguments, secretly or openly), the fights, fights, fights. I am like my father; I have his argumentative nature. But this horrified me, so I repress it and instead become passive, withdrawn, unable to assert myself or feel comfortable around other people, especially my father and his relatives. It's as if I'm afraid my pent-up hostility will finally blow open. Rather than let this happen, I control my emotions and behaviour around people to the point where I stop feeling altogether, and thus I act unnaturally. I am aware of how closed I must seem to others. I cannot talk about myself. I actually don't talk much at all about anything, except with my mom and with my close girlfriends. I've built up a wall to control my destructive tendencies, but life is pretty empty when you're the only person enclosed within a wall. Sometimes I don't think anyone can see that there is a person in here, or they don't see the real me. It's time I changed myself in this respect.

I also have to change the way I feel about my father. I haven't worked out even my basic feelings toward him. They're such a mix. I admire him more than anyone, yet I am disgusted by his previous apparent cruelty to my mother. I might be angry at him, too, but I can't think about that because it makes me feel so guilty. I feel guilty because I've avoided him for so long. I moved in with my mom for good, many years ago, and I think both he and my mom always thought I'd eventually go back to splitting my time with both of them. I never did, and it must have really hurt my dad. How else could it have looked? I didn't want to live with him. I loved my mom more. How could I be so cruel to feel that way?

Being around him also possibly reminds me of my repressed hostility, as well as stirring up this mix of guilt and shame. So I avoid him, which makes me feel worse, thinking about how he must feel, being forgotten, abandoned, tossed aside, by the daughter he helped raise.

June 13, 1992

There's a festival going on in the park nearby, and it's pouring rain, absolutely pouring. Musicians and writers and storytellers and construction volunteers have worked so hard to put this together, and there are barely any people out to enjoy it. The rain is too penetrating and cold. That's exactly the story of my life: There's an exciting world out there that people have worked hard making, but I can't enter it because in my eyes it's always raining. I stay wrapped up inside myself, but the rain still penetrates. It's really only dark and wet inside me; if I left that behind and made my entrance into the world, I'd probably be surprised.

July 18, 1992

I always think, when I'm in a good mood for a change, that I will continue to feel fine and that I'm cured of the depression. Then before I realize it, I'm back in the self-centred, confused, terrifying, masochistic world of my own making, my hole.

It hit me harder this time than I could take. I said to myself at first, "You just have to try harder to pull yourself together." But I can't do it, which is depressing in itself because it confirms that I've failed at everything.

I've tried calling Family Services many times but the person I should be talking to is always at a goddamn meeting or on lunch break. Private psychologists never have weekend or evening office hours. I can't stand it any longer, certainly not until August.

My mom's sister came to visit, with her kids, the boy is 11 and the girl 5, for a week. I thought I would go insane trying to look normal on the outside for these guests of ours, and I finally snapped when my mom got mad at her sister (over something disgustingly trivial – how to cook noodles) and then swore at her. I know there is tension between these sisters and I thought there would finally be a confrontation. No fucking way I could handle that without an anxiety attack (that's my usual reaction to arguments between relatives) so I left the house, even though we were all sitting down to eat. (I probably would have thrown up at the table anyway; I can't eat these days without feeling sick, especially when I'm agitated.) I walked out of the house without anyone knowing it and without any money or ID or keys. I got as far as the playing field at the local school, then I stopped and cried. I hate crying where people might see me. I hid my face against the fence and wished I didn't exist. Then of course, I noticed my half-sister's husband and my niece walking down the street so I took off quickly. It was like my dreams of escaping. I walked to the Chinese Gardens to calm down, then decided not to go back home for a few hours. If they saw me like this, in such a mess, I would feel more awful. I asked someone for a quarter and called home, pretending to be fed up with them all and trying to sound angry at my mom, so she would think that was why I was staying out for the evening.

I walked to the library downtown. I read a bit on mental illness. I got quite hungry. I felt worse. I decided to just do what I've wanted to have the guts to do for so long was to talk to a psychiatrist, immediately. I walked toward St. Paul's Hospital and it occurred to me that my fascination with this hospital, and hospitals and medicine in general, could have yet another root. I want to be close to a hospital and to doctors because I feel safe then; I am somewhere I can get help.

After remembering that our next door neighbour works at Triage in Emergency at St. Paul's Hospital, I changed my course to Vancouver General Hospital. I knew it would take an hour to get there on foot so I doubted I would get far, especially being so hungry. But as I walked over the Granville Bridge and looked down at the water with a strange feeling growing in me, I decided to make it all the way, no matter how long it took me. To make this quick (I'm tired and menstrual cramps are bugging me), by 11:00 p.m. I was talking to the Emergency physician about my depression and the need to hurt myself somehow. It was such a relief to let it all out, even though I felt stupid and inarticulate and the doctor seemed impatient. He gave me a referral to the Psychiatry Department out-patients' clinic which I could phone the next day for an appointment. I went home (got a free bus ride – I must have looked ragged enough) and had to phone my mom from the neighbour's house because I had no keys. She was pissed off that I'd woken her up at 1:00 a.m. and that I had so rudely and abruptly left the house earlier. I lied to her, yet again, saying I spent the evening at the movies with a friend. This all happened two days ago, Thursday.

On Friday, I told my boss I had a headache and I took Friday afternoon off. I called the out-patients' clinic from a pay phone and was told to call back in an hour because the receptionist was in a meeting. I called back and was told to call in another hour, very sorry, etc. etc. Why the fuck is it so hard to get hold of a counsellor?

Finally I got through to the right person. Actually it was the wrong person, but I only realized that after I'd already spent ten minutes answering questions as the woman filled out something or other. Some questions were quite personal, and I felt uneasy because an old man had sat himself down on a nearby bench for a smoke. I hope he was hard of hearing.

Anyhow, the woman finished the form and said that I could make an appointment for September. I thought I would crumble right there. I couldn't talk; I thought I'd cry like a baby. I reminded her that I'd seen the doctor in Emergency the night before and he thought I should see a psychiatrist within the next two or three days. She paused, then said, "Oh, you should be speaking to the therapist, so and so – let me transfer you." The transfer took a good minute, then a very kind and sympathetic male voice came on. He asked me all the same questions I'd just been asked, but in such a gentle way, I didn't mind. Then he asked me how I would feel if he told me I would have to wait until September for an appointment; would I feel bad? Yes, I said, that would worry me. I wanted to say the thought freaked me out. He said he could squeeze me in on Tuesday. Then he thoughtfully explained what would happen during my first visit to the clinic. I was stunned. I thought I would just sit down and start talking with a psychiatrist about my depression. What he told me made it sound like I'd be applying for a job. First, I meet with an "initial interviewer" who asks me a set of general questions. Then three (THREE???) psychiatrists interview me for about forty-five minutes. Then I go to a waiting area, and fill out a questionnaire, about fifteen minutes. Then between 10:30 a.m. and noon I'm asked more questions by someone and at some point, everyone who has interviewed me meets and discusses my "case" (without me present, of course) and other cases, I imagine. They come to a decision about what kind of treatment I should get, then tell me their recommendation. I asked the therapist on the phone if this will guarantee me a session or more with a psychiatrist for actual treatment, but he evaded the question. So I may go though all this and still not get help. But this is the closest I've ever come, so I feel relieved. Also very nervous.

July 28, 1992

I'm afraid to write for some reason. But if I stop writing in here, I might feel as if I can confide in my therapist enough that writing in here is unnecessary. I don't want to give this up, even if the writing becomes less precise or thought out. (I can't think precisely very well. My grammar is not good.)

None of this is what I mean to write. I was thinking of Anais Nin and her psychoanalysis and how she was encouraged by Dr. Allendy to give up her diary-writing as if it were a neurosis of hers. I won't stop writing. It's not the same at all as talking. Yet already I've confided things to a near stranger that I've never written in here. When you say something, the words are transferred to the other person, the listener. Then they are gone, or actually kept privately inside the listener's mind. Written words don't have that kind of transience. They're permanent and harder to hide.

I shouldn't have waited ten days before writing again. I don't feel at home in here anymore. What am I going to do? I mean with everything. I have two weeks before my first session (actual therapy session) with the therapist I'll be seeing at the Vancouver General Hospital out-patient's clinic. It's felt like a long wait thus far, and two more weeks?? I don't know if I can bear it sometimes. I want to scream or complain or break something, or curl up and die. The reason they couldn't schedule me in earlier is because both the psychiatrist and the therapist (she's an R.N.) are on holiday now, and they were quite booked up as it was. I'm very much relieved I didn't get put on the three-month waiting list. But I sometimes can't stand getting through the day minute by minute. It feels like three years have gone by since I was interviewed and registered at V.G.H. I didn't think I would get any worse, at the time the appointment was made. She repeated the date to me, August 10, several times and pointed out on her calendar that it was over three weeks away. Now I realize she was giving me a chance to voice my worries about how I would get through this eternity, but at the time I could only feel grateful and relieved I was given an appointment at all. I should have asked what to do if I couldn't stand it any longer and if I thought I might give in to the urges to hurt myself.

Trying to keep some semblance of sanity to my behaviour is harder than I thought possible before. I have to avoid people in order to avoid arousing their suspicions. I have too much silly pride to admit to anyone my fears and illness, and I would also hate to hurt my family, especially my mom. She has enough to deal with right now, without having to learn that her only child has a mental illness.

I'll be starting on the anti-depressant Luvox or perhaps Zoloft, shortly after my August 10 appointment. I hope, hope, hope it works. It will take a few weeks of pills before I will know if it is going to alleviate the depression. So that's more waiting. But on August 10, I'll ask my therapist if there's somewhere I can go if I get desperate. She might suggest admitting myself to the hospital, as the Emergency physician suggested on July 16. But I don't want to go that far. How would it look to the Medicine Selections Committee and Medical Dean of any university if, in my file, it stated that I'd spent time on a psychiatric ward? It's risky enough that I've been diagnosed as clinically depressed. It freaks me out sometimes that I might have just blocked off several career paths; I don't want to erase those dreams yet. I still want to be a doctor or a researcher – one day when I'm a functioning person.

It takes me ages to do anything these days. Just writing these few pages took an hour. I feel like I'm wasting my time, my days and weeks. Physical pain is such comfort compared to the emotional and mental hell I'm in. I often can't think logically, and can't convince myself this will ever end.

August 2, 1992

I have too much damn pride to admit to relatives that I have a depressive disorder. I'm used to being viewed as a strong, successful person. Today I weaseled my way out of a beach BBQ (it's my half-sister's daughter's third birthday) but I know they expect me to show up for at least a couple of hours. Can I handle even that? These dilemmas are my own fault, I realize, for being too afraid to tell anyone I have this illness. I've trapped myself into a corner. I can't socialize, I can't even wash the dishes; I have nightmares, I can't eat, I am down to 102 pounds, my head aches, and I know I should get some exercise but it's too hard to keep moving. I don't want to feel sorry for myself, but I admit I would like someone to put their arms around me and say, "You poor thing." I was never a very persistent, invincible go-getter, even in my best moods, so now I am really a hopeless case. I just can't try hard enough.

I began this diary bitching about menstrual cramps. There is a similarity between physical and mental pain in terms of how awful the desperation is when you can't stand it any longer, you can't see how you can make it through another moment, yet you don't see an end in sight. Depression takes away hope as well, which is about the only thing that got me through dysmenorrhea each month. So what to do?

August 6, 1992

To begin, I wanted to be able to say I'd successfully undergone psychotherapy and behold, I'm a new person. However, I know that the miracle worker is the anti-depressant drug, and the therapy is secondary in its importance. So I am starting this diary on the night of my first dose of fluvoxamine. As a biochemistry student, I should have some appreciation for the wonder drugs that have been developed to treat mental illnesses. But I'd rather be thankful for a sympathetic, skilled psychotherapist than for a chemical. Everything in my life seems to come back down to chemistry, the science I refuse to care about because it has nothing to do with life, but of course, my disgust really comes from my fear that life is nothing more than chemistry. The fact that I am taking a drug that will probably change my mood, increase my motivation and sociability, and affect every aspect of my life as varied as ability to concentrate, desire to eat, and capacity to hope for a better future; this does rather laugh in the face of my anti-mechanistic view of life. We are controlled entirely by the chemistry in and between our cells. If I were religious I might be able to believe otherwise, but without that type of spiritual faith, I really only have my childish beliefs in an omniscient force that loves everyone, in other worlds, in dreams and fantasies. And right now the concentration of certain neurotransmitters in my brain is increasing subtly, a change which within a few weeks will alter my feelings, my mind. Is there a mind and a brain? It would appear that only the latter exists, and it is what is responsible for creating the former. We believe we have minds because the chemicals in our brains trick us into thinking this. "Trick" is the wrong word, because these chemicals have no motives or cunning. It must just be a fluke that they allow the organism they constitute to believe that is has a mind – and a soul. It is all an illusion. Funny that this idea actually relieves me in a way. Or maybe the fluvoxamine is starting to exert its sedating, calming effect on me. Actually, I don't know if Luvox (the trade name) is sedating or not. I researched anti-depressants at the biomedical library at the university but didn't find information specific to fluvoxamine because, at the time, I didn't know the generic name. Drugs aren't indexed under their trade names very often, I found out during a very frustrating five hours at the library.

I could ramble on for a while about nothing, but I realize after careful introspection (practising up for the imminent psychotherapy) that I am just putting off going to sleep. I'm nervous about having taken this drug. I also get anxious before sleeping if I start to think about having nightmares. How many times have I been raped in my dreams, and what does this mean, and is it my mind creating these awful scenarios, or just some misfiring.

August 12, 1992

Two of the possible side effects of Luvox are somnolence and agitation. I think I've been experiencing both. I'm tired a lot, but also tense and anxious for no apparent reason, especially during the night and in the morning. It got so bad the night before last that I ended up in Emergency at Vancouver General Hospital after a group of teenage guys found me in an apparently drugged state in an alley downtown. (It had felt like I was sleepwalking. I have little memory of how I got downtown.) They thought I had taken LSD because of my panic and confusion. They called an ambulance and off I went to the hospital. I always wanted to ride in an ambulance, but all I could think about then was keeping my eyes shut and trying to rationalize my terror.

The doctor and nurses were extremely kind to me. They asked me questions about my depression and medications, and I told them about the traumatic incidences when I was about 3 or 4, and if I felt this terror was connected to those experiences which I'd suppressed for so long. I spent the night there, and in the morning a psychiatrist came to see me. It helped to talk to him about everything, even something horrible that I've never written about here. He said that other patients of his who had been sexually abused as young children had a similar reaction of post-traumatic stress later in life. (The anxiety that night began after "waking up" from a very vivid nightmare in which the molester told me he would come to kill me because I'd told about the abuse.) And the doctor said I have a long road to recovery ahead of me, but he was confident I could make it. I told him I want to go into medicine and we talked about that for a bit. He didn't give me any indication that these problems I have are going to prevent me from achieving that goal (i.e. if I successfully deal with them). But I didn't ask the question straight out.

The anxiety started to come back as he asked me more questions about the abuse, and I told him I didn't know who the abuser was, but I believed it occurred over a one-to-two year period, when I was 3 and/or 4. I started having flashbacks of the incidents and of the previous night's confusion and panic. I couldn't stand the feelings and I said I couldn't go on, I had no energy left to cope. He patted my arm and held my hand and I actually felt safe for a moment. But I knew I had to go out into the real world and face the day, and the next day, and the next. He told me to call my therapist whenever I needed to talk for a few minutes. However, I know that my therapist is very busy and is also a part-time graduate student at the university so that wouldn't be a feasible option. He also said that if I needed to, I could come into Emergency again and a psychiatrist would see me within a few hours (if it's daytime; otherwise, I have to spend the night and see him the next morning, which wouldn't be possible if Emergency was very busy, I imagine).

Tomorrow it will be a week since I started Luvox. It's been the worst week of all, but the medication should have some effect in another week or two. In the meantime, I have an appointment with my family doctor on Friday (she's prescribing the Luvox) and with my therapist on

Monday. I'm beginning to feel awkward around her. It was after my session with her Monday that I went berserk. Talking about these issues – depression, abuse, anxieties and phobias – is important, but it's also much harder than I thought. It makes me afraid because it bring back memories. Each time, I remember a bit more and it gets more horrible. One of the nurses was very helpful. She comforted me and said that eventually, talking will make it all seem less scary. This is going to take some time, I think. But maybe the worst is over with.

And hey – I managed to write it down finally! I was sexually abused when I was little. Now it's in writing. I can't ignore or deny it anymore. I have to face it, a little bit at a time.

I feel half-dead most of the time. Oh well. That means I must also be half-alive.

Still can't get the courage up to tell any relatives and friends about any of this. I nearly called my best friend, Jan, on Monday as the anxiety was increasing. Maybe within a few days I will be able to tell her.

Today's the first day I feel like I'm going to get through this alive and, someday, happy.

August 15, 1992

I'm living in two realities now, one in which I do usual things like chores and shopping and playing tennis with Jan, and another in which I see and feel everything differently, as if in a dream. In some part of my mind, I'm 4 years old again for a moment. Then I'm 19, and then 100, looking back and wondering if that was the same person. I'm not lying to myself anymore, and that is the one thing I feel good about. I pretended the abuse never happened, and I wondered where all of my problems were coming from. Now I've let the secret out. I even told Jan a couple of days ago. That was a relief. She's such a good friend, so supportive.

A while ago, I wrote in my diary something like this: What if I told you that everything in here was a lie? That my carefully written-out life story was a pack of lies? It's time to end my diary now. I can't keep this charade up. THE END.

I was close to admitting the secret at that point, by expressing it in written words. Nothing in my diary was a lie, but because I left out the one important secret, all the truths were negated. Writing it down then would have been too hard, though. For once it was easier to tell somebody rather than write it out. And it took me fifteen years to do this. Oh, well, better late than never.

Jan suggested I tell Vicky, my other good friend, too. That's a good idea. Tomorrow might be my opportunity. We're going to the park to play volleyball and tennis. But other people will be there, too. We'll see.

I must be improving – did I actually write that I was back to doing my usual things? A couple of weeks ago, I was barely functioning as a living, breathing person. The Luvox must be starting to work, and I think I also feel better because I've decided to confront my blocked-out memories. The problem still remains of how to remember it all. I recall some vague details, but it's like waking up from a dream whose plot and characters elude you but whose general atmosphere is still vivid in your memory, as well as a few odd details. I'll ask my therapist on Monday about how I might try to recall more.

August 18, 1992

I'm up the coast with my mom. I did tell Vicky about being molested; at least, the little I remember of it. She was simply writhing in anger at whomever it was who did it. I wish I could feel some anger. I feel closer to her than before now that I've told, rather than awkward around her, which is a relief.

My session with my therapist yesterday went well. I felt more alive and could talk more easily and extensively. I told her my general mood and appetite were improving, and that I've decided I want to remember all of the abuse, not just vague feelings. I hate these flashbacks, too. I had a new one during the session. I was looking at her arm while talking, not really seeing her arm or noticing that she had a watch on. Suddenly his arm flashed before me: he had a gold (?) watch on. Her watch must have triggered my memory. (The arm, etc. is described in a list I'm making of the flashbacks.)

I asked her if there is a way I could remember all of it at once, and she said yes, through hypnotherapy or drugs that induce a hypnotic state. I would have to see a psychiatrist outside of the clinic for that. I said I was very interested. She said this was a courageous decision I was making, but warned it might be better to regain memories gradually. She convinced me to wait another five sessions (i.e. five weeks) and see how far I've come by talking with her. And she gave me an article on sexual abuse (a long one) to read, warning me it was quite disturbing. I didn't find it too shocking, however. It was basically what I expected to read. A few things surprised me, and some relieved me, too. I made some notes about the article on a separate sheet of paper (with my flashback list).

Today – actually last night – I started to express my feelings about the abuse through writing and drawing, for the first time. My therapist had suggested I draw a picture of one of the images that has been coming to me. I did that, but I don't love sketching, so I then tried writing a simple poem. Today I started a short story (entirely autobiographical, but written in the third person to create a bit of distance). I've enjoyed writing it to such a degree that I can't believe I've waited so long to do this. It's unpleasant, even creepy at times as I'm recalling things and deciding how best to express them in words. But the feeling of release and of self-control I periodically get as I finish a section and read it over makes it absolutely worthwhile, and therapeutic, too.

Aside from diary-writing, I haven't done much writing (especially creative writing) in the last year or so. Maybe this is the end of my creative block. Which would mean something positive has come from these horrible experiences. I hope this is also the end of my memory block.

To be more specific about the molestation: It occurred over perhaps a six-month period, but possibly went on for two or more years, until I was 4 or 5. I know it wasn't happening when I began grade school. I assume the abuser was an acquaintance of the family, but I have no idea who. Yet.

August 19, 1992

A couple of hours ago, I finished the short story. It's not really a story in the true sense of the word. There is no real beginning, middle, or end. But there is some sense and meaning to its flow. It was a very rewarding experience, because I expressed thoughts and feelings I haven't ever before, and because I created something. I've felt overflowing with words the last couple of days. Tomorrow it will be two weeks since I began the Luvox. I believe it is having an effect.

Last night before falling asleep, I had two startling thoughts. First I remembered being 2½ with the measles, lying in the shack up the coast on the same bed I was in last night. I described this in detail in the story. Here I'll just say I had a dream while 2½ of being molested. So it must have begun earlier than I thought.

The other thought: I suddenly remembered somebody who might have been the one who did this to me. It's so obvious, and so horrible. I'll discuss it with my therapist before I write in here about it. I can't remember, no matter how hard I try, who it actually was. This is just a guess.

August 20, 1992

There will still be bad days now and then. It will get harder as I remember more about being molested. But I have the Luvox as a sort of safety net. Before I had made up my mind to deal with the abuse and try to remember it all, my therapist said to me that if I did decide to go through therapy with her, I would have a safe place to do so. It's a relief to know I have a safe place to do my recalling, because sometimes I get urges to be reckless and do something that will physically hurt, in order to shut out the emotional hurt. But I won't do that in her office, obviously. I'm writing this to avoid thinking about my self-destructive urges. But I'm reminded every time I happen to glance at my left arm where the scars are still visible. Until they fade, I'm wearing long sleeves when around other people. The psychiatrist in Emergency asked me if I ever cut or scratched myself to relieve tension. I couldn't believe he knew to ask this – I thought I was doing something totally freakish that no one, not even lunatics, do. I guess I'm not unique. Reading the article from my therapist is reassuring in the same way because I could accept that my general usual behaviour is a reaction to the abuse and is a pattern typically seen in people abused as children.

The psychiatrist asked to see the scars and I showed him, feeling like a small child making a confession. He touched a finger to my arm and stroked the scars for a moment absent-mindedly as he began another question. It was kind of like a parent who wants to make a scraped knee or a bumped elbow feel better. They care, and that actually helps relieve the pain – in my case, mental pain. I was afraid to leave the hospital that morning (I had to obviously, or my mom would start to wonder where I was). I felt safe for the first time in ages. The psychiatrist and the nurse stayed with me through the anxiety attacks which hit me like electric shocks, and they talked to me and convinced me I was strong enough to make it through the day, and the next day. I swear I don't know how I would have gotten through that episode without them.

But that was ten days ago. Things are better now. I look forward to the next therapy session, a week from today. I hope the week speeds by.

August 24, 1992

How does one stand this? How have other people made it through this hell??? I almost wish I could get hold of drugs or at least try some marijuana.

I hate anxiety attacks. First a shooting headache, then weakness, tight chest, racing heart, shudders, fear. Afterward it's like being in a coma. Can't think or move.

Keep forgetting whether it's Monday or Tuesday. Who cares. Well it matters because Thursday is the day I see my therapist this week. She's on holiday today. (Mondays are the usual day I see her.)

I need to do something. Dreamt of desperately wanting to kill myself last night. I had killed someone else earlier in the dream. I was slithering along the ground, insane, mumbling, trying to tear my chest open with my fingernails. I want to change the way I feel. I need an escape. Long walks, writing, reading, talking to Jan and Vicky just don't help now.

I don't know what to do.

I could go to Emergency and wait three hours to be told there isn't room, I can't stay the night. I'd rather satisfy my urges to do something bad. Evil. Yesterday evening I saw a friend's new apartment. Twenty-third floor in the West End, incredible view of the city, water, mountains. As we watched the sunset all I could think about was how nice it would be to jump.

August 26, 1992

I just played some pieces on the piano. Now I'm listening to my k.d. lang tape. I haven't let myself indulge in music in ages. I must be improving. I really felt good playing "Sarabande" by Handel, the way I felt when writing up the coast.

This song of k.d. lang's takes me back to the last year at university. The struggles, the fun and excitement, the long hours (and finally the misery). It's possible to feel this creative thrill again! I can't believe it. The feeling I have at the moment is what I used to feel when I was 12 or 13, a wonderful ecstatic kind of joy that hit me occasionally.

I've missed it. I'm glad it's back. The torture I felt on Monday ceased gradually after going for a walk with Jan. I spent a few hours at her place with her and her brother and his friends. Being around that lively, hilarious group was what I needed.

* * * * *

Today I really felt all right, even quite good at times. Saw my family doctor this morning and told her this. She's keeping me on 75 mg, since I have no side effects at this dosage. She was glad I was improving. Then she talked for ten minutes about her daughter who is at McGill University. I think she didn't quite know how to talk to me about the details of the depression, etc., so she avoided the subject. I was irritated at first because I'd spent an hour getting to her office (slow buses) and mostly she yakked on and on about her family. I couldn't get a word in edgewise. I did try. But I couldn't feel irritated for long, because I understand that it must be very difficult talking to patients about subjects like mental illness and sexual abuse when you've been trained as a medical doctor and you're used to treating broken bones and heart failure and the like. I think medical students should get more training in psychiatry than they presently do.

Tomorrow at 3:00 I see my therapist. As usual, I feel nervous because therapy is still unfamiliar territory to me and because saying certain things out loud makes me realize how horrible they are. But, like the Vancouver General Hospital nurse said, "The more you talk about it, the less scary it gets." I'm finding that the actual act of saying things out loud, such as describing a flashback where I was made to perform oral sex, is extremely uncomfortable, then the realization that I've said it is terrifying. This only lasts a few seconds; then I feel a bit of relief and I calm down. Over the next while, hours or days, I feel better and better about having spoken out loud about the things that have happened to me and the way I feel about them.

I'm going to tell my therapist that I've had a thought about who it might have been. I'm sure I'm wrong. But it's better to talk about it then try to decide. Remembering the abuse is impossible, except for some bits and pieces. I need to remember, and I have to know who it was. I think sodium amytal or sodium pentothal would be the best way. I should try non-drug induced hypnosis first, I guess. My therapist wants to wait another four weeks but I need to know sooner. It's much worse not knowing.

August 28, 1992

I'm living a double life. In one, I am preparing for third year in biochemistry by buying textbooks, arranging schedules, putting together scholarship applications, and thinking about who I'll run into on campus. I'm at the university's Sedgewick Library after having picked up my transcript of marks and returned some notes to Jan. This is me, the student, the 19-year-old person who envisions herself as a doctor one day. Actually this is a pretend person, the "me" I would have been if, if, if...

The "me" that is more real now is the 19-year-old person who was molested until she was 4 or 5 years old and who has now plopped herself down into the world of doctors, psychiatric clinics, therapists and psychiatrists. She isn't a premedical student; she's a patient.

These two roles I'm playing don't (at the moment) interfere with one another, so I'm not concerned. But it sure feels different, having exposed a side of me that's been hiding for fifteen years. I feel naïve and childish at times, as if I'm back to a 4-year-old mentality. For instance, with the therapist yesterday, I felt vulnerable and stupid, unable to clearly articulate my thoughts and having frequent terror attacks. I'm fine until entering her office, and then suddenly I'm a frightened little wimp. Of course, this transition must in some ways be therapeutic, maybe by helping to take me back to when I was little, letting me remember. But I didn't remember anything more during that hour. At one point, I felt so doomed and freaked out that I mumbled, "I want to die." As an absurd explanation of this, I went on to say, "There's a presence in this room." It really felt like that, a peculiar kind of energy around us that chilled me and made me try to slouch even further into the chair as if by keeping low I could evade it.

"Is the presence good?" she asked.

I paused for a moment, not to think about my answer (for crying out loud, do I look like I'm experiencing a good presence around me???), but to ponder whether I hadn't maybe heard this conversation in a movie before. I try to watch out for the moments when psychotherapy raises life to a high (and false) drama.

So...

"No," I whispered.

"Who is this presence?"

"I don't know." Somehow, the air conditioner's whirr had something to do with it. This was too bizarre and unpleasant. I stopped trying to answer questions or think of something coherent and relevant to say.

After a long silence during which I wrung my hands and tried to move my seemingly leaden legs a bit, (while she watched me with an inquisitive look on her face which, to my dismay, seemed not to show any real concern for me), she asked, "Are you afraid I'm going to hurt you?"

This was an interesting idea. I was too ashamed to admit it, but it did feel like some of the sinister presence in the office was emanating from her. I said what I figured she'd like to hear: "No. Of course, it's just coming from me. These feelings are only inside me – this must have been how I felt when I was being molested."

"Or maybe when you thought of telling someone about the abuse?"

"Yes, that's possible."

Indeed, it sounded very sensible. Telling someone about this "secret" even though fifteen years after the abuse ended, brought back the feeling of being haunted by his threats not to tell.

I left her office feeling like not much had been accomplished, and feeling like an idiot for not making more of this precious hour I get each week. She must think I'm a little crazier than she initially believed, now that I've talked about an evil presence. It's funny how much it matters to me what she thinks of me. It's like I don't yet want her to see me as Lara the patient; I want her to treat me like the phony Lara who copes with everything and is an honours student. But I can so rarely play that part around her.

Yesterday evening I decided I needed some more life experience, of a different variety than what I'd been getting as a student, daughter, friend, patient. Or maybe I just needed to escape for a while. Institutions sometimes make me feel very stifled (but usually I feel safe and protected in places like schools and hospitals). Being in the clinical environment of a psychiatric ward or the out-patients' department kind of depressed me yesterday. I craved a sense of self-control, power, and freedom. So just after midnight, I left my house ostensibly to sleep over at Jan's, and headed downtown instead. Dressed in old jeans, runners and layers of black shirts, I hoped to look at least a little like a street kid.

Main and Hastings [the centre of Vancouver's Downtown Eastside] never looked so inviting. I wanted Skid Row to be my home at that moment. I felt so strong and self-sufficient, not in the least bit frightened. It occurred to me that I was testing myself in a way, trying to prove I was a tough kid who could deal with a tough past. I wanted to chat with and get to know some of the street kids and prostitutes on Hastings Street, to get an idea of how other young people have dealt with shitty pasts, and to try to make myself feel a little anger about how unfair it is that kids are treated so horribly that they choose the streets over their homes. I'd had a problem trying to feel any anger about what happened to me. As someone stated in the article my therapist lent to me, "I was still too scared to feel anger." Well, the fear was in my memory (I'd been terrified only a few hours earlier that day in her office) but I felt invincible and totally unafraid at the present moment. The adrenalin was running high. It being a Thursday night, it was only moderately active near Main and Hastings. I tried to start a conversation with some hookers who looked about 18, by asking them if they knew where I could get some hash. Maybe not the best question to start off with, but I thought it would made me sound genuine (I had no desire for hash, of course; I had a natural high last night.) They eyed me suspiciously and pointed down the street. I tried again by saying I arrived in Vancouver a few days ago, etc. etc. but I guess I didn't look shabby or spaced out enough to really be a street kid or a potential prostitute, because they just wouldn't open up. You can't trust anyone when you're working the streets, I guess.

Fed up with trying to "research" youth prostitution and drug use, I started noticing all the johns circling the block. With disgust (and maybe a bit of amusement) I realized that the thought of getting into one of those cars aroused me a bit. Now with an adrenalin high and a slight sexual arousal, I started to walk slowly along the curb, making eye contact with the drivers. A pickup truck stopped. The window on the passenger side was closed so I had to open the door to speak. I can't remember our conversation now, but I basically said: "Whatcha doing? Cruising around, eh? I'm just out for a stroll myself."

I didn't want to give the impression that I would screw him. Once I was in the truck and we were moving, he eyeing me with a broad grin, I said, "I'm not a hooker. Sorry. I'm looking for a friend who's working the streets down here." I manufactured that lie on the spot, figuring he'd offer to drive me around to look for her, which he did. I wanted to stay in the car a little longer, and see what happened. I'm stupid enough to do it. This was just great. I felt in absolute control of my life. I'm sure my therapist would call my actions self-destructively reckless, but I really knew what I was doing.

* * * * *

I will say that last night's escapades left me feeling stronger than before, in control of myself, responsible for my body, mature and intelligent, and also left me with an appropriate amount of disgust and anger for the adults who manipulate and abuse children, so often without realizing the great harm they are doing.

YES, I FELT ANGER!!! And pity and scorn. I am not powerless. I can make changes, improve the system; there must be ways. SOMEHOW. Through public health, maybe. I can't expect to do anything through social services or the justice system, but as a doctor, I might be able to help. (I say that because I would never make a good social worker or lawyer, but not because nothing can be done through those avenues.)

I'm still on that natural high from last night. I've had three hours of sleep in the last forty hours and I feel great. Better than great. This energy is unbelievable. Energy and confidence. I've been lacking both for so long. I can think of three possible reasons why I'm feeling like this: (1) Luvox really is a miracle drug; (2) Feeling healthy anger at last about being abused and towards the abuser has transformed me into the person I should have been or would have been, the real me ("through anger comes action" – something like that from the article, I think); or (3) I don't have unipolar depression after all – I'm manic depressive.

I wish tomorrow wasn't Saturday because I should call someone – therapist or psychiatrist – about the possibility of (3). I don't think I'll be able to sleep much tonight. But who knows. I'm going to read now.

I saw Jan tonight and told her all about last night. She thinks I'm crazy. What the hell will the therapist think? Who cares! This is MY life!

August 29, 1992

School starts in nine days. What happens then? I don't feel like a university student at the moment. I can see it now: pre-med student by day, hooker by night. Why do I have this huge urge to go back to the streets again? I must be nuts. It gives me the illusion of having control, but it's too fucking dangerous. I should be thanking my stars I wasn't raped Thursday night.

After the man drove me around awhile in his pickup truck and I made an effort at small talk, he offered to buy me a pop. I accepted. To my surprise, he actually answered my questions about why he comes down to Main and Hastings, what he likes about sex with prostitutes, how often he does this. He started to open up even more, and during the next two hours, he told me his life story. I won't repeat it here. Depressing stuff. I couldn't see any happiness in his self-conscious smile. His name was Monty and he must have been about 30. He was a tugboat operator and he lived with a woman he felt nothing for. She physically abused their two kids. At one point he spent three years in jail for drug involvement. He no longer uses. I wondered, though. And so on and so forth.

He told me this while we were parked in a field by the waterfront near the grain elevators. There was no one within shouting distance but I wasn't nervous because it was so obvious that Monty was a lonely unhappy person and really needed someone to talk to. Sex would be nice, I'm sure he was thinking, but all he tried on me was a kiss. I said, "No, I'm not a hooker, remember." He stopped. What a feeling of power and self-confidence that gave me, to be with a man in a car far from anyone and to know I wasn't going to let him hurt me or do anything I wouldn't like. A very therapeutic experience, I believe.

After an eternity of listening to him and trying to act as therapist under the guise of street kid, we had an interesting interruption. A port police car pulled up behind us, lights flashing. The port police are really paranoid about drug trafficking by the waterfront. The policeman ordered us out of the truck (separately), and interrogated us one after the other. I had told Monty I was previously an arts student at a university but now was bumming around. Of course, I had to tell the cop the truth. When he asked me what corner I was working, I replied, "I'm a pre-medical student." He apologized by explaining that there was a lot of trouble in this area, so he had to check everyone out. After a zillion questions, he gave Monty back his drivers' licence and then asked him if he had any tattoos. (We were back in the truck by now.) I was getting bored so I said very loudly, "Boy, do I have to urinate." The cop said, without looking at me, "What a coincidence. I'm all finished here." After he left, I tried to talk Monty into heading back downtown. I wanted another experience with another man. So finally he finished his life story and he realized I really wasn't going to give him a blow job, so he dropped me off on Pender Street somewhere. I headed back to the corner that was calling me lustily.

A Chinese guy in a sports car pulled up and insisted I get in. I was a little suspicious. He looked like a pervert. The 20-year-olds are the ones to beware of. I declined and eventually he stopped following me. Then a black man in an expensive-looking car caught my attention. "What are you doing out here at this time of night?" he asked.

I said I was looking for a girlfriend. He said hop in and he'd help me find her. In the car, he asked me for a description and I made one up. "I know exactly who you mean," he said. I muffled a laugh. So we drove around and he told me he owned the hotel at Hastings and Carrall as well as a condominium or two. He then proceeded to tell me his life story, or at least his rise to success after arriving here penniless from Jamaica a few years ago. He bootlegged until he had enough money to invest in real estate. He's gone from homeless bum to wealthy and respected pervert. Only he didn't say pervert. But I had suspicions he was a pimp as well as a hotel owner down here on Skid Row.

He took me back to the bar at his hotel and gave me a wine cooler. Then he spent quite a while lecturing me on shaping up, getting off the streets, avoiding drugs and, above all, "Don't sell your body!" What a joke. He ended up taking me back to his apartment and inviting me to bed with him. I declined, and he didn't make a deal out of it. He fell asleep on the couch within twenty minutes. I slept on the other couch. Or I tried to sleep. I was bored again; I craved more. But it was 5:00 a.m. and the apartment was warm and quite classy and comfortable. A lot nicer than sleeping on a bench in Victory Square surrounded by drunks and hookers. So I snoozed on and off until 8:30 a.m. He woke up then, too, and insisted on making me breakfast. He got very demanding about wanting me to spend a couple more days with him, or even live with him ("and make babies," he said with a chortle). I just smiled and said little. I didn't want to anger him. When he asked if I had a boyfriend, I truthfully said no, but he thought I was lying and almost blew his top. There was something very strange about him, despite his moralistic lecturing, so when he went to the store for some milk, I wrote a quick note thanking him for his company and I took off. He lived on Francis Street near Commercial so I had a short walk home. And that was the end of my night of "research."

My energy is back to its usual low level. The elation and rush must have been a result of the excitement of feeling free and street-smart. "STUPID is what it was, you idiot," Jan said to me when I related the story to her last night. She doesn't understand how strong I felt while out there in the night. I love the city. I needed to try to understand what makes men view women's bodies as objects, and sex as a substitute for happiness. I got to experience what it's like to be an object, a meaningless piece of flesh. And I got to stand up for the rights of my body and protect it, refusing to let men treat it as an object even if they obviously thought of it that way.

My therapist gave me the name of a very good hypnotherapist (a psychiatrist outside of the clinic). I'll bet the waiting list is months long. Until I can see him, I'll continue with the therapy with her even though I'm sick of our useless sessions. I doubt I'll tell her about Thursday night. She's very nice, but I want to talk with someone who's a bit more willing to make intelligent comments and say something rather than respond in the boring, predictable way she does.

On Monday, I'll call my family doctor, asking for a referral to the hypnotherapist. Tomorrow, Sunday, there's a party at Vicky's. I don't know if I'm up for socializing. We'll see. I'll hide out in her room upstairs if I can't stand it.

* * * * *

Bored.

Saturday evening and nothing to do. That's not true of course. There's housecleaning, course preparation and scholarship applications to get off. And I intended to call up my dad and see if he'd like to go to the "Twin Peaks" movie that's finally playing. But I haven't seen him in weeks, and I don't feel up to that tonight. I'm itching to go downtown tonight. Maybe try Robson Street where the classier hookers work, or even Davie Street. I'll just observe this time. No getting into cars. We'll see. Who knows.

Maybe call Jan? No, she'd want to lecture me about the "crazy things" I did. And it's probably her dinner time. If I call her later, she'll try to convince me to come over when I would rather go out into this amazing city. I can feel the energy in my body already. This is going to become like a drug for me. I wonder what I should wear. Not anything too scruffy, or I'll look out of place for Robson Street.

The bare truth is: I need adventure, no matter how low-grade or sleazy. I want to feel alive. The idea of returning to university or partying at Vicky's house or going through therapy just doesn't do anything for me. Perhaps I'm attempting to relive the sexual abuse of my childhood. But this time I'll be able to defend myself. This is what I need to experience. Even if the experience is a traumatic one, at least it will be better than feeling dead inside.

September 4, 1992

Effects of the abuse:

For as long as I can remember:
• feelings of dread and hopelessness, combined with the belief that I was completely alone and no one and nothing could help make these feelings go away. These feelings came especially in the mornings when I woke up and was still lying in bed. If I stared at the curtains, the feelings

intensified. As I got older (9 to 12), I had the additional feeling of confusion, like there were a zillion things I couldn't understand and this made me feel small and helpless.

• nightmares and sleepwalking. Until I was 6 or 7, the dreams would be of monsters chasing me up and down stairs and elevators. I would be in an apartment building or in my own home. I would feel terrified and have the urge to get out of the house or building and run away. I never actually saw the monsters (I never looked behind me). Their presence I could feel very strongly without seeing them.

• timidness and self-isolation to the extent that people would ask my parents if I were autistic on first meeting me. When I was about 3 and started going to a new daycare, my mom tells me at first I played all alone and would not speak or acknowledge anybody, or participate in anything. I behaved this way in new situations or when meeting new people (e.g. meeting my mother's partner when I was about 5 or 6).

• the habit of throwing my belongings around when I got upset. I had frequent tantrums, until the age of 5 or 6 – as if by breaking my favourite toys, I would feel better.

From the age of about 8 until 12:

• fantasized about running away from home and living on the streets. Believed I would be absolutely safe on the streets. Couldn't think of any reason to leave home, however, so I never did run away. Fantasizing gave me great pleasure and relief, though.

• periods of time lasting a few hours during which I lost motivation to do anything at all. I would complain of boredom to my mom, but actually I knew there was plenty to do. I felt incapable of doing anything. Nothing mattered. I was depressed, although I didn't use that term at the time.

• I did cruel things to kittens, cats and occasionally slugs and insects. To kittens, I would separate them from their mother when they could not see, and place them on the staircase. They would meow in a way that cut through me and hurt me terribly but I felt driven to continue doing this. The mother cat would always retrieve the kittens in her mouth at first, but later she stopped bothering to. When the kittens were older, I did more things to scare them. I put them on high ledges and watched them fearfully jump. I growled at them and cornered them. In between these fits of rage and cruelty I would treat the cats with love and affection. I felt very guilty about my cruelty.

- the nightmares were similar to the previous ones but now I would be chased by a man who intended to kill me.

From about 13 onward:
- developed crushes mostly on much older men/father figures (who obviously were not available)
- felt more and more uncomfortable around my father, but couldn't understand why. Eventually stopped spending half my time with him, and instead lived full time with my mom. Also felt uneasy around my dad's side of the family, for no apparent reason. Felt guilty that I avoided them.
- in my one fairly intimate relationship, after we nearly had full intercourse (which was pleasurable), I could no longer enjoy his touch or kisses. I stopped feeling anything. I broke up with him because of this.
- became interested in the subject of child abuse, but didn't let myself think I was. I watched TV movies about the subject and read books in private.
- nightmares: now I would be raped as well as being chased. Sometimes I would watch other people being killed or drowning. In some dreams, I was drowning. In some, I tried to kill myself.
- episodes of depression lasted longer, from several hours to several days.
- strong but unexplainable interest in hospitals, doctors, psychiatry.
- after an incident where a trusted friend of the family kissed me and touched me, I started feeling nauseated when eating (this has continued, but I have periods where it goes away for weeks).
- panic attacks that didn't seem to have any source (except the one I had the day after the man mentioned above came on to me). Often the anxiety came while eating a meal with family or friends. As much as possible, I avoided eating at the same time or place as the rest of the family.

From about 16 on:
- fantasies of throwing myself in front of a car (attempted once).
- from about 17 or 18 onward, felt depressed most of the time, with a few hours (in the evenings usually) during which the depression lifted slightly or even completely.
- continued to over-achieve and be a perfectionist, as if by excelling academically I could make up for the empty parts in me. I felt I could gain people's approval best by really achieving in school and in other competitive areas.

- wanted to develop relationships with guys but felt incapable of maintaining them; physical touch was either frightening or produced no feeling whatsoever in me. Felt increasingly guilty about not being able to enjoy this aspect of the relationships, and I always broke it off with the guy or pretended to lose interest in him shortly after the closeness between us developed, even if I'd spent months hoping to win the guy's heart.
- at 19: After entering therapy (initially only for depression), began having flashbacks of the molestations. Sometimes I feel terrified during the flashbacks, and sometimes I can feel nothing at all, even though the pictures that flash in front of me are horrible. Often I get the feeling that I must have separated myself from my body during the abuse so that I wouldn't feel it as much. I can remember doing this later, years after the abuse ended, when I would be lying in bed in the dark.
- sometimes have the notion that I must be insane.
- feel guilt about a lot of things, especially about avoiding my dad as much as I can. This may or may not be connected to the molestations. (I couldn't remember at this time who the perpetrator was.)
- cutting the inside of my arms because it gives relief and the physical pain helps to blot out the mental pain.

September 5, 1992

I'm rather dissatisfied about my sessions with my therapist. I do feel better after talking with her, but from the little I know about therapy and from what my gut feelings are telling me, she is not receptive enough. I might as well be talking to a tape recording or getting therapy from a computer. She asks standard questions each time and has virtually nothing to say about my responses. She just goes from one predictable question to another. I try getting discussions going about issues I need help understanding, but she keeps everything at a surface level. She doesn't help me to understand more than I currently do. All the therapy accomplishes is letting me voice my feelings and memories. That's better than nothing, but I don't need a registered therapist to do that. I could talk to my cat, for God's sake, and get about as far as I'm getting with her. Nonetheless, she seems to be a kind person, a maternal woman. It bothers me that she lets no emotion show on her face and that her voice is a monotone. (I can't read her, but she can read me – it's eerie). But at least she's a human being who listens non-judgementally.

I mentioned before that she gave me the doctor's name (the hypnotherapist/psychiatrist) and phone number. Well, after I received word that an appointment had been set up for Tuesday to my utter relief and joy, she told me that she talked to the doctor and they both thought that hypnosis would not be appropriate at this stage. I should let myself remember naturally. FUCK THEM. They don't know the agony I am going through, wanting to heal but not knowing exactly what I need to heal from; not knowing if I was just touched or if I was raped; how long did it go on for, and who the hell it was. Am I accusing my grandfather and my father of doing something horrible that they actually did not do??? I feel awful about this. I need to know the truth, the sooner the better. Somehow I have to convince this new doctor that hypnosis is the right thing for me. My therapist didn't actually cancel the appointment that had been set up; she said it wouldn't hurt to talk to him this once.

She makes me mad. She recommends a hypnotherapist and then tells him I shouldn't receive hypnotherapy yet. The disappointment and rage I feel at being let down like this is immense. I feel so damn stressed out now about seeing the doctor because this time with him will determine whether I will be "allowed" to go through hypnotherapy yet. It's crucial that I be articulate enough to let him know how I feel, how important it is for me to remember. I'll beg him if I have to. I'll scream and shout, throw things around. Like I would do when I didn't get my way as a little kid.

I'm not going to be passive about this. Shit, I have five fucking days to get through before I see him. Shit, shit, shit. Homework, laundry, dishes, nightmares. How do I fit it all in? Goddamn. How do I act human and natural when incest is on my mind twenty-four hours a day. I'm such a phony. I smile at school, behave like everyone else, and it's as if that's not really me. I'm actually off hiding in a corner or in the closet, praying I'll be safe. I hate this existence.

Tomorrow I could call my therapist and bitch. Where would that get me, though? She wouldn't actually say anything of relevance. She'd let me voice my anger and then bring the "conversation" to a close and hang up. I want someone to turn to who will empathize. I don't think that's too much to ask for. I can't make any progress if I'm being treated as if from a distance with sterile gloves. Who am I? I want to be a person in her office. All I am is a voice that is listened to and acknowledged but in the most minimal way. Because this "therapy" is being covered under Medicare, I have to take it or leave it. I can't shop around because I'm not paying for it. Of course, it's wonderful not having to pay. But how far am

I going to get with her? I still sometimes get the desperate feeling that there's no way I can cope any more, that I need to be hospitalized or I'll lose control. I can conquer this feeling now, but it does recur. It takes a lot of energy to suppress it. The weekend approaches. That freaks me out, as usual, because I get worried my energy to cope will run out and I'll have nowhere to turn (except Emergency which would be pretty pointless).

Fuck. Shit. Fuck. I hate myself.

September 11, 1992

Time to organize things a bit. Firstly, it was my own choice to get into therapy. No one's forcing me to stay in it. If it really is useless, I can just stop. I don't feel like stopping, though, so there must be something worthwhile about it. Secondly, as mad as it makes me feel, I do not have the right to demand a certain kind of treatment and expect to receive it. You can't go to a doctor and order them to give you a shot of morphine because you supposedly have pain in your arm. They're going to make absolutely sure you need the morphine. So of course, the therapist and the doctor are hesitant at rushing into hypnotherapy with me, not being sure if it would make things better or worse. They have my best interests at heart. I can feel angry at them, but it wouldn't be right to voice the anger since they're only trying to help me.

On Tuesday I must pull myself together and appear calm and collected and rational before the therapy session at 2:30, then proceed to the psychiatric building at University Hospital to see the hypnotherapist at 5:30, hopefully composed enough to articulate my feelings without sounding psychotic. I'm ready now. How the hell do I wait another four days?

* * * * *

It's time to put down on paper an incident that has affected me in many ways since it occurred, when I was about 4. It is the incident I wrote about in the past in terms of my mother dying and my father not helping her. This wasn't really what was happening, but that's how I thought I perceived it at the time. There is more to it than that, I think. I didn't realize this until last Sunday night as I was trying to get to sleep. I went over what I remember happening, walking through the memory carefully and slowly, which I can do now, but it used to be too terrifying to attempt. Here's what I remember:

My mom, dad and I are sitting at the kitchen table eating dinner (actually I don't think it's in the kitchen; I think we had a dining room of sorts). I am about 4 years old. My parents are still together, but it must not be too much later that they separated. The table is round and wooden. We are nearly finished eating. My mom is drinking a cup of coffee. Some coffee grains must have been in there, because she started to choke. She ran to the bathroom at the back of the house. My dad and I remained sitting at the table. Finally I went into the bathroom and asked her why she was coughing so much. Of course I knew, but I wanted her to assure me she was all right. She motioned for me to go away. I went to my room and sat in the corner against the wall. It was dark. Shortly after, my dad came into my room. As far as I knew, he had not paid any attention to my mom in her distress. He crouched beside me. I said that I was scared. He said, "Me, too."

And then there's a blank.

I know some time passed, but I don't know what happened. Everything else is vivid in my memory except for what happened after my dad sat beside me. Later I remember all of us back in the dining room. My mom is okay. She makes some comment about a coffee grain going down the wrong way.

The strongest feeling I have from this incident is terror. I was mortally afraid. WHY??? It's not like I hadn't seen someone choke before. I didn't really think my mom was dying, although I was very worried about her. It just doesn't add up. Why has this memory, or at least a portion of it, stayed with me so long and had such significance? Why has it caused me to develop an obsession with first aid and insist on playing doctor with my friends when I was little? Why do I still feel like I'm drowning in dread and fear whenever a family member chokes? And why in hell do I feel my vaginal muscles and the insides of my legs stiffen painfully when I witness someone choking? By reading a first aid book, especially the section on choking, I actually got sexually aroused. What is going on here? Am I being far-fetched in making assumptions here? First, I feel my grandfather may have molested me repeatedly. Now my father, too??? I know it can go from one generation to the next like that, but how could this happen at all in my family? My perfect little family? I often think I must be insane, or perverted, or cruelly ungrateful to accuse them of this. I mean, I have no proof, only vague feelings and

117

memories, and some flashbacks that don't help much except to freak me out. I have to find out the truth soon, or I will go crazy.

I love my father. (Why have I always felt a bit uneasy around him, to the point of avoiding him and the other relatives on his side, and feeling really stressed out whenever I'm forced to see them?) My father was wonderful with me. He was always kind and gentle; he played games with me and read to me; he took me on walks and bike rides, and he sang me to sleep at night. Why did I feel I absolutely had to stop spending time with him and instead live full time with my mom, when I was about 13, becoming a "woman," starting my period? He never pressured me into anything, he was always understanding, he never tried to pull a guilt trip on me for wanting to spend more time with my mom. On the phone he would say, "Your bed is still here and all made up; the room is full of books and boxes but we could move them out if you wanted to come and stay for a while." And if I said no, he wouldn't say anything more. Why the bed? Why did he always mention my bed, and always keep it made up even when the rest of the room was converted into a storage space, and it was obvious I wasn't coming back? Why did I write in my diary occasionally that I couldn't stand it at my dad's house, and then list a bunch of trivial things like there wasn't enough space and my room was situated poorly, and there was so much dust. Come on, Lara, what was the real reason you would become extremely depressed a couple of days before you moved over to your dad's after finishing your two or four weeks with your mom, and feel alive again and incredibly relieved when moving back to your mom's? Why did you once break down in sobs and cry for an hour on your bed at his place, the day of your move there, after having spent a long while trying to suppress the horrible feelings inside you in the bathroom with the door locked? When he asked you what was the matter, you said, "I don't know. Leave me alone," and that was the truth: you had no idea why you felt the world was ending. Were you blocking out some memories from a much earlier time, or was it a recent memory? I've read that abused children sometimes "learn" to forget what happened to them immediately after it happens, or even while it is happening. I do remember feeling separated from my body, as if I wasn't really present. So I didn't have to feel it or remember it. Was that when I was 4? Or also later? I have no way of knowing at the moment how long the abuse went on, because I may have been forgetting it as it happened.

My worst fear right how is that my dad may somehow find out what I'm accusing him of, and my grandmother may find out what I am similarly accusing her late husband of. I would never forgive myself if I were wrong. And it would be hell to live through if I'm right. So. The sooner I remember what really happened, the sooner I know which option I get.

I've seen my dad once since Sunday night. We went to see a movie (ironically, we saw "Twin Peaks: Fire Walk With Me"). The core of the "Twin Peaks" story-line which I've never mentioned here before, despite the pages and pages of obsessing I did about "Twin Peaks" television series, is incest. A girl is being molested and raped by her father, but she does not let herself become aware that it is HE who has been doing this to her since she was 12, until it is too late. She gives her molester another name and face because the truth would be too horrible. The girl's name is Laura. I guess Kyle MacLachlan wasn't the only reason I felt a tie or bond of some sort to that television show.

Coming home from the movies, my dad mentioned something about the movie not being terribly good compared to the earlier "Twin Peaks" episodes on television, but that at least the theme of incest was well presented and was an important, relevant issue. I looked at him as he said this, and his face was beautiful and gentle. I felt so badly for thinking he could have done anything to me. All I wanted was to love and comfort him, protect him because he looked vulnerable in a way.

He saw someone he knew on the bus, and they talked about his radio show. The man was going to read some poetry on the show. My dad wanted him to read it this coming Sunday as planned, but the man suggested waiting until the following week because then he would have time to make extra copies of the poems for my dad to look at and follow as the man was reading them aloud. At this suggestion, my dad erupted. An almost psychotic look came into his eyes, and he spat out that he would not have time to read along, that it would have to be this Sunday, that they had already agreed, etc. etc. You would have thought the man had threatened to do something horrible like blow up the radio station. My dad goes berserk like that now and then. He has a violent temper. My earliest memories are of him and my mom arguing fiercely. He loved to argue. His whole body changes; he takes this aggressive stance and his arms wave and his eyes glare. He shouts and yells. Actually, in the last few years, he's controlled himself much better. Which is maybe why it's easier now to feel a kind of pity for him.

So I have two pictures: one of the perfect family who loved and nurtured and supported me all the time; the other of a mixed-up family, some of whom sexually abused me and others who must have known this but ignored it. The first picture is the one I've totally believed up until a few weeks ago. I must be psychologically twisted to have even imagined the second picture. That's crazy. I'm crazy. These people loved me! I know it. Everybody knows it. Shit, shit, fuck! What is wrong with me? God I hate myself.

I had a dream about six years ago of my father dragging me out of school one day and forcing me to watch a pornographic movie with him at his place. I had very resentful feelings about what he was making me do; I felt it was almost hate. Another time I dreamt he was chasing me or something. I can't remember much of the dream but I do recall telling a friend at school about it who responded, "You must have some serious problems with your father."

I answered, "That's the funny thing. I don't."

A year or two ago I wrote about a dream I had of him trying to stab me with a sort of spear (it looked like the knife sharpener we have, and it is rather phallic-shaped). I grabbed a poker to protect myself. I jabbed him around his chest area and his genitals. My mom and several other people are standing around, watching this. I feel panicked. I think he wants to kill me. I feel my poker penetrate his skin several times. Then my feelings shift. For the first time in the dream, I am fully aware that it is my father. (In my writing about the dream the morning after, I said that at first it seemed like it was either my father or my half-brother, but after further reflection, it was more likely my father.) After that realization, it becomes apparent that he had intended no harm towards me, he was only playing a game. I have hurt him badly in trying to defend myself, and the other people around begin to tend to his wounds. "I am overwhelmed with guilt and grief," I wrote. "I realize that I hurt him terribly; he thought I was simply playing around, too, when I had actually thought he was a burglar or a crazy murderer and I had to protect myself from him."

I can't be crazy. This dream is trying to tell me something did happen between my father and me, as much as I hate to believe it, and impossible as it sounds. I love my father. Wait a second – I remember writing in here once that I just couldn't love him, that it was unfair you were expected to love your relatives just because you were related to them. How do I really feel about him???

Whenever I think hard about the possibility that he molested me, I feel desperate, panicked, and especially self-destructive. According to the dream description and "analysis" I wrote on January 9, 1989, the first time I cut myself up and down my arm was a little bit before the night of the dream (I assume a few days to a couple of weeks before). I said I did it because I felt awful about not being very nice to my mom when she was trying to help me with some chemistry homework. And I wrote: "Another way of looking at the dream is this: by hurting someone I love, I also hurt myself." This is exactly what's behind the self-destructive feelings I get when I think of the fact that I'm accusing my dad of something so horrible. I feel so much guilt that I could hurt him with such an accusation, and so I need to hurt myself.

I know he loved me. That has nothing to do with the molesting. He did love me, and still does. It's very hard for me to feel genuine love for him, though. But maybe I should leave love out of the picture for now. It's not the issue here.

It's raining. My mom and her partner and I went for a walk in the dark before it started to rain. The wind made it chilly. I can't feel the bond between my mom and I that I always used to feel. I was always so emotionally dependent on her. Now I feel so distinctly separate from her. I can't share any of what's happening in my life these days with her yet (except for the usual things like school and social events).

Funny, I feel very secure and safe at the moment, in my cluttered, cozy bedroom. My cat, Rupert, sleeps soundly on the wool rug. I'm also feeling hungry. I'll go eat something and go to sleep. Please, please, please let my dreams be revealing tonight.

September 16, 1992

I have ten whole minutes before I head off for university. I was too tired to write anything last night, so I'll summarize now:

The therapy session went okay, although I can't remember what exactly we talked about. Oh, yeah, I talked about the "choking incident" and about my relationship with my mom and with my dad. She asked me, toward the end of the session, why I felt there was such a urgency to remember what really happened and who it was. I repeated again that for me, remembering is an obstacle I need to overcome before going on with the healing process. And I can't stand wondering if it was my dad and/or my grandfather or just a friend of the family. The therapist can't understand this, she says.

Then I went back to the university and had a bite to eat. I walked to the psychiatric building, past the Acute Care Hospital and Emergency, places I've always hoped to be training in one day. (What am I doing here as a fucking patient???)

As soon as I walked into the building (after ten minutes of hunting for it), I felt comfortable. Maybe because it was a academic environment as well as a clinical one. The doctor was very good. He's a middle-aged Oriental man with a very nice way about him when he's talking to people. (I noticed him with some of his students while I was in the cozy waiting room.)

He agreed that hypnosis would be all right if I wanted it!!! I was so relieved. My next appointment with him is next Tuesday. Meanwhile, there's school.

* * * * *

It's going to work better with the hypnotherapist at University Hospital, I can tell. Just one hour made a big impact on me. Of course, he mostly asked questions, but not in a mechanical, monotonous voice. He actually talked with me. He made comments; he didn't just jump from one very personal question to another. When he got to the questions about my schooling and he asked me what area I was studying, I told him. And I said that I had thought of going into medicine but now I had a lot of doubts about my capability in such a field. He said, "Why? Your academic record would suggest you would be capable."

"I'm good at reading textbooks and writing exams, but I don't think I could function in the real world in a job where interaction with people is so important. I have a hard time forming close friendships. It's like there's a barrier between me and other people. I can't open up very easily."

"There might be a reason for that, right? You're protecting yourself, and you had good reason to at one time. As you work through the memories and your feelings, that barrier will come down."

I looked at him in disbelief, but also with a huge amount of gratitude.

"So, you're keeping your career options open?"

I said yes.

Will I actually, really, one day be a doctor??? I really do want to; the desire to practice medicine never goes away. It's my self-confidence that fluctuates.

I wanted to ask him if he's worked much with sexual abuse survivors. He even gave me the opportunity at one point, asking me if there was anything I would like to know about him. But I was too shy. I did ask him about hypnosis, though. He explained it to me. My question about his experience with sexual abuse victims was answered this morning when I saw my family doctor about raising the Luvox dose to 100 mg. She said that the doctor had called her and that he sounded like a very nice man. They had a long conversation and apparently he has a lot of experience with "this sort of thing" (I believed she meant suppressed memories of sexual abuse). She commented that she'd like to meet him in person. So it really does look like I've been very fortunate in getting a referral to him and in seeing him so soon. I hope it's all right if I continue with him for a long time. This would mean discontinuing my therapy sessions, I guess. I'll talk with my therapist about this. It would be great for me to have two hours a week of therapy, but I don't imagine it works well, because of the obvious problems inherent in seeing two medical practitioners simultaneously for the same problem. If I have to choose, it will be the doctor over my therapist. I feel more comfortable after one session with him than after five with her.

During the first two sessions with him I will learn how to go into a hypnotic state (he will teach me self-hypnosis) and come out again. Then if I feel ready, I'll try retrieving and exploring some memories and flashbacks. The most important thing is to feel safe as this is done, he said. I wonder how exactly it will work! He asked me if I ever sleep-walked and I replied that I have. I told him about going downtown one night in a sleep-walking-kind of state. He said that sleep-walking is a kind of natural hypnotic state, and that I would probably be a good subject for hypnosis. But of course I'm worrying that I won't be able to do it. I have a lot of faith in him, so I'll try to trust that this will work.

Before meeting him, I worried that I would find him attractive, as I find many older men in the field of medicine. However, that wasn't the case this time. I feel I can trust him completely, but there are no physical or emotional feelings in me at the present time that would suggest I'm going to grow attached to him.

From the doctor's window, I could see an ambulance parked near one of the health buildings. I found myself staring at it now and then. How ironic to see one at that moment of my life, just as I'm realizing why ambulances have been symbolic for me for so long. But of course I'm in the medical area of the university so it shouldn't stun me to see one there. I keep wondering if I'll ever work somewhere where it's an everyday experience to be around sick people and maybe even ambulances. I want it to be a normal part of my life. But right now it all still has a touch of magic to it, a symbolism I'm in awe of.

September 17, 1992

Guilt, guilt, guilt. Why can't I love my dad? Why did I have to hurt him by avoiding him, by wanting to live only at my mom's? Why do I pretend not to notice him when he rides by on his bike? I feel so much pity for him. I wish he could have had a different daughter, not someone like me. I've been so cold and ungrateful. I can't stop thinking these things sometimes. This happens when I can't believe he could possibly have molested me, and I hate myself intensely for ever having thought it happened. How and why am I so cruel? I wish Tuesday would hurry up and come. I hate this shit, and myself.

* * * * *

Something worthwhile actually did come out of this shitbag of a day: I had two flashbacks. One was of a dream I'd had about being in the artists' studios where my dad and I lived for a time. There were so many doors and rooms. I felt worried, trapped (that is, I recalled feeling that way in the dream – during the flashback I was basically emotionless as I often am). A child or two children were being hurt in some way in the room next to the one I was in, but I couldn't figure out how to enter this adjacent room. After this all went through my mind, I was aware that I've had many dreams of being in those studios, and there's usually anxiety and sometimes terror in them. In fact, I dreamt about the place about a week ago, but I'd forgotten. In the dream I was there with my mom and we were running from the police because we'd stolen something (cocaine, I think). We pushed through the large wooden swinging doors that opened onto the staircase leading down to the front door, and a whole mess of policemen were facing us with their guns pointed at us. End of dream.

As I wrote this down just now, some feeling about that staircase came back to me. First of all, the swinging doors scared me. And it was always so damn dark going down the stairs. They weren't carpeted, just concrete or wood or something, and dusty and grimy. Because of the metal strips attached to the end of each step, a clacking noise was made when anyone walked up or down the stairs. This echoes into the shadowy high ceiling. The doors go whoosh-creak-whoosh-creak and then bang, BANG as something funny happens to a hinge.

I seem to be running down the stairs, away from something. I'm being chased? I get to the heavy front door but I can't get the bolt or lock

124

undone to open it. He's coming down after me. I can hear the whoosh-creak and the clack of his shoes. It's dark, the door won't open; he's got me. [*Recalled later, and written in the margin:* He is saying to me, "Don't run. Why are you running away?" It's my father's voice.]

Is this a dream I had? If not, it's the longest and most whole memory I've had thus far of the suppressed events. There's something about it that makes it feel more real than a dream. Maybe it was a nightmare based on something that happened.

"At night I dream of monsters chasing me down staircases, through corridors, up and down elevators. But I am never able to get a good look at the beasts," is what I wrote in my short story about Catherine. This sentence was toward the end of the story, when she is recalling what it was like to be 4 years old. I wrote that section in the first person. By the end of the story it was easier to say "I. "

So the significance of the stairs is verified. There were also corridors in the artists' studios, as well as in the apartment building my grandparents lived in. That's where the elevators were, too. The other flashback was of an apartment building and I was walking through the door into the wide, carpeted hallway from my grandparents' apartment. The hallway is spacious, well-lit, clean, a bit stuffy-smelling, and there are large windows to the right. I think I can see trees outside. Despite the pleasant surroundings, I feel anxious.

These flashbacks are startling when they occur, but very reassuring later on. I couldn't be making this all up. These "instant memories" are too real. But – incest??? It couldn't happen in my family. My family is good and loving, politically correct and educated, intelligent, compassionate, and supporters of the peace movement. They're good people, and they've nurtured and supported me all my life. It's not like I was neglected or deprived in any way. It's hard to believe something like sexual abuse of any kind could occur in my family. I don't think anyone would believe it. I've also read that this is often how it is in families with incest. "Who would have thought?" It's especially excruciating when you're wondering if it happened in your own family. I must be the crazy one; that would make more sense than my loving, gentle father and grandfather molesting me. It's simply more likely that I'm mixed up and perverted. I really wonder if I am, sometimes. But then there are these dreams and flashbacks and the fact that I have virtually all the traits and problems listed in that "Incest Survivors" book I flipped through at a bookstore the other day, under the heading, "If many of these traits describe you, you may have been a victim of incest who, like many others, has forgotten the abuse." Some of the points to check off, I hadn't realized, had a connection to sexual abuse. They all applied to me: I was stunned. I can't ignore these things, even if none of them is absolute proof I was mistreated by a family member.

September 20, 1992

Another dream took place at my dad's house (his old one, the little house behind the studio, in the alley). I was reading a sort of joke book that had some jokes of a sexual nature in it. One of the jokes listed a bunch of slang terms for various types of sex. This gave me an idea for a plan to find out if my dad might have been the one who molested me in the past. I read this joke to him (we were in the kitchen together) and then said, "I'd sure like to learn how to do some of this stuff," referring to the list of sexual acts. I hoped to learn something from his reaction. This is what he did: He smiled and said, "Really? Oh, good!" and went into my bedroom were he pulled down his pants and underwear, waiting for me to join him. He bent over in a position that clearly indicated he wanted to have sex of some kind with me. As I watched him do this, I felt sadder than ever before. I began to cry, because I knew then that he HAD molested me, after all. He saw my tears and smiled kindly, saying, "Oh, are you not ready for this yet?"

"But you're my father; I'm your daughter!" I wanted to scream at him, "You molested me when I was little, didn't you?!?" But I decided that now wasn't the time to confront him. I ran out of the house and down the alley. Trees must have fallen down because the alley was strewn with trunks and branches that were difficult to climb over. I scratched my bare legs on the prickles and thorns that were strangely growing out of the tree trunks. The sight of the scratches and the stinging from them reminded me of the cuts I had made on my arms.

I continued to run, feeling so much grief I thought I'd burst. At this point I woke up and was immediately aware that this had only been a dream, although it seemed very real while I was dreaming it. I noticed that I wasn't exactly sweating as I usually was after dreams like this, but actually I wasn't really scared in this dream. The overwhelming emotion was sadness at this horrible realization. I was breathing quickly as I had been in the dream while running. I lay still for a while and thought about these dreams. Oh, God, oh, daddy, it was you, wasn't it? That's what some part of me is saying and I feel more inclined than before to believe it. I had cried in the dream, and in the previous one had felt intense anger. But I couldn't cry or feel angry now that I was awake. This was frustrating. I tried to go back to sleep, but couldn't. I kept reminding myself that this is Sunday, and Tuesday I will be in the safety of the doctor's office. I did eventually to back to sleep and slept until 11:00 a.m.

*****

Sometimes I feel like a little girl again. I hug my teddy bear to get to sleep at night. I feel helpless and powerless. I used to crawl into my mom's bed at night to feel safe. But what did she do? Did I tell her, and did she ignore me? I can't believe she would do that, but the dream with her in it certainly seemed to be suggesting that. Drowning has always been a symbol or metaphor for my worst fears, and I know now what those were and why I have recurring dreams of drowning.

Something else gnaws at me. I have the creepy feeling that my dad climbed naked into bed with me and that he would invite me into his bed and make me fondle his genitals. The thing is, these very vague memories are of us in the little house in the alley. I was 6 or 7 or maybe 8 when we moved in there from the studio. This makes me wonder if the abuse went on longer than I previously thought, like maybe until I was 12 even, and I was forgetting the individual incidents as they occurred. I keep thinking about the time I broke down sobbing on my bed at his place. I was 11 or 12. The strain, the inner tension, was unbearable. I couldn't stand it any longer. I couldn't bear being with him at his place. Why, why, why? I don't think I consciously knew at the time.

September 30, 1992

My stomach unknots to moan and my chest squeezes out a tear. I can't cry, and I think that if I could, it would help release some of the tension and pain.

I've narrowed this situation down to two possibilities: I am a functioning person who has a mild psychotic disorder verging on schizophrenia which has caused me to think that incest occurred in my family; or, my father and perhaps my grandfather molested me – my father maybe until I was 11 or 12.

During hypnosis yesterday at the psychiatrist's office, I was able to remember my dad attempting intercourse. I was jolted out of the hypnosis at one point because it was too frightening. I think penetration might have occurred and this sensation might have been what made me jump. But I'm not sure.

I felt so close to crying several times with my therapist and with the psychiatrist. But it wouldn't happen. I wanted to let it go. Damn it, I want this out of me.

Yeah, I'm demented. No way this could have happened between my dad and me. I'll say this to my therapist next Tuesday, and I'll also tell her about the "knowings" which I guess are also a product of my schizoid brain and my crazy nights out on Skid Row with the hookers, and also my stubborn belief in my imaginary world, Kawiakee (yes, I still believe I was sent here from Kawiakee by the supreme being, Goshiba, who will one day return me to my real home and I will once again be Ayesha Cema-cusha). Life on earth sucks.

I don't want to function any more. I want to give in and be a vegetable for a while until my energy and optimism come back. This would be hard to hide from my family, however. (Dear mom, I'm having a wonderful time on vacation here on Psych Ward 3. Wish you were here.) Shit. I feel like shit.

October 1, 1992
University Hospital, Acute Care, Psychiatric Service

Now and then I believe in the demented schizoid possibility, because reality keeps slipping between my fingers, dropping. I see shadows and also bright scenes, and I don't know any more which is the world other people call reality.

I am in a room with a large picture window, curtains pulled to absorb darkness, brass lock glaringly visible. I'm in a closed space, a closed system, a self-contained room. No air from the lighted sane world can seep through to my little box. The night sounds penetrate, though, and I cringe when each car passes because I am now isolated from that majesty and freedom. I am soundless, colorless, dimensionless, a shadow like those cast on the floor by the lamp shining on a putrid green plastic chair.

I am in a hotel, an apartment suite, a dormitory, my own room, my grandparents' apartment, a waiting room, a ship cabin. I could be in Kawiakee. Actually, I'm hiding in the shadows of the strong, real world.

"I am half sick of shadows, said The Lady of Shalott."

A man named Brett knocked on the heavy wooden door of my dark space and asked if I might perhaps like a snack and some juice. I declined politely. I'm hungry but I can't venture out into the plastic chesterfield room of garble and talk and agony. The pain is not palpable in the areas where many gather. Each person is distinct and even unusually different from the norm, but altogether they blend into a homogenous human melting pot. The anorexic looks like the schizophrenic who is chatting normally to a drugged psychotic who could be my biochemistry professor. The bulimic is trying to calm down the anorexic but gives up and instead howls with laughter, reflecting the psychotic's pin-black eyes.

I would blend in, too; like overlapping shadows one identity is lost among others. I want to remember Lara Gilbert, but she cannot be present in this world. I left her outside in the night sounds and trees to wait. Every evening she will whistle to me from the wet green grass below my cell and beckon. I can never manage to break the brass window lock, so I just stare and wrap the curtains around my shapeless body. I might be nothing. I think I'd like to be a sound. Then I could penetrate through walls and windows and connect people.

I'm lost, in a 10'x14' box with no openings. I need an infinitesimally small space to exist in without being lost, a singularity. For now I'll slip into the nothingness of half real shadows – two shitty dimensions instead of three.

October 4, 1992

I'll be blunt today. I'm depressed and unhappy, listless, anxious. Waiting. The weekend has been like a feverish dream: slow, confusing, monotonous, bewildering, stagnant. No sessions with the psychiatrist or medical student interns. Many of the patients are out, either off the grounds if they were allowed a day pass, or on the campus (with an escort or friend, of course). So there is very little activity. The nurses chat with the patients who are still on the ward, but that's about all that happens.

Tomorrow is Monday, and I am supposed to have come up with a plan, i.e. to have made a decision about whether to tell my mom about the incest and if so, when and how. Of course it would come down to this, but somehow I thought that I could go on hiding everything from her for a few more years. I told her I'm staying with a friend who lives in residence on campus. The lies would have to continue and get bigger if I don't tell her soon. On Friday, two people helped to nearly convince me to tell. My roommate, Margie (she has obsessive-compulsive disorder, and she's one of the strongest, toughest people I've ever met – God, I admire her) told me she was fondled by her stepfather for a number of years. She never told as a child because she wanted to protect her mom and the marriage. But as an adult, she got her last chance when her mom developed cancer. Margie told her before she died, and she says she would have felt just horrible the rest of her life if she had waited until it was too late and her mom was dead. Anyhow, Margie is not one of the two people I mentioned (that is, she has helped me come to a decision but this was last night, not Friday).

My plan is to tell my mom (at the hospital) on the day before I am discharged, sometime next week, I think. I will ask her not to tell anyone else (except a therapist if she chooses to see one) until I am ready. I'm definitely not ready for my dad or grandma, etc. to hear about what I remember. Just thinking about seeing the look on my dad's face makes me suicidal. It makes me hate myself. (Maybe I just have a strong sense of hate that I am afraid to direct at him???)

The weird thing is that everyone I talk to is encouraging me to tell because then my mom, etc. could be supportive and I do need support now. But I don't want her support. It could be I have some anger toward her: I don't want to accept support from her now when she wasn't there for me before. But to be honest, I don't think she knew about the abuse, ever.

My worst fear is that I may be wrong; I may be making all this up. My dad may never have harmed me in any way. I may be the mixed up one. Well, if he denies that he molested me and I believe him, then that's that. I'll apologize to him and say that I'm a bit psychotic.

The following is a letter addressed to her mom, dated October 2, 1992 and inserted into the journal. Also noted in the upper margin: Never Sent

Dear Mom:

This is a very difficult letter for me to write. I think it would be harder to say this to you in person right now, so I'm taking the "easy" way out. Before, I didn't want to tell you because I love you so much. Now I've realized, with the help of friends and therapy, that because I love you and because we have such a strong bond, I have to tell you. I'm so sorry I had to keep this secret from you for so long and I hope you don't feel hurt by this. I've been hiding some of my feelings and lying, too. I was afraid of the consequences of telling the truth. I haven't been fair to you, and I'm very sorry. I also was afraid of hurting you and putting you through hell. I didn't think it would be fair to do that to you, when you have been such a terrific, supportive, loving mother to me. You have always done so much to boost my confidence and make me feel good about myself, and you've encouraged me in every way. I'm so grateful for how positive and understanding you've always been. I think you are the strongest person I know. I hope I can be as loving and supportive when I have children, and be able to give a lot of time to them, listen to their problems, help them out, and really be friends with them, the way you have been with me.

What I have to tell you about has to do with what happened to me when I was little. I'm sorry it had to happen, because nobody should have to experience it (but many do) and I'm sorry you have to deal with having the knowledge of what happened to me, because you were in NO WAY responsible.

In the last five months, I've grown increasingly depressed, but up until two months ago, I didn't understand why I was feeling this way. I hid my feelings from you because I was afraid of having to answer questions like "Why are you feeling this way?" when I didn't know the answer, and also because I had too much damn pride to admit I had a problem. Two months ago I started having vague memories of things that had happened years ago. Up until then I had totally suppressed these memories. My recollections grew clearer, and in the last couple of weeks I've recalled the basic things that make the general picture complete (but there's still a lot missing in this picture). This is what I've remembered:

My dad sexually abused me when I was young. I think grandpa may also have molested me when I was very young.

I've been in therapy for almost two months. I go for an hour or two once a week, and it's been very helpful. My family doctor has prescribed an anti-depressant for me, which I've been taking for two months. It has helped, too. However, yesterday I felt too overwhelmed by the memories that were coming to me, and I felt unable to cope at all. I've been admitted to University Hospital. I will stay here for about a week, I guess. I'm getting a lot of support; the nurses and doctors are great. When I feel strong enough to continue coping, I will go back to my day-to-day life at home. And I'll continue seeing a therapist. I hope you will consider this, too.

I've felt like shit, like total hell, and I've been confused and sad and guilty. But you've showed me by example how to be optimistic, and I will not ever stop hoping that things will get better.

I love you very much,
Lara.

October 6, 1992

I'm in an extremely different mood now than I was on Sunday. For one thing, I'm angry at my new psychiatrist.

She spent fifteen minutes with me yesterday (bringing our total time together up to an impressive twenty minutes) and obliterated all hope of mine regarding a successful confrontation with family about the incest. She spoke quickly, coldly, almost sarcastically to me with a stupid grin on her face the whole time. She hardly let me get in a word. Paul and Lynn, who are my nurses on Monday, were also there but she didn't give them an opportunity to speak either. The two nurses each helped to shift my attitude from "I'm never going to tell my mom" (Thursday, the day I arrived) to "I'll tell her in a few days, while in the hospital, and with the support of the staff" (Sunday). That psychiatrist bitch said I was heading for a psychotic breakdown, that I would "crack" and end up a permanent psych patient if I continued to focus on my new memories of my past, and continued exploratory therapy with the hypnotist doctor and my therapist. She said I would have to suppress the memories, not talk to anyone (including friends) about the subject of abuse, and avoid everything that might trigger new memories such as reading about it, writing about it, etc. etc. Otherwise I will waste a couple of years of my life as a psych patient, and my academic life will go down the tubes.

I interrupted at one point, almost in a state of shock from this advice that was the total opposite of everyone else's advice, to say that I'd come to the difficult decision to tell my mom all about it. However, this would require that I deal with her reaction to what I tell her. I wouldn't be able to avoid dwelling on the subject if I were living in the same house as my distraught mother. But it would be very difficult financially to move out. Her response was "Then don't tell her now." She told me to get on with my life, block out thoughts of the abuse, and get into a secure relationship.

I wanted to scream, "I can't do any of this until I deal with this problem!!!" but no words would come out. I left the meeting feeling like shit. As we walked out of the meeting room, I caught Paul's eye. I could see he was trying not to let much expression onto his face, but I saw my frustration reflected in his eyes. It was nice to know he felt for me.

So.

Today, I haven't met with that same psychiatrist (surprise, surprise) or with Paul (who is in Victoria, for how long I don't know). I feel like I'm being ignored. Tomorrow I'm being discharged. I would like to leave tonight. I'm getting more depressed by the minute by staying here. A few minutes ago, the psychiatric aide or assistant or something came to see me, the first person today. I voiced my frustration and confusion, and he tried to get me to see that the psychiatrist was right ("She's a very good psychiatrist"). I guess she was right in saying I have a strong stubborn streak (she spat this out after having spent a total of ten minutes with me!) because I cannot accept that her advice makes good sense. I'm not trying to dwell on the problem!!! My mind is consumed by the memories because it's trying to let them out so they can be dealt with. Pushing the memories back in is just a ridiculous piece of advice!

Get on with my life??? Jesus Christ, how can I possibly do that? She said I should get immersed in school and socializing and the normal things 19-year-old university students do. I've been trying to pretend to be normal all my life, while feeling strange and depressed and unhappy. Am I supposed to continue hiding these feelings and live a phony life?

I'm so frustrated. I see ahead of me several years of depression while I slowly go through the "superficial" therapy that she recommends (yes, that was the term she used). I can't face that. I feel more suicidal now than I did when I came in here last week. Did I mention I'm to leave tomorrow?

The nurses gave me the impression I'd be permitted to attend classes this week while at the hospital. The psychiatrist, to my astonishment, refused to let me go (this was Monday morning as I was preparing to go to chemistry class). I can't understand her. If I'm supposed to get on with my life, why didn't she let me go to classes? I think she's as psychotic as I am. One last thing: From Thursday to Saturday, during which time I followed her instructions from the meeting with me on Thursday afternoon, to avoid all thought and talk of the "problem," I got increasingly worse (physically and mentally). I blacked out more often, had more hallucinations, and felt awful. Suppression does not work. I let some thoughts through on Sunday and things started getting better. So. Great advice, doctor. Thank you so much.

Dinner is served shortly. I'm sick of everything. I would like to kill myself. But one thing the psychiatric assistant said did make sense: I have a lot to look forward to. I've got to keep that in mind. There IS a future ahead, somewhere far in the distance, that could actually be quite good.

And for the present, I can't concentrate on school; I don't care if I fail everything, and I'm very depressed.

* * * * *

Probably my last entry from the psych ward. I'm afraid I really bitched earlier today. I just never realized how hard this would be for me to live through. I've got to stop feeling weak and instead see myself getting through each day and each week with strength and courage. (Yuck – talk about corny!)

I walked all through the University Hospital this evening after dinner, and it gradually sunk in that my most important goal, to become a doctor, is only attainable if I face the hard times ahead and make a pact with myself to live through them. It's easy to die. If I keep on living, I can tell myself I've faced a challenge and come out on the side of success. Then I can go into medicine with confidence and a sense of accomplishment, rather than feeling incompetent like I do these days. I know I really do want to spend time, probably a lot of time, working in a medical environment. It feels more and more like it would be the right place for me.

Now – to get to that point, I obviously have to keep up with my studies. I have a reason to care about them. At the same time, I still feel I need to have a way out of this hell if I can't take any more. Not that I'd necessarily take that way out, but if I know it's there, I won't be as desperate. Does that make any sense – that keeping suicide as a last resort, but still a resort, staves off the desperation???

October 11, 1992

"School is very important." Repeat ten times and go back to reading the textbook. Read a page. Feel sad. Wonder why. (What's sad about oligodendroglia and Schwann cells?) Ignore the feeling. Turn the music louder. Read another page. Get half-way down and stare at the page for five minutes, thinking about literally nothing. Jolt "awake" again and try to continue, but feel totally stupid and useless. Sit back in chair and pinch arms and rub temples. Thoughts wander to quick and easy ways one might kill oneself. Glance at the textbook. Repeat "School is very important " ten times. Try another couple of pages.

134

It's good that I have some sort of focus. If I weren't in school, I would feel much worse, I'm sure of it. But I'm not going to whiz through the next couple of years of undergrad studies with flying colors. As long as I keep my average up to 80%, which is about what medical school applicants need, I will be happy with my standing. And as long as I can keep from falling too far down into my dark hell, I will be satisfied with living each day as it comes. I'm prepared to live a few years with this kind of mentality. It's better than stopping school for a time to focus solely on the abuse issues (which would drive me psychotic, according to that psychiatrist) or pushing back the memories completely and plunging myself into my former academic lifestyle, as an unfeeling, emotionally empty person.

October 16, 1992

I've made a few decisions while I've been in this "up" mood:

(1)   I will live at home for another year, possibly two years, even though I'm secretly itching to move out (as if that would solve anything! It would be like running away, just to avoid all contact with family). Then I will apply for a student loan so I can either live in residence at this university (or another university if I transfer) or rent/share a suite close by the campus.

(2)   I will not tell my mom or any other family member anything about the abuse or what's been going on with me regarding therapy, etc. until I am independent (i.e. living on my own).

(3)   After completing a B.Sc. degree in biochemistry (probably another two years after this year, since I want to take an extra year to fit in more biopsychology, physiology and psycholinguistics), I will apply to medicine. If I don't get in, I'll try working a year or perhaps starting grad studies, then I'll apply again. If I do get in, I may enter the combined Ph.D.-M.D. program after my first year medicine, or maybe I'll do a straight M.D. and later go back to school for grad studies. Or maybe I'll love medicine so much that I'll forget about doing a Ph.D., but I doubt it. I think I'll always want to do both – practice medicine and do research. It will mean at least another nine academic years after this year, plus several years of internship and residency. But I feel happiest in school, so this is more of a plus than a bother.

(4)   I'm going to get involved in volunteer work again, at a medical clinic nearby or at a mental health facility if possible. Just three or

four hours a week would be very valuable experience, and probably quite interesting, without cutting into my study time too much. Of course it's also a must if you want to get accepted into medical school!

October 24, 1992

I feel freer, much less bound and suffocating than ever before. I can even nearly imagine total freedom. I can picture it; it exists ahead of me; at some point in time I will meet with it. I'm running to catch it, and I love the feel of the wind against me.

I'm letting more out with my therapist. This is helping. I can truly call our time together "therapy" now. In a few days, I will tell her more about the "knowings" (I introduced the subject last week).

Before, I had decided I could never reveal these things to her because I would have to face her psycho-theorizing and analyzing. Now I think that maybe she would believe what I have to say: I'm not crazy or schizophrenic; I do have "knowing" experiences.

November 7, 1992   .

The last two weeks have been very encouraging. The Luvox is doing wonders; the therapy is helping immensely; I feel so different from how I felt during the shitty summer months. It's cold outside now, and crisp and slightly overcast. Last night it rained and rained. I love the transition between fall and winter.

Still keeping really busy. My midterm marks have been great, which is amazing to me. I somehow squeeze in socializing, piano, working out at the fitness centre, and visiting art galleries. School is very absorbing, and the enormous amount of work is a little frightening, but being able to do a lot of other things gives me a strong fulfilling feeling. I love everything I'm doing. I'm still waiting to hear from the Food Bank. Expect to start work there in a week or two, later than planned, but good actually because my midterm exams will be over by then.

Things are going great, but there are some problems still:

I can't seem to decide if I should volunteer at the Gastown Medical clinic. It's a tough decision. If I don't I will work with the Strathcona Mental Health Team. Or maybe I can fit it all in. I doubt I'll have the time. But I love being busy. What should I decide?

Now and then I get strong urges to go to Main and Hastings (Skid Row) again and stand on the corner in the middle of the night, waiting for a car to stop. I want to sell my body, turn on a man, have sex with a stranger. I've confessed this to my therapist and I told her about my night out. I didn't want her to think that the therapy was somehow the cause of this obsession of mine, so I lied and said I'd been doing these things for a year-and-a-half now. Sometimes the thought of returning to the streets disgusts me, and sometimes it is so alluring that I have to give in. I'm being reckless and impulsive. I have to stop this soon, but it's like an addiction.

The week before last, I spent an evening with a friend of mine. We went to a nightclub. It could have been a really fun night out, but I did something really stupid, which I'm afraid I might do again. I took a tranquilizer and a sleeping pill as well as several of my anti-nausea/ anti-anxiety pills and a few pain killers, before I left to go out. I wanted to be relaxed for the evening. Well, I was a little too relaxed. After consuming several drinks at his place and at a restaurant (according to him – I have only a vague memory of all this) I was quite out of it by the time we got to the club. After about twenty minutes there, I passed out. I ended up at St. Paul's Hospital, and then he took me home. I didn't tell him about the pills I took – he assumed it was the combination of alcohol and Luvox that made me pass out. He was pissed off. I was depressed. I don't know why I do these stupid, impulsive things. The day after, I had what the doctors called a dystonic reaction. My jaw, neck and back seized up and went into painful spasms. I couldn't talk (my teeth were clenched) and could move my head only with difficulty. My mom drove me to St. Paul's and there was a different shift working, so no one recognized me from the night before. Somehow I got across to the doctor that I was taking anti-depressants. (I think I recall writing LUVOX in the air with my finger.) This was after several minutes during which the doctor and nurses stood around me, puzzled, and wondered aloud what was going on with me. I was confused as hell, too. "Is she having a stroke?" one of them wondered. Finally someone asked me if I was taking any medication, and I "told" them (but I didn't mention the tranquilizers, etc. which surely contributed to the dystonia). The nurse said, "Aha! That's it!" And they spend another few minutes congratulating each other on their diagnostic coup. Finally I was given an injection of Benadryl and told that I was having a dystonic reaction, a possible side effect of my anti-depressants. I was grateful that within a few minutes my muscles relaxed and the pain went away. I was also grateful that these spasms could be explained simply by the Luvox, so I didn't have to confess about the other pills I'd consumed. I asked the

137

doctor not to tell my mom that I was on Luvox. So my mom thinks I had an allergic reaction to something. Phew.

November 16, 1992

A long, high-pitched, drawn-out wail, like a scream, can be heard from two blocks away (on Hastings Street). The agony. Probably a prostitute. Could have been me. I wish I could scream right now.

Dad, do you know what you did to me? How can you look me in the eye? How can you get up every morning? I hate you and I still love you and feel responsible for you. If you're not happy, I feel it's my fault. If you were to get depressed and commit suicide, I would blame myself for not preventing it. I have this crazy idea, very deep-rooted, that I have some kind of power over you, a kind of responsibility, for your welfare. That's where this guilt comes from. I feel so fucking bad about the thought of you finding out I know – that I remember the abuse.

I'm afraid you'd feel so bad you'd kill yourself, and it would be my fault. The reason I see you depressed now and then is because I no longer live with you; I've abandoned you. The guilt I feel because of this is tremendous. But what I've come to realize with my therapist's help is that this feeling of power I have is distorted; it is not valid. Somewhere along the way I got the idea that I owed you something, that it was my duty to keep you happy (sexually or otherwise) and now I can't get rid of that crazy feeling.

(The rest of this entry is in large chaotic handwriting - Ed.)

Goddamn you, get out of me
you demon   you shit   you asshole
I hate you   I hate you

I HATE YOU

You raped me   You hurt me
and you pretended none of this happened.
You held me tightly in bed so I could barely breathe.
You entered me... and moaned. "Oh, kiddo... "
you said and I cried.
"Please don't please don't
I love you anyway It's OK"

It's NOT OK. I won't let you ruin my life.

At night I want to be cuddled and rocked like a baby. I hold my teddy bear tightly and rock back and forth on my bed until I fall asleep. It's as if I'm a little girl again, feeling lonely and afraid.
I don't know who to be
    Pre-med student?
       Incest survivor?
        Prostitute?
          Psych patient? Crazy person, schizophrenic,
          Hallucinating maniacal delusional paranoid schizoid
          NUT
I FEEL LIKE DYING

It's 11: 00 p.m. but I'd like to go for a walk. I take late night walks quite often. It brings me back over the line to sanity. But not tonight. I will go to sleep now and wake up tomorrow with a sunny smile on my face and go to school and write my BioChem 301 midterm exam and then go to a dentist appointment and then come home and who knows what.
    WHO KNOWS?

Maybe I'll take some pills (this has become a bad habit but it's not like I OD or anything; just take enough to knock me out so I don't feel anything for a few hours).
    Oh, moan, bitch, complain

    I want to go someplace wonderful
       like Kawiakee, Paradise
         I want a perfect world

I'm tired and depressed

November 19, 1992

The day after that last entry, I did indeed write that midterm and go to that dentist appointment and both went very well (bizarre or what!) and I actually feel good at the moment. Saw my therapist today, and together we uncovered some pretty fundamental truths about humans and life. Or maybe I should put it this way: she helped me accept that there are possibly no real truths about anything; reality is relative. The astounding thing is that I feel more optimistic now than when I went to her office at 3:00 today. This is because of her answers to my questions: "But nothing really matters anyway – people live awful lives and then

139

they die, so how can I accept this world? Why can't I imagine a perfect world and live in it in my mind? Would this make me insane? Do you believe things are real – objects and people and everything – is it all really real? Is the traffic we hear outside real?"

I babbled on and on in this pessimistic manner and she responded by saying yes, she does believe. She believes in her reality, and she believes that it has significance. What she does on a day-to-day basis is generally consistent (though at times unpredictable) so she can count on it; have faith in it, and she does believe her actions are meaningful. She believes in the traffic behind the sounds. "And I can hear something else, too; I'm not sure what it is. A sort of clanging? It's stopped. There – it's started again. Can you hear it?" I nodded and smiled, looking into her large dark eyes. There was a strengthening of a bond then, kind of an acknowledgement that we have an understanding of one another's perspectives.

Hearing her proclaim her faith in this reality was so encouraging to me, I could have cried. This is what I needed, someone else to validate what I perceive around me, someone strong enough to accept the world as it is and believe in her own existence; I am linked to this faith through her, despite not being strong enough myself to hold it independently right now. Things are real to her, and she is someone I trust, respect, and like. Therefore, I'll put my trust in her take on reality and tell myself there are other people, her for instance, who have a strong grip on things. So I can trust things, too. The distortions I perceive really are just distortions.

"Is there a universal reality?" she asked herself at one point, rewording a question I had put to her. I forget her answer to this. But knowing she cares enough to formulate the question is encouraging to me.

"Am I hopeless?" I asked at one point. She said no (of course).

Do you want to grow up?" she asked at another point.

I said no automatically, "No, I'd like to stay about 14 if I could." Later I changed my mind. I said that yes, I would like to grow up.

She then said, "The question I have, is who are you? Who is Lara? And what do you want to be?"

"I don't know; I don't even know how to start finding the answers to that."

"You could start here, in therapy," she said. "You could start by making some important decisions."

Well, I made one decision after our session, which I will announce to her when I see her next Tuesday. I do not want to be a prostitute any longer. That is one identity I want to toss aside. The urge to tackle Main and Hastings is gone (at the moment at least and if it returns, I will fight it for all I'm worth).

The reason is, I was raped last night. I'll relate the incident later, but in short, a wealthy, respectable man picked me up just off Hastings and the deal we made was a blow job and eat-out (oral sex on both our parts – no pun intended).

After that was accomplished in the car (lovely big one with plush seats and cellular phone) I said I had to go but he insisted on mounting me. This he finally accomplished despite my refusals, by pushing me down and against the door (my back is killing me today) and holding me tight, pumping me quickly. It was so painful. My flesh was screaming between my legs. I kept saying NO, and he finally stopped, disappointed he couldn't fully penetrate me. It just wasn't physically possible – I was too "tight" – but he got in far enough to make me bleed quite a lot. Got in me anally as well. I'm pretty sure he didn't ejaculate, so I don't think I have to worry about STDs. And he insisted he was sterile, after I raged, "Where's the condom?" So I doubt I'm pregnant. But I will worry nonetheless. I'm going to make an appointment to get tested for AIDS soon.

It's a relief to say "I won't go back and do it again." I sure hope I can live up to this pact.

Anyhow, I made $20 last night from that creep and so I'm going to get a perm on Saturday (which will cost about $60).

November 24, 1992

Welcome to Hell. Earth. Planet. Home. Brain. Get me out of here.

It has been one awful day, just because of the way I've felt. Must be the morning-after pill they gave me at Shaughnessy Hospital. All that estrogen. Hormonal chaos inside me. Feels like really shitty PMS. Anxiety, self-hate, exhaustion – actually it feels much like the time I took quite a few steroids (the anti-nausea/anti-anxiety pill that turned out to be the cause of my dystonic reactions). I'm not surprised I feel a bit drugged today, what with the effect of the morning-after pill, the Luvox, and the eight caps of tetracycline I'm taking daily for a week (to attack any possible infections of gonorrhea? or chlamydia? or syphilis? – any two of these three). Tomorrow I'll need some Anaprox and Gravol for menstrual pain as the estrogen does its work. Life stinks.

But life goes on. STRESS. Oh, God this has been a grueling week. I was too tense and cranky today to make my session with my therapist a productive one. I'm so far behind in chemistry it's scary. The Christmas exam is Dec. 8. I might fail. I'm unhappy and afraid. The stress created by not letting my mom know how I'm really feeling is harder to handle than ever.

"How much longer are you going to keep all these secrets?" my therapist asks. "Will your relationship with your mom ever be a genuine one?"

"There can be no more heinous threat to our children than sexual exploitation. It robs them of their innocence and can inflict lifelong damage."

Lloyd Axworthy

Chapter Six

Age Twenty

November 26, 1992
Birthday, Age 20

My father went hunting in a second-hand shop for my birthday present and found an incredible antique stamp album, full of old and historically fascinating stamps. We turned the pages together in awe and I thanked him, all smiles. We hugged. He recommended several current art exhibits downtown; he described the cold frosty weather of the day I was born in crisp, then melting words, poetry, music. I thanked him for my birth.

(Most of this entry is written in tiny scratching handwriting - Ed.)

Daddy who did what he knew was wrong, would hurt, would frighten and confuse me, did it anyway because he couldn't control his feelings, impulses, sex, sex, sex. Dad who kissed me on the lips today as he said Goodbye and Happy 20th, who then moved his lips down to my neck and shoulder and left a red blotchy mark there. Who are you? How? Does it mean there is no pure good nor a real Utopia here or later or ever?

Once yesterday on my bed I felt a flash of real suicidal desires, but it passed quickly and I stopped my writhing for a moment to ask myself, surprisedly, why I let it come at all. Never ever – even if I think I'm too weak to handle the pain. That's just cowardice. I'll hold on, because I have my friends and my therapist and in a sense my mom to hold on to. And my desires, ambitions.

In the midst of birthday wishes, he handed me a typewritten page (a photocopy, that is) of a piece of poetry/prose he wrote today, with a handwritten note, ending in "I lost my virginity at 20!" My father. I'd like to offer myself to him now, in entirety: take me all; just accept me and do what you want with my body, penetrate and caress and kiss if you'd like. I don't really care – there are no feelings in this flesh now – they're hiding.

OH   HEY   WHO CARES

I think tonight I will tell my mom. Oh, God, I can't believe it. I think I'm ready.

December 16, 1992

My mom knows now. But before that happened I did something extraordinarily stupid: I overdosed. For sixty seconds last Thursday evening I really wanted to die. I took about 30 pills (Luvox, Cogentin,

Gravol, Anaprox, Benadryl) and then in horror realized what I'd done, and tried to throw it all up. Didn't work, so I called Jan and tearfully confessed what I'd done – then to Vancouver General Hospital where they gave me a drink of charcoal. I thought that was that, but I guess I had already absorbed a lot of the pills because I went into a long delirium; I was incoherent and hallucinating and God, what a shitty experience. Spent the next few days in the Psychiatric Assessment Unit (PAU) where I told my mom what was going on.

Now everything's changed: our relationship, our life, etc. etc. No more secrets. It's a relief, and it's also fucking chaotic and stressful. Saw my therapist yesterday, and again today with my mom, then I had a short session with her supervisor, a psychiatrist. He and my therapist made it very clear to me that they will not offer me therapy regarding suicidal impulses; that is, if I continue to behave suicidally, my therapy with her will be terminated. At first this hit hard because I felt like I was being abandoned when I needed help most, but after a while I realized that it just isn't fair to my therapist what I did; she's putting a lot of effort into helping me live a better life, so my trying to end my life conflicts totally with this therapy. They told me that I can return to the PAU at Vancouver General Hospital whenever I feel self-destructive again, but the issue of self-destructiveness will not be addressed in the out-patients' department between my therapist and me. I said that was fine. So I will continue with her after all, which is good. Also, my mom will start individual therapy at the out-patients' clinic in February (long waiting list) and my therapist will recommend a good family therapist for us. So some positive things have come out of this stupid, stupid thing I did last Thursday. I still regret it very much. I wish I could turn back time.

Mood is still all over the place, up and down and up and down. Feel afraid and fragile, then confident and strong, then out of control and insane. Confused, stressed out, tired. And, Oh God, there's Christmas to deal with.

* * * * *

My mom and her partner (who also knows now) is taking everything really hard, naturally. Not only does she have to learn her daughter was molested by her former husband, but she also has to deal with her daughter's attempted suicide. What an imbecile I am. I can think of a hundred easier ways to have broken this to her. Oh, well, what's done is done.

146

December 19, 1992

Living with the secrets out in the open (in this house, that is) is about as difficult as I thought it would be. The ambience in the house is tense, unhappy, angry, grieving. My mom's partner, my mom and I are being supportive of one another, but there's so much emotion in the air that I sometimes wish I were 1,000 miles away. It's getting better, though: every day it feels a little easier to communicate for me and I can see that my mom is handling the initial shock more easily as time goes by. But she wants to be near me or at least know which room of the house I'm in, all the time, and will not let me leave the house (e.g. go to the bank or mail a letter) without accompanying me. This over-protection is understandable, and I don't bitch about it. There's a lot of guilt on both sides; she feeling awful for not having protected me when I was little; me feeling awful for putting her through the agony of last week's overdose. But I'm being more honest with her now, and what an incredible relief that is! The stress of lying is just not worth it.

* * * * *

Naturally things are a bit strained regarding my dad who has knocked on the door and phoned, trying to see me. He doesn't know what's going on, so I almost felt sorry for him when they slammed the door in his face yesterday, saying "We're not home. Lara's not here." I'll phone him tonight so he doesn't get suspicious. None of us wants to confront him yet (but I'm starting to like the idea of one day getting out my rage and just telling him how much he's ruined my life). I imagine that within a few weeks, my mom will be as used as I am to acting and pretending around other people in order to hide what really is still a secret.

It gets better, not worse from here. I have support and love from my mom, her partner, and friends, and I have my therapist and my doctors and the hospital to turn to when I need to.

Secrets, secrets – I learned for the first time a couple of days ago that my mom was physically, sexually and emotionally abused as a child. I knew her household was a mess because of her alcoholic parents, but I had no idea she was abused. She has also broken the news to me that depression does indeed run in the family (her mom and her uncle, among others). After telling me all this rather shattering stuff about our family, she added, "There is also a tendency towards genius running in the family" which, I guess, she meant as a consoling note. From what I've observed, however, genius and insanity are pretty much equivalent and I'd rather have neither in my ancestral roots.

* * * * *

I wrote something today, at a point when the chaos inside me seemed about to explode me – this poem kind of fell out of me, and the relief afterwards was like finally being able to cry hard when you've been unconsciously holding the tears in for a long time.

The little girl floats
Up with sparkles and bubbles in the drink
Her father holds
his hand weightless on her golden head
and hair is swimming in the amber drink
Wet hands on head   her hair dripping
Separates and drifts above him
No more a part of tangled strands in
yellowed fingers
Now apart   Far gone   Faint the smell
of stale smoke and beer.

Wrapped around her head now
Lifting pulling pressing down
He separates her dampened hairs
into glass fibres that float around
his drowning eyes
Framing the picture, she weaves him up
into a cocoon
Breathing his anger, she lifts herself above
the tangled flesh
Now wrapped tight, closed hands and mouth
He doesn't want to let go yet
"Touch me once more, angel"
Saliva drips from shining lips
"I am your father, child"

The bubbles break   hairs unwind   he's free
She falls from her floating perch
Gives in;

But one day will untangle her small limbs
from his
And weave a net of words around him
Leaving him bound
And separate from her,
Still his daughter
But apart and free.

> Memories to focus on maybe:
> - staircase
> - choking incident
> - grandparents' house (snoring) and hallway
> - flashbacks of legs spreading apart and penis against me
> - pressure in my behind – dream (measles)
> - curtains
> - my dad in my bed or me in his, at little house

December 20, 1992

Sometimes chicken soup tastes so good, it's unbelievable. And everything else is just right, too. You don't even need to think about the concept of hope; you can take it for granted. Life is good. I'd like to read a hundred books tonight, write a novel, play the piano till my fingers fall off, plan my medical career, organize my room, file the mounds of papers on my desk. All this fantastic energy – and I have to go to sleep. Dammit. But my mom intends to wake me up at 8:30 sharp so I need to go to sleep now, whether I feel like taking on the world or not.

My psychiatrist assures me I'm not manic-depressive. I'm sure he's right. These episodes of super energy and confidence and creative impulses are too short-lived to be called mania – I rarely actually carry out any of the more outrageous things I plan during my "rush" because it's all over so soon, like a roller-coaster creeping up that hill and pausing one glorious moment at the peak before crashing down.

Back to the usual me – depressed and cranky. I wish mania was my default emotion, and not depression.

149

December 23, 1992

Gone down. Feel like shit. Not telling my mom because she's already upset enough. God, I hate these swings. Why can't I stay up? All over the place. This sucks.   suck   suck

                                        I could call the Crisis Line
                            from downstairs where my mom (in bed)
                                    could not hear. Or just go to bed and
                                sleep the fucking night away. Okay, if it
                        takes more than an hour to get to sleep, I'll call.
              Knife   cut   kill   hate
                    me   me   me   FUCK

December 25, 1992

Merry Christmas
Yesterday was okay, even with my evening spent at grandma's with dad, et al. But today I'm down in my pit again. Oh creation, oh life, give thanks; "life is too precious" the family therapist said to me after learning I'd overdosed. Precious pile of shit and pain. I belong in a grave.

I must concentrate on my upcoming second term of third year at university. Starting January 4, I'll be back in the academic macrocosm of the university campus and I must play the part of science student, pre-med keener. I only show masks to the world. And to myself as well. What they and what I want to see.

Who the hell am I? I'm a floundering animal in a mound of shit at the bottom of a deep pit in the reeking dark.

December 30, 1992

I'm making big changes and it feels chaotic inside and out but I believe my decisions are good ones, this time. If I am lucky enough, I'll be able to jump on a vacancy in Gage Towers, one of the university's residences, on January 4. I've been to the Student Housing office and they expect some rooms to come available over the next few days. So hopefully I'll be moving out! I will finally be somewhere where I will need to grow up, where I am free to control my own life. As wonderful and supportive as my mom and her partner are, I realize now that as I matured from an adolescent to an adult, I was being treated as a child. Every little thing going on in my everyday life was monitored and still is, except the things I worked very hard at keeping secret (seeing my

150

therapist this summer, for example). I was given the feeling that if I deviated at all, hell would break loose, so I did what was expected and lived what appeared to be a free, happy, normal life, but which was actually under rigid control. I'm breaking loose now, and I'll miss home for sure (already I feel painfully homesick) but I certainly will not miss my father's side of the family. I am leaving this neighbourhood, and leaving my father and his family. My father is a cruel, violent man who hurt my mother and me almost beyond belief. My picture of him as a gentle, compassionate person is an illusion. He worked hard at creating it for me, but I know more now and I see through it. I know how he took advantage of me and used me sexually when he pleased, and simply ignored me (and my mom) when he wanted to. All through my mom and his seven years of being together (married common-law), he was having affairs with other women, my mom finally told me a day ago. He would leave in the evening and return at 5:00 the next morning, and this would occur even when my mom and I needed him most, such as when I was only a few days old, or when my mom was left alone with his father (my dad's dad) who made frequent aggressive sexual advances toward my mom. My dad also coerced my mom into sex whenever he felt like it, whether or not she was willing, and once he got angry at her for trying to break up an argument between him and his sister and he threatened her with a knife. My mom says I was 3 or 4 at the time, and witnessed the event.

Who do I see him as? As a doting father who would like to see more of his busy daughter who rarely calls him up, that ungrateful child. I felt so guilty for not being loving enough to him. Goodbye, guilt!

My mom said the other day, after telling me these secrets she'd kept so long, that I may have been pining for him when we were apart but he wouldn't be thinking of me at all. He'd be seducing as many young women as he could, and sleeping with them. She also said that she had a good five hours more worth of stories about how awful he was. Then she said that when they finally separated, she was a basket case.

> Bastard   Fucking bastard
> You asshole!
> Liar!   Hypocrite   Sleezebag
> Shit-filled creep

Oh how shaky I feel, like I'm hanging
from a thread.
I need more stable ground.
I want out of my twisted family.

January 7, 1993

Moving into Gage Residences this weekend!!! I'm so excited. My
mom and her partner are supportive of my decision to move out, but also
sad that it had to happen this way, during this not-so-happy situation.

I'm nervous, too. Changes tend to take a long time for me to adapt
to. But I think the university is the best place for me for the next four
months – away from my father and away from the downtown streets at
night. I'm going to keep things together this term. I'm making
connections again with high school friend and prom date, Jim C. I think
there's the possibility of a real relationship.

January 23, 1993

I've never felt so safe and comfortable anywhere as the way I feel
living here at Gage Residences (except perhaps up the coast). I'm free! I
love my room and its view; I love the presence of other young adults all
around. Despite the fact that I share this place with five others, I feel like
I have more privacy than I ever had living at home. I do miss my mom
and the house (and my kitty, Rupert!) and I worry about my mom, but
this move has felt like just the change I needed.

Friday morning I found myself in Emergency at the Vancouver
General Hospital, wondering why I had cuts and scratches all up my
arms and on my chest, and confused as hell as to how I got from my
room on campus to a park at the foot of Main Street* (where apparently a
police car came across me curled up and semi-conscious). The
Emergency doctor thought I'd overdosed again so I was forced to drink
down charcoal (possibly the worst stuff in the world to try to swallow)
despite my insisting that I'd taken nothing except two Gravol about 8:30
Thursday evening for an upset stomach.

In the morning, the doctor asked if I wanted to see the people from
psychiatry but I declined, not wanting to spend any time in the
Psychiatric Assessment Unit. I took the bus back to the university at 6:30

---

* Not far from where her father had lived when she was a child - Ed.

a.m. Friday morning, shivering cold (only had a light sweater on – how I survived the night in the park without freezing to death is beyond me).

I called my therapist Friday afternoon to relate the strange events of Thursday night, and she suggested I come in to see her on Tuesday so that we could spend a session talking about my actions that night and my memory loss, before this coming Thursday which is the BIG DAY: I'm going to confront my dad about the abuse, at the psychiatric out-patients' department where I regularly see my therapist. She will be observing behind a one-way mirror, i.e. both my dad and I will know she is near by and monitoring us but it will feel more private than if she were sitting right with us.

I'm looking forward to getting the confrontation over with. It will be a big step toward detaching myself from his side of the family and their pattern of abuse, and towards finding out who I am and how I want to grow and change. Also, I expect the feeling of telling my dad what I think of him and showing my anger will be a gratifying one.

January 29, 1993

Yesterday was supposed to be the day I confronted my dad, but a few days ago my therapist's secretary called to say she was off work this week because of a death in the family. I'll hear from her on Monday, apparently, to arrange a new appointment. Thank God I hadn't called my dad yet to ask him to meet me at her office.

* * * * *

University Hospital, Acute Care, Psychiatric Service

I don't know where my faith in life has gone. All I can put trust in are the mountains out there. I have to go back to Kawiakee soon, I'm being told by Goshiba. I will be going home at last! My real home. I will be Ayesha again.

How to explain this to my therapist? And to "family"? To my therapist I will attempt to explain everything so she doesn't view my "death" as a suicide but as a transformation and releasing of the soul so it can return to its original home. The only way to accomplish this is to discard my present body and allow Goshiba to guide me home. To family, I will leave a letter explaining this and apologizing deeply for how this "experiment" of Goshiba's may have hurt them due to its early aborting. If the experiment isn't aborted soon, i.e. if I am not returned to

Kawiakee, the poisons of Earth (which I was sent here to neutralize with Goshiba's guidance) will penetrate my Kawiakun spirit. This disruption will create an imbalance in the collective Kawiakun life force large enough to destroy Kawiakee in the way the Earth is being destroyed by humans on it. In effect, my poisoned spirit would infect Kawiakee with Earth's disease, for which there is, as yet, no cure. The Earth needs to be healed. But it will have to be done in some way other than through a Kawiakun spirit with an Earthly body which is by nature flawed. Its strength is going. I have so little physical energy these days. Spiritually, however, I am very alive!

Before my journey back, I will carry through with my confrontation with my father, which will hopefully be next week. He needs to learn that his actions have consequences, and that he will be prevented from harming other children the way he harmed Lara.

February 11, 1993

I've been in hospital ten days now. The first day was in Vancouver General Hospital Emergency where my therapist took me after the psychiatrist talked to me and decided I was really out of it ("confusional and dissociated"), so he wrote out a form that meant I was committed to hospital for reasons of mental illness. I had simply tried to get through to him the situation with Kawiakee: I had to discard my body. I guess I sounded psychotic. Anyhow, from Emergency I was transferred to the Psychiatric Assessment Unit for three days (where I was in December, but now the unit has been expanded and is quite pleasant and comfortable).

On the second day I was there, a male nurse assaulted me in my room (partial penetration occurred) which just freaked me out. I went berserk after he left the room, him saying, "I'll come back later" and pulling up his pants. I threw stuff around; I swore; I let out the anger and it was great. What wasn't so satisfying was when the head nurse came into my room (another nurse had already given me an injection to calm me down) and immediately started defending the male nurse, saying my "story" had loopholes in it because, at the time I said the assault occurred, he had been in the lunchroom. Well. To first be abused and humiliated by someone I initially totally trusted, and then to be told I was making it all up by another person whom I trusted and whose concern should have been for my well-being, not his (I was the patient after all) – this just made me furious. I demanded I be transferred to

University Hospital as soon as possible. In the meantime I made a statement to the police who came to the Psychiatric Unit to interview me. Then they took me to Shaughnessy Hospital where the sexual assault system is in place. I was medically examined and any evidence (e.g. hairs, blood, semen, all the clothes – I mean pajamas – I was wearing at the time) were taken in the systematic way it's done now. The examining doctor was very kind and gentle. That was a relief. Anyhow, with the psychiatrist's help (I had called my therapist to bitch about the situation in the Psychiatric Unit where a male nurse roams the patients' rooms looking for a good fuck), I was transferred to University Hospital a couple of days later, which was a Friday evening. Tomorrow it will be a week here. I am feeling okay, but swing down occasionally still and feel self-destructive off and on. My psychiatrist here prescribed Loxapine for me, an anti-psychotic drug, and he took me off the anti-depressant Luvox. I am not too sure if he knows what he's doing. Just because I have a spiritual basis to my life which doesn't fall under any of the traditional categories, e.g. Christianity, Buddhism, Islam, etc., doesn't mean I'm schizophrenic. I hear Goshiba telling me what to do, guiding me, so now I'm called a schizophrenic??? They really aren't sure what's wrong with me. They would so much like to make a diagnosis because that's the whole point of medicine sometimes, unfortunately.

On the 18th I'll be given a series of psychological tests (including the ink blots and all that – what fun), as if the tests will solve the question of "What's wrong with Lara?" Sorry to sound so cranky and ungrateful; actually I'm relieved to be here where I'm safe and looked after. I need to stay at least till next Friday, February 19, they say, but I do have the option of leaving earlier on my own accord because I'm no longer "committed" to stay.

A few nights ago I got fed up with the place and left in the middle of the night (how I evaded the security guards is beyond me – must have been Goshiba's guidance). I went to a place with bushes and trees around, only a five-minute walk from the hospital, and waited for a signal. I was told to look into the sky for strength. I stood with Orion on my right and the Big Dipper on my left, and the gloriously full yellow moon directly above me. I was infused with strength from the Kawiakun life force. Ayesha is strong enough now to last a little longer before the decision to "discard the body" has to be made. This extra time is needed because I still haven't confronted my dad (it will have to be by phone, hopefully this weekend) and because Lara does not want to be discarded. Part of me will return to glorious Kawiakee, but Lara has more to do here on Earth. The reintegration of the two intertwined spirits will have to occur without harm being done to either Ayesha or Lara. I want to continue life in this world, as fucked up as Earth is, because I (like every human on this planet) have a responsibility to pull our planet towards health and peace. And, hey, maybe it's possible! Not an instant cure, but a nudge now and then by all of us could seem to give quite an effective pull away from the precarious tilt we're at now. Perhaps I'm just being optimistic because I'm high on medication. Anyhow, I'm enjoying this high and I think I'll keep this relatively harmless method of mood-lifting in mind for when I crash again. I'll try Gravol if I can't get Ativan easily enough. Twenty-five Gravol pills put me into a lovely snoozy delirium a couple of weeks ago (although my heart rate zoomed up to 150 – probably not terribly safe).

Tomorrow I hope to get an "off-campus pass" so I can go the "Biological Basis of Language" conference at Simon Fraser University (downtown site) after my classes and lab. Been looking forward to this for a long time: lectures on neurological bases of language impairment, dyslexia, genetics of language disorders, etc.

February 27, 1993

On Wednesday I met with my father and a social worker and a nurse from the hospital, in the social worker's office. This was the day before I left the hospital. If I'd planned it better, I would have scheduled the confrontation a few days earlier. Oh well. It actually went OK. No shouting. He didn't admit to anything, mind you.

March 5, 1993

What's the point? Life sucks. And then there's biochemistry. How the hell can I care about fucking biochemistry? But it relates to real life, to our lives; it can make lives better. Neurotransmitters and lithium, myelin and multiple sclerosis, jumping genes and antibiotics. But I have to keep my faith in biochemistry and genetics because… because… some things have to change. There's too much misery. If I just give up and do nothing, I have no chance of helping to make any changes in the future. Life is crappy. Let's clean up the crap. God I hurt; we all hurt; let us go; give us peace.

March 13, 1993

The only thing to do that is bearable is to look at the water and layered mountains. Golden ocean, submerge me.

It would be so easy to give up! The end would be so sweet – for me, that is. Obviously suicide is not fair to the people left. If I didn't have my mom and close friends to think of, I would end my life in a minute. It's what I want; it's the only way to escape the pain of insanity.

And I have the means right here in my drawer:

23½ Luvox - 50 mg tablets

14 Sertraline - 150 mg

15 Loxapine - 10 mg

Oh, and 3 Gravol and 4 Ibuprofen. To be sure, I could buy another 60 or so Gravol tablets at the campus pharmacy.

One way to avoid leaving family and friends in pain would be to kill them before I kill myself. Now that would really be self-centred! The idea is appealing, though. But how do you kill someone without a gun? Poison? Gather them all together in a house and make an explosion occur? Stabbing? Fire?

I'd like to blow up the whole world. Goodbye planet Earth.

The next best thing to killing myself would be to allow myself to be killed by someone. The best place for that is around Main and Hastings. But I've roamed that area plenty of times at night, and nothing's happened to me yet. If I gave it a few days, however, maybe it would happen. I could just sit in an alley for a few days and wait. No, that would be pointless.

March 15, 1993

The urge to walk out into the night is so strong. I want to fly. But no, I will not take any drugs. I'll just let my own innate insanity take me wherever it wants to go. The moon, hay, sea, tree, silver fish – I can survive, I know and I will. Under the sycamore tree there lies a body all broken and sticky with blood.

March 21, 1993

I know how to get a gun. One of my roommates in the residence has several guns and rifles at her parent's home in Coquitlam (her father likes hunting). There's still the question of how to use it. I have no idea how guns work. Another option: While at my family doctor's a few days ago, she gave me about 60 more Sertraline tablets (50 mg each) because she had some extra free samples and she knows how expensive they are to buy. This was kind of her, but she sure ain't too bright – giving a depressed person (who has previously attempted suicide by overdosing on medication) an extra large amount of prescription pills all at once???

Oh, well. Actually, I'm doing better than I have in ages. I'm actually functioning: catching up at school, socializing, sleeping all right, seldom crashing down. Suicide still seems very appealing, mainly because I know I have a place to return to: Kawiakee. I just want this life here to be over, so I can move on. But I can't do this to my mom. NO.

Things to do here on Earth first:
- go sailing with David
- spend summer evenings at English Bay with my best friends
- travel
- gain enough knowledge and experience that I can make a difference somehow in this place we call home
- try to accept it when my thinking doesn't make sense, rather than despairing over this insanity – perhaps it will enhance my life, not hinder it.

Tomorrow evening, David and I go out. He is a 24-year-old man I met at a party a week ago. I asked him out. Just felt something special there, maybe. At least give it a try. Will it work out? Will I like him even more as I get to know him better? Will he like me? Even if the attraction is mutual, would I be able to maintain a serious relationship? I'm not sure exactly what I'm getting into.

March 28, 1993

If David proposed to me tomorrow, I would accept. We were meant to be together; I feel it in my bones, in my soul. Something special, indeed. Since our first date last Monday, we've been going out almost every other evening. Last night we went to a BBQ at Peter's house (a friend of David's) – left for the BBQ at 6:00 p.m., spent a few hours there and then came back to my place where we watched television and talked and enjoyed each other in every way imaginable until 4:00 a.m. – possibly the best feeling I've had in years came over me while I rested, nestled in his arms, my head against his chest in which his heart sang out to me...

This week has been dreamlike, sometimes lovely and lazy and other times confusing and frightening as I see myself trusting, depending on, and clinging to a man. In a sense I feel more vulnerable now than when I sold myself on the streets, maybe because then I was fully expecting to be hurt and mistreated and thus prepared for it and accepted it when it happened. But now I want to imagine this relationship David and I are forming as being perfect – but is that possible? Isn't there always some perversity, pain, cruelty in relationships? When I think of the possibility of this with David, the dream-like state I'm in becomes more like a nightmare: I feel lost and groundless. Indeed, I have had nightmares the last couple of nights, about performing absolutely brutal experiments on frogs, inflicting so much pain and misery on the little creatures that I writhed in horror and guilt, while still being driven to torture the animals out of scientific curiousity. Would I hurt David that way if I let myself go? I'm afraid I'll drag him into my screwed-up world of chaos and confusion and masochism.

April 5, 1993

A milestone today: my last session with my therapist. In a couple of weeks I start group therapy. Endings and beginnings, as she said. One thing I'm afraid will never end is my tendency to feel like the core of my mind is in chaos and I have no way of ordering the confusion. Fear, despair, horror, disgust, hopelessness and what the hell are we all doing here on this fucking screwed-up planet and fuck there is no point to anything.

"But there is a point," David says to me. He holds me tight to him and strokes my head.

* * * * *

Well, I guess you can look at a hospital and see the negative things – the patients suffering and the families mourning – or you can see the positive side, the small but amazing steps people can make with the help of inner courage and modern medicine; the caring that never ceases despite how depressing or hopeless a case may be. Defying logic, we all care; whether there is a point to anything or not, we keep holding on.

It just isn't all fun and games like I thought it would be, is it? Life is a challenge, not a fun game. I worry about the future, about how I will possibly cope with a regular job in the real world after I'm finished with school; will I really accomplish what I've dreamed of doing? Writing, researching, doctoring – or will it be one psychiatric hospital after another, a useless existence, a wasted life?

I want to do better than just exist. Oh, God – please let me keep on going and get somewhere, not just stagnate. Oh, help. Fuck this mind of mine, that hurts me from the inside. Shit the hell – goddammit – God this is not nice, this sucks – I want to cocoon myself, give up all responsibilities.

Look now, I'm walking in the fresh air of freedom. I am who I desire to be and not a concoction of another's needs – a real presence. Sunrise over the mountains, a new day, a fresh beginning, the end of night.

May 9, 1993

I'm hyped up, buzzing with energy. Very edgy, or rather on the edge – in a wild frenetic state with despair below on either side. It's a fine line to be walking. Rationality out the window; I could do anything.

My new place (a room in the Fairview Student Housing residences) is great – very small but I've filled it with just the right amount of my good old familiar stuff, and lots of photos and posters on the walls. Fairview is a beautiful complex of townhouses for students – nice atmosphere, lots of greenery right outside, a sort of European air to the quaint courtyards. I share a suite with three others. We have two floors which is great. Lots more space than in the other residence. Well, here for four months then hopefully into the less lovely but more centrally located studio apartments for fourth year students.

Exams came and went – marvellously well considering how much school I missed this year. The one exception to my nice marks was in Biochemistry 303, which unfortunately is my most important course. It was my last exam, and I was pooped out. I so wanted exams to end.

I recently told David that I didn't think we could build a good relationship, considering the problems I am going through. So that was that with him (but we're still friends! He's a great guy). Meanwhile, Cam was finally indicating that he does like me. So the two of us ended up studying for the biochem exam together on the 27th the night before the exam. Of course it was hard to focus on the books. I stayed up all night (Cam took a few cat naps) but it didn't help. Anyhow, I got 55% in that course – but Cam and I got each other. I like him a lot, and I feel better about putting him through my "hell" than David. Cam knows I've got a lot to work through. It was in the psych ward where we first met last

October – he was a volunteer. He's going into psychiatry. And yes, that's one of the (many) reasons I'm so attracted to him.

Irony of ironies, we both (coincidentally) registered for the same summer course, "Abnormal Psychology!"

* * * * *

"We love you, we want to help you," said my half-sister on the phone when I called her in February. But what I'm hearing from other people is that my dad is telling family and friends that my accusations are false, that the abuse was all in my imagination. I'm afraid a lot of people will believe him. I do not feel like a part of that family any more at all. They probably think I'm nuts. My own half-sister doesn't even believe me. ("I believe you think you were abused, Lara, but come on now, let's be serious. How could that have happened?") I don't KNOW how it could have happened, or exactly when, or in fact in what manner. I still have trouble believing myself. When I start to feel that I must be imagining all of it, I get crazy and suicidal from the guilt and self-hate. What kind of disgusting monster am I, to openly accuse my loving father of such a thing, and greatly upset everyone in the family? I'm selfish and egocentric, attention-seeking and cruel. Oh well. I'll probably never be able to prove I'm right about the abuse, so I have to decide whether to trust myself or my dad. It would be a lot simpler to kill both of us. Yup, I'm nuts.

May 14, 1993

The hours are unreality. Today is one of those days I'm just not fully awake. I can't snap out of it. It's a dreamy, unhappy, moody state of being with a constant undertone of anxiety. When I slip into this way of existing (which happens less and less frequently, thanks to all the therapy I've had), I must have some control, probably unconscious, over the transition from alert to un-alert. Some part of me must want to attain a state of un-alertness, a safe place of numbed feelings and slow movements. But I don't think I like this way of feeling at all. I wish I would stop slipping into it altogether. But I guess the urge still comes. When the transition can't be accomplished on my own, I employ the aid of a handful of pharmaceuticals. But I've resisted the urge – the craving – to do that for three months now. I want to be present, be in control, and take responsibility for my own health and safety. Ayesha, my other self, still begs me to end my life here but I resist that, too. I have a responsibility to other people.

If I could just get rid of that responsibility somehow, then I'd be free to leave. I want that peace, change, new world, relief, so badly I've even thought of killing all the people who would be sad if I died, so I could then kill myself. Number one on the list would be my father, because my suicide would really upset him regardless of how indifferent he has been to my well-being all my life. And because I hate him. Next would be my mother who has suffered more in her life and put up with more pain than anyone should have to. Next my grandmother, and so on.

Let me count the ways:

15	Loxapine x 10 mg
23	Luvox x 50 mg
44	Ibuprofen x 200 mg
3	Gravol x 50 mg
32	Zoloft x 50 mg
117	pills in total

Enough.

It's not so much depression as wanting this stupid game to end. There's nothing worth continuing for. I don't get pleasure out of things. I'm grumpy and uncooperative and incommunicative with family. I'm useless and without the motivation to become useful. I'm bored and I want to stay that way. Death would be the ultimate boredom and freedom.

In an effort to jolt myself out of this fog, I'm starting volunteer work in Emergency tonight. I don't believe I'll feel any better after two hours being useless and in the way, but I made a commitment.

May 19, 1993

I used to think I was a cold, distant, ungrateful daughter because I couldn't bring myself to enjoy being near my father. I used to feel very guilty that I never missed my father when he went away on trips or when I stayed at my mother's place and thus didn't see him for a few weeks at a time. In fact, I wouldn't even think about him; it was as if my memory of him would vanish when he wasn't around.

It was a feeling of relief to be away from him, but coupled with extreme guilt and self-hate. I denied, to the very core of my being, that the reason I didn't really like my father was because of some failing on his part. The wrong-doing simply had to be on my part. There was no question about it: as an adult, a "care giver," an authority figure and a daunting personality, my father must automatically be in the right. Therefore I was in the wrong.

Now I'm 20 and now I finally realize, as an adult myself, that my disliking of him was a result of his cruelty and coldness, not mine. Feeling uncomfortable around him didn't mean I was an abnormal child; it meant I sensed danger even though the source of the danger eluded me while I continued to block, or unconsciously deny, the sexual abuse that was taking place.

Now the memories I have of my fear of him and my secret guilt tell me that I was protecting myself, through denial from the knowledge of what was happening to me. An unfortunate consequence of this denial was my shouldering his guilt, internalizing his self-hate, as if it were my own. The distinction between my emotions and his seemed blurred to me, perhaps as a result of his manipulation and abuse of me or maybe because of my denial that he was doing anything wrong. I developed the tendency to take responsibility for other peoples' feelings and mistake them for my own; there were so few emotions that truly came from inside me to be expressed freely that maybe I just needed to fill this void with some thing, so I chose to internalize the feelings of important people in my life – my parents, close friends, even pets. I could feel the sharpness of their anxiety, fears, sadness and insecurities in a sort of larger-than-life manner, meanwhile denying any emotions originating from my own mind and soul.

Now I'm asking my own feelings to come out and at least peek at the world. Doing this makes me feel vulnerable and exposed. But I will no longer deny who I really am; my past is mine, my beliefs and emotions are my own; my goals are my own. I am not someone else, a different persona, an alien being, or a fragmented personality.

I am an individual human being and there is a boundary between myself and others and it can be a flexible and malleable one. Through this boundary or personal distinction I can send ideas and expressed feelings to be witnessed by other people, and they will know I exist and that I'm not an empty shell.

* * * * *

That self-serving, self-righteous, self-centred bastard can be assured that virtually every deeply-rooted problem and unhealed wound I bear today is the result of his abuse of me. I am a damaged person, pretty

163

screwed up, obsessed with the idea of suicide, and it is his fault. As a child and adolescent, I was and still am to some extent an overly shy, cautious, distrusting person. I've always been wary of making new friendships, and my attempts at relationships with members of the opposite sex have been utter failures. With strangers I am flirtatious and at times promiscuous; with boy friends, I am "stiff and unaffectionate," in their words. Whether it is with a strange man in his car or with a close male friend in my bed, sexual intercourse is frustratingly painful. I feel denied of a basic human pleasure. I cannot enjoy sex.

I have grown-up feelings not quite real in a very unreal world. When I appeared happy and outgoing, I was really just playing along with this game called "life," knowing I would eventually have a break. When I was unhappy and withdrawn, I was actually fed up with the game and was longing to bring out the end myself. My psychiatrist says I am chronically suicidal, thus while there will be bad days when I'm very close to killing myself, there will be better days, but the suicidal feeling will still be present, just smaller in intensity.

Fighting to get through a single day, let alone planning for the future, is an exhausting task and I owe this struggle and the pain associated with it to one person: dear old dad.

May 27, 1993

How I have taken responsibility for myself:

I am living on my own, supporting myself. I am in charge of my daily living, and I try to make decisions that improve each day – simple things like deciding to grocery shop for some special items so I can try a new recipe, and larger things like planning my future schooling and budgeting for the upcoming academic year.

I recognize that I alone am responsible for my own feelings and my health. If I feel lost and depressed, I allow myself to admit this and respond to the feeling, e.g. by spending some time doing quiet, pleasant activities like reading or walking with a friend. When I feel self-destructive, I take the initiative to seek support before acting on my impulses. I call a friend or the crisis line or I go to Emergency at the hospital. It has taken me a long time to assume responsibility for my suicidal feelings – it has really only been three months that I've been responsible in these terms. It's the hardest thing I've ever tried to do, which makes sense because an important thing is at stake – my life.

Some of my feelings about not wanting to take responsibility are:

It seems easier to leave it up to others to take charge of my well-being and to decide whether I should live or die. It's true that sometimes I'm too mixed up to be the sole person deciding whether I should end my life. But I can't depend on others to control my impulses forever; I have to take care of myself or else there is really no point in being human and alive. I don't want to give up all responsibility and spend a large part of my life being protected by the medical system – and yet, existing in the psychiatric ward of a hospital often seems more appealing than existing outside on my own. I crave protection: I want to be taken care of like a child, as if it would make up for the past.

Some of the ways I am not leading the life I would like to lead:

I would like to be in an intimate, long-term relationship rather than dating sporadically.

I wish it wasn't so hard to hold down a simple part-time job.

I wish I was ready to apply for medical school now, along with my classmates and peers.

I wish I was excelling at school like I used to.

I wish I could spend less energy on convincing myself not to commit suicide, and more energy on the above things.

May 31, 1993

The last thirteen days have been a roller coaster ride – some great, some bizarre, some awful. Friday night I broke my three-month-sober period by taking a bunch of Gravol – went berserk for twenty-four hours. I'm not in control. Tried to kill myself by eating foxgloves today. Got a stomach ache, that's all.

Let's be serious here. I'm not coping. I'm going back to Emergency tonight. I have to keep on going, if not for anything else but to protect others.

June 1, 1993

No beds available in Psychiatry so they discharged me from Emergency. I was practically begging to be admitted. Don't the bastards believe me when I say I'm out of control and I want to kill myself?

Ayesha is going home.

It's my life, my responsibility.

No one but me is to blame for my suicide.

I love all my family and friends, and I know I am well loved.

I'm so sorry I'm being selfish but I need to end this now.
Peace.
Death is better than insanity.

> The end of my life here,
> but only the beginning
> somewhere else.
>
> AYESHA.

June 4, 1993

It looks as if the health care system is leaving the choice up to me for the first time, and that scares me. I'm taking responsibility for myself for once. I can't get into the hospital or even see a therapist in the near future. This week I told six different health care professionals that I need help because I'm suicidal. Each one sent me to another. The doctor who was filling in for my family doctor while she's away was extremely nice. On the 3rd, I went to see him and said things were rough, and was there any way I could get counselling soon before I go and make another attempt. He spent a good 40 minutes with me, checking out possibilities. He called the S.A.F.E.R. group (Suicide Attempt, Follow-up, Education and Research) and the Community Mental Health Team. Because I am an out-patient at the Vancouver General Hospital in that silly group "therapy," I am apparently not eligible for counselling through either of those systems. Fuck the stupid group. FUCK! SHIT! The doctor said he wanted me seen that day somewhere, and he said the hospital may be the place. I said I didn't want to be hospitalized – I'd changed my mind since Monday. I want to learn to cope on my own. We talked a bit more and I finally said okay. He said, "I'm not asking you to consider hospitalization – I'm telling you." I liked that firmness. He then checked out the situation at the Vancouver General Hospital's Psychiatric Assessment Unit and must have been told on the phone about my problem there in February when I was assaulted by that male hospital worker. He said, "I guess you wouldn't want to go there… " and I said only as an absolutely last resort. So what was left was this: he told me to go through Emergency at University Hospital and see a certain doctor who would be expecting me. So I did, and that doctor asked me some questions and seemed quite unconcerned. I relaxed, too. Suddenly, the urgency of the situation, which no one else seemed to sense but me, has been creating the drama inside me. If I want to kill myself, I can just go ahead and do it. OK.

I said to him that actually I felt comfortable now with everything and I knew I would make a rational decision. He said I could call him on the 18th to see about setting up sessions with him – he was booked up but could maybe fit me in, in a few weeks. He also said I could call him or come to Emergency before the 18th to talk to him. I said I'd rather not live on an emergency ward. And he said I could ask for counselling at Student Health Services. So I went there immediately and saw another doctor, who gave me a number to call the next day to set up an appointment with a psychiatrist there. So today at 11:30, I met with the psychiatrist. He was a good fellow and asked the usual questions in a very sensitive manner and I answered them as I have the dozen or so previous times I've been assessed by a psych worker. After quite a lot of pondering and checking the appointment book, he said that there was an opening next Thursday. I said great – I'll take that.

*****

Last night I bought some heroin at Main and Hastings. (That's a whole story in itself.) It should be enough to do the job tonight. I have a syringe and I've been practising getting it into a vein. This will be the first time I've used an illegal drug. I thought heroin would be a good choice because there's been some very pure stuff sold recently and many users have accidentally overdosed. I'm going to listen to Chopin's nocturnes. In about three hours I'll be ready.

June 6, 1993

God forgive me for being so weak. I'm going to focus on living now, not dying.

The heroin didn't work. It might have, but some people saw me in the woods near this housing complex Friday night, stumbling around. I was trying to bury the syringe, etc. so it wouldn't look like suicide, but my balance was off and I must have looked like a nut. After a while, I couldn't stand up.

Two paramedics tried to get me into an ambulance but I ran (or rather crawled) away. Got covered in dirt and pine needles, bruised all over. They did get me eventually, and took me to the hospital where I was given Narcan and released this morning.

The agony I'm feeling right now is so awful. I want to be stronger, but I don't think I can be.

Anyhow, I won't attempt suicide again until I make another attempt at getting better. There has to be a way to kick depression.

June 12, 1993

One whole week without trying to kill myself(!), thanks to the psychiatrists at Student Health Services, who have been very understanding and encouraging. The two of them met with me Thursday morning for an hour. I was feeling low but stable; no more plans to die. They said that I would definitely get weekly individual therapy with one or the other of them, and that it was good that I'd sought help and kept the appointment with them that morning. They were probably wondering if I'd show up, because they'd called my place at residence and got no answer since I've been moved to another housing complex during the repainting, without a phone. Noting that I'd been all over the place trying to get help the week before, one doctor said, "The system has let you down, and I imagine you lost some trust in it." He was also referring to the sexual assault at Vancouver General Hospital in February.

They were concerned about my present safety and spent some time trying to convince me to spend a few days in hospital. I finally agreed although I didn't feel I needed hospitalization then (the previous week would have been nice, thank you very much). Off to Shaughnessy Hospital I went, and gritted my teeth through twenty hours in there before asking to be discharged. The psych ward there is not pleasant.

So I checked out Friday morning, against medical advice. Much relief at getting out into the sunshine and open air, and back to campus where I'm resuming my normal routine (minus the job and volunteer work which I decided to quit). I've never left "against medical advice" before but this time I knew that what I needed was to return to a relatively normal, independent daily life.

June 29, 1993

Been doing strange things lately – unwise, unhealthy, stress-producing things. Life was okay for about a week after my last entry, then I tried a little heroin, and chaos ensued. The pleasure and release I got from it was so powerful that I decided I needed it to get through each day. I stopped using it a few days ago, and I don't plan to start again (at least, not until I know I can use it in a controlled manner). Drug addiction costs you your judgement and your money and your friends and, God, just about everything.

Withdrawing was unpleasant. I still feel physically shitty and very tired, but maybe I'm also catching a cold or something. As for mentally, it ranges from wanting to die (maybe if I tell my mom that I am going to commit suicide and explain that it is the right thing for me, then she'd cope better afterward?), to resigning myself to keep on plugging through. Plodding on. Whatever the expression is. I know I have to (the rational part of me knows) because someday I'll make something out of myself and my existence, and there will be a reason to live after all. Yeah, right. The psychiatrist wants me to consider going to group therapy only, having it be my only treatment. The group therapist told him that the group was intended to be the patients' primary treatment. I can't believe this. I feel like I've been abandoned already. I need one-on-one counselling right now. Why won't they listen? I'm so afraid. It's 1:00 a.m. and I'm exhausted even though I slept ten hours last night. My sleep has been restless lately, unhappy dreams and waking up in the middle of the night cold and wet from sweat. But still, sleep is a sanctuary for me and I thank God I can spend part of each day in a lowered state of consciousness.

June 30, 1993

Put on a happy face; grin and bear it; cheer up; keep your chin up; look on the bright side; hang in there; don't give up now; hold onto your hat; show us your smile; turn the other cheek; don't be a wimp. I used to be pretty good at all that. Where the hell did my spunk and drive go? I still have the ability to put up a facade of contentment and appear happy, but when I used to do this it would often have the effect of lifting my mood. Putting on a happy face helped me feel happier and forget my negative feelings. But now, putting on a happy face is just flipping on a mask. I remain the same underneath. Confused. I can see that there is a slight possibility that the rest of my life won't be meaningless to myself and to others. Just that inkling of hope should be enough to convince me it's worth striving for. I just doubt – very strongly doubt – that I'll ever make the effort needed to reach meaningful goals. I'm a-motivational, apathetic, lazy, restless. Now and then I have a "good" day – I get the laundry done and run some errands as well as reading and socializing. But most of the time I'm so inactive it's disgusting. I hate myself this way.

I'm supposed to be dead now! This is nuts. I'm still alive; I've got what they call a second chance (or I guess by now it's my third or fourth chance) and I'm still taking life for granted. Pooh, pooh to the miracle of life. This attitude is shallow. There is depth and spirituality to life. I know first-hand about other "dimensions" or realities, and about the unexplainable powers of the mind. But something must be spiritually missing from me if I still see no value in life. Other people, though certainly not everyone, feel enough drive and find enough value in life to keep on going without contemplating suicide every single day. I must be abnormal.

The rest of the world isn't giving up, saying what's the goddamn point?   shot   jump   hang   O.D.   slash   goodbye I wish I could change myself then maybe I'd have faith in the possibility of changing the future – everyone's.

One more week till I see the psychiatrist (no session tomorrow because it's Canada Day). I'm going to state it plain and simple: in my opinion I need further individual therapy. (Inside, pleading, "Oh please don't set me loose; don't abandon me. I need this. I need you." And outside, stating, "I'm feeling unstable.")

Keep up that old facade. Put on that happy face. "Things aren't so hot, no. I'd like further therapy, please, thank you." ("God, there is no reason to live – please, doctor, you're my last chance. Please help me find a reason to live.")

(This section of the entry is in disordered and disjointed handwriting - Ed.)

Living in a half-dream
is better than not living at all.
Kawiakee
you are with me all the time.
I don't need to be dead
to experience your magic.

Dead

dead   dad   dyad   done

    deed   dying   deaden   end

                dead end

                                  dad

July 6, 1993

Either I'm really inept at trying to take my life, or there's a reason for me to keep on living. (Yeah, right!)

I'll get it right next time. I'm going to prepare a few more things, clean up and organize my belongings, write notes/letters to family and friends, buy some more heroin and decide on a nice, green, solitary place.

What will it be like after? Cool and light and a place where hope is justified.

Tonight   I'm   going   to
                                    call   Goshiba

July 18, 1993
Psychiatry, St. Paul's Hospital

I wish the roots of happiness and sadness were fully understood. It's frustrating not knowing why I have no faith in this world while most other people do. My personal belief is that they are deluded into ignoring the plain truth: this planet is in a mess and there is so much more misery than joy. The only way a person can live day by day contentedly is by "overlooking" the pain around them. And anyhow, the pain inside oneself can be enough to deal with, let alone the pain of the homeless and mentally ill and prostitutes on Skid Row; the pain of starving children in Somalia; the often silent pain of oppressed peoples, minorities, women; the unheard pain of forests and whole ecosystems being destroyed. I have a lot of admiration for the people who are working to solve local and global troubles but the immensity of the problem is too great – it's naïve to think that the little that's being done here and there is going to bring about solutions. I don't see any hope for this civilization of ours; maybe if the human race were eradicated, the Earth would have a chance. After all, we act as if we are the only living beings here, or even if we acknowledge the presence of other life on the planet, we believe we are superior and so only we count. But the richness and diversity of species is outside our concrete cities. The only way to preserve this life and to respect the miracle of its very existence and evolution may be to eliminate our species from the picture, before we destroy everything. Something went wrong in the evolution of Homo sapiens.

Maybe I'm over-generalizing because I've become increasingly aware of something wrong within me. The psychiatrist said that depressed people see the world through a negative lens or filter. Is my pessimism unjustified? The strong feeling I get is no; my hopelessness is justified, and the optimists of this world are deluded. I envy their delusion; obviously it allows people to live their lives and say, "I know I can't change everything and solve all the world's problems, but I can do my little bit and be satisfied with that."

So my belief is that what's wrong with me is I can't put "blinkers" on and just be happy, coping with little things and maybe contributing in a bigger way one day when I have the education and skills. I can't accept this way of life. I don't have any rose-coloured glasses to put on – the view through a lens or filter that the doctor spoke of is how I see other people living. Depression isn't clouded judgement or a fog or a negative perspective: it's the clear, truthful, unbiased attitude towards this awful place, this world. It's the "happy" ones whose views are clouded.

I've heard the opinion, in general and with regard to myself personally, that people abused as children often develop depression as adolescents or adults. I don't argue with that theory at all, but I think my ideas about depression fit in perfectly with this cause-effect hypothesis. The fact that my grandfather forced me to have oral sex and anal intercourse with him, and that my father fondled and raped me until I got the guts up to move in with my mom – these events pretty well tore those rose-coloured glasses off me and allowed me to see the real world, early on. Some people speak of lost innocence, but if anything was lost, it was the ability to close my eyes to the negative aspects of our existence – I mean existence in a collective sense – us as a species, as a planet, as a solar system, as a/the universe. Innocence is a delusion, but a necessary one. Maybe my eyes are wide open to everything, but the effect of this has been to incapacitate me. Instead of facing the challenges life presents, I've lost motivation and energy and interest, while still being aware that those challenges are there. I feel guilty for not even putting the effort into the small things – I can't even do the laundry and cook, let alone organize my life and contribute in some way to society. All I've been doing is taking, taking, and here I am again in the hospital, taking up a bed and nurses' and doctors' time and causing worry and pain for my mom. I'd be better off dead, and I wish my family would understand this so that when I am successful with my suicide, I won't have caused them even more problems. If I could prepare them for it in a better way... I've tried writing goodbye letters that explain my point of view, but I know that alone won't be adequate. I'll be letting a lot of people down and creating unhappiness, but since I can't create happiness while I'm alive and depressed, useless, non-functioning, dying is not going to be so wrong. I'll be causing fewer problems in the short term by ending my life now than I would cause in the long term by living. And maybe, if there's an afterlife, there will be some way I can make up for the pain I've caused – who knows what happens and how the spirit or soul exists and interacts with the physical world.

I feel like I was meant to end my life from the very beginning. When I was young and believed I was really Ayesha from another world, Kawiakee, I also believed that before I became an adult here, I would return to my real home. The voice I heard in February, saying, "Ayesha, discard your body and come home" made perfect sense (but of course I realize that hearing voices is not very normal). So maybe my childhood fantasies and "imaginary" world have a real basis. Who knows. Maybe I'm Ayesha with a calling to obey, or maybe I'm a screwed-up, disillusioned depressive with a crummy past and faulty neurochemistry. I don't think there is an absolute truth, to anything. Either way, I have to end my life. Forgive me, mom and God (whomever) for only saying I don't know how to make up for what I'll do. I'm really, really sorry.

July 22, 1993

There are a lot of apparently inconspicuous, nondescript people here on the ward whom few observers would suppose were suffering inside. The vast majority of the patients are female. Many of us learned not to admit to pain from an early age. Pain is part of woman's role. As usual, on this psychiatric ward, there are a couple of nurses who are not well either. But, gee, one just has to grit one's teeth and do one's job. Anger, coldness, distance from these nurses is not questioned. They're doing their best in a system that does not tolerate weaknesses in women taking on the traditional role of nurturers.

I hate this time of morning. I have to face another long, shitty day in this place. I mean this world. There's nothing particularly bad about this hospital; it's this planet I want to escape from. Since 3:00 this morning I've been murking over the situation, the options. As always I end up wishing I had no bonds or ties to any other people, so that ending my life would not affect anyone. In my stupid, selfish way I am angry at the people who care about me because they make my decision harder. I feel forced to keep on living in order to please others. Not that I offer anything by living, but all the effort they (family) have put into giving me life and helping me grow has to be considered. I owe them something. But the way I am now I can't give anything to them, anyway.

In the last year I've brought a lot of confusion and unhappiness to my family, and I'm tired of being the "problem person" of the family. Things would have gone so much more smoothly for them if I'd never been born. But being dead is not the same as never having been born. Maybe it would feel the same to me, but, of course, it wouldn't to my parents.

God, I just want out of this fucked-up world and my fucked-up mind. Tomorrow I'll start having electro-convulsive therapy which is supposed to straighten out my mind but that's not going to change the state of the world.

Nurse just popped her head in – "Hi. Just doing rounds. We do rounds till 7:00 a.m." In other words, I won't be disturbed after 7:00. Well not exactly. At 7:30 we get the "wake-up call" and at 8:00, the "breakfast call" (a patient volunteers to go around knocking on each door). At 9:00 we line up for medications, getting vital signs checked beforehand if necessary.

July 31, 1993

I'm in St. Paul's Hospital, Psychiatric Unit. Been here for two weeks. I escaped from the University Hospital's psych ward on July 11th and spent that night in a hotel room downtown with a couple of people. I tried to overdose on heroin again, but one of them called an ambulance. I came to, in St. Paul's Emergency, with a tube down my nose. Spent the next hour throwing up charcoal. The doctor had called my mom; I'll never forgive him for that. They certified me again and kept a close watch on me. I didn't go AWOL again. I've been started on another anti-depressant, desipramine, and I'm also getting electro-convulsive therapy (ECT) three times a week. ECT somehow alleviates depression in 90% of the cases where it's tried. I felt an immediate increase in energy and appetite. It appears to be working! I'm getting restless and bored being in the hospital. I get a daily 1½ hour pass to go out with a friend, which helps. In a little while, Jan is coming over and we're going to the beach. I want to enjoy some of this good weather before school starts.

The one annoying thing about ECT is that it screws up your short-term memory. Over the last few days, I've had frightening moments where I've forgotten basic things like what year of university I'm going into, whether or not I've gone to court yet regarding the sexual assault at Vancouver General Hospital, and which chapters I still have to read to prepare for my Abnormal Psychology 300 exam.

My memory should start solidifying again when the treatments stop – I have only four more to go. I'll be discharged in about two weeks, which gives me only three weeks of holidays before school starts. Actually I'm looking forward to school. Hopefully I'll be moving into a bachelor apartment and not the crowded quads. Also, hopefully, I'll get my full student loan.

When I think hard and serious about life, I still don't really want to stick around. But I know I have to, anyway. After so many people have put so much effort into making life more bearable for me, it would be really ungrateful to go and end my life after all.

August 10, 1993
(The following entry, written at 2:15 a.m, is in tiny, disorganized and almost illegible handwriting - Ed.)

> Please excuse my sloppy work
> Please excuse my sloppy work
> Please excuse my sloppy work
> No, I'm not going to write 500 lines
>   of this crap
> I went AWOL again two days ago. All my clothes were
>   locked up here
> What went wrong?
> Parents often respond, "Oh, she is going through a phase, at times
>   unpleasant."
> I'm sedated and not very in

August 12, 1993

I don't know how or why, but my mood has bolted upward over the last couple of days. It happened so suddenly; it was as if a switch had been turned on. I'm still certified (committed) which is a drag because the weather is gorgeous and I can't go outside to enjoy it. But I am enjoying my shift in mood. I don't know exactly (nor does my doctor) what to attribute it to, but it's probably a combination of electro-convulsive therapy and desipramine. Because the last week was so rocky for me (up and down, up and down), this psychiatrist might start me on lithium on Monday, the 16th. I hope I don't have any bad reactions to it. Chlorpromazine, a tranquilizer, was given to me several times a day until I convinced the doctor that I was having side effects (tense jaw muscles, inability to swallow or speak clearly, and especially hallucinations. I saw baby spiders everywhere – in the sink and bathtub, in my bedding and in my closet). Apparently, these are called anticholinergic effects. So, now I'm on a more subtle tranquilizer – name is something like flupenthyxol.

From about Tuesday onward (after I went AWOL and was brought back and strapped down in restraints), I've started thinking more about school and how much I'm looking forward to September. If this good mood is here to stay, I predict it will be a fabulous year at university for me. I'm craving success in my studies; this year I'm going to enjoy my courses and strive for good marks.

I got to know another patient. She had just been diagnosed as manic-depressive. For two sick people, we sure had a lot of fun together! She's very bright and articulate, and in law school. She was discharged a week or so ago. I've been getting a little bored here, now that she's gone. There are several other females here in the 19-25 range. St. Paul's Hospital is the clinical centre for eating disorders in the city. But I don't feel entirely comfortable around them. They're so serious.

The 4th year medical student under my psychiatrist's supervision just now came in to say goodbye (it's the last day of her psych rotation) and also to wish me luck and encourage me to keep working toward medical school. She said she knows of some medical students who had dealt with depression and were doing well in medical school now.

This reminds me that I have some investigating to do; to find the right university to do my Master's in neurolinguistics. Initially I thought McGill would be best, but I shouldn't make hasty decisions about these things. Since I'm doing two more years for my Bachelor of Science degree, I have a good amount of time to make a wise decision.

August 14, 1993

I feel like a prisoner here in the hospital – it's been over a month now that I've been certified. The electro-convulsive therapy and drugs have pretty well brought an end to my depression – thank God for that. I don't know how much longer I could have stood it. But now that I'm feeling better, I'd like to get back to my normal routine – back to my place at the university, buying textbooks, getting ready for fourth year. And all I can do is read, write, and watch television. I'm so bored.

August 17, 1993

I'm afraid that being so bored here is going to bring back some of the depression. Have to keep thinking positively. I only have a few more days here and I'm back on my own. Yesterday I was decertified and given community access (I can go out, i.e. leave the hospital for a time, if I'm with someone). I celebrated by going window-shopping at the mall with Jan. It was fabulous to be "free" again. I keep myself going by looking forward to little things: for instance, today my mom is coming over at 3:30 and we're going for a walk. I just have an hour and twenty minutes to kill.

I'm so thankful that I made it through this summer alive. Thanks especially to my nurses and doctors who have been so terrific. I'm going to send them a card after I'm discharged. I'll probably get a weekend pass which means I can go home for the weekend, then I check back in here on Monday and if everything's okay, I am officially discharged. So I really only have three-and-a-half more days of boredom to wallow through. Of course, I'm actually grateful to be bored because it means I'm no longer depressed. I'm through the electro-shock therapy (which was no big deal, and totally painless) and now I get a tricyclic anti-depressant, desipramine, as well as 900 mg of lithium daily. The lithium is an extra which may help stabilize my mood. Normally, it's given to bipolars (manic-depressives) but it can also work for unipolars.

It's now 2:25 p.m. Time goes by so fucking slowly here in the hospital. It helps that there are three other young women my age here (they're all in for anorexia) but I didn't hit it off marvellously with any of them. But it's company. In the evenings we watch movies on video (Karen picks up movies every day) and that helps to pass the time. I have mega-amounts of reading material but I'm finding that one can get to a point where one has done enough reading for the day.

One more hour till my mom gets here.

Another goal: write the Psychology 300 final exam which I missed. I think I'll try phoning the professor.

August 20, 1993

I'm out on my weekend pass! I'm staying at the Fairview Housing complex tonight (it's strange but nice to be back at this place) then tomorrow, Jan and I are going to the beach. Then I'll spend Saturday night at my mom's and go back to the hospital Sunday evening. Monday morning I'll be discharged!!! I'm so happy to finally be HAPPY! Goodbye depression, for a long time I hope.

* * * * *

In my opinion, I have bipolar disorder, not unipolar. I am manic-depressive. My manic episodes are short-lasting and "hypo" rather than "classic." Other symptoms I've had fit in perfectly with what the book* on the subject described. My anxiety attacks, heart palpitations, and upset stomach are also symptoms of manic-depression! Also, this disorder tends to be passed through the mother's line. Patients often have family histories with bipolar relatives on the mother's side, and alcoholism is common too. My mother's mother and her uncle had/have manic-depression. The uncle was diagnosed; my mother's mother committed suicide before she could be diagnosed or helped, but the stories I've heard about her match the disorder well. She had violent, almost psychotic outbursts, between which she would be very low and unhappy. She drank heavily (this, too, is typical).

Other forms of self-medicating are common, too – e.g. my tendency to take 20 or 25 Gravol in order to calm myself down; and, of course, my brief fling as a heroin user.

That night I took to the street and got into the cars of strange men, and spent the night at a man's apartment, was without question a manic episode. That was totally unlike me, to have such poor judgement and be so bold and flirtatious.

And in the last two months, before I was hospitalized, I somehow blew $2,000. I bought a lot of clothes and ate out a lot. I don't know how I spent it all exactly. I know that I didn't spend more than $300 on heroin. Spending sprees are common in mania. I think I had a depressive episode peppered with manic moments. This recent episode of mixed-up highs and lows was my worst experience ever. I'm surprised I'm still alive. The number of times I've tried to kill myself – it's amazing I'm still here. I must have a guardian angel.

---

* "A Brilliant Madness – Living with Manic-Depressive Illness" by Patty Duke and Gloria Hochman, Bantam Books, New York, NY, 1993

178

August 23, 1993
Back at the Fairview Housing Complex!
(Discharged)

I'm back at home. I feel so strange! A good kind of strange. It's gradually sinking in that there are good times ahead – also tough times, but the good ones will make life worth living. It's so bizarre having my mood stabilized finally! I still feel small fluctuations in mood and energy, but only occasionally. These changes scare me a bit because if the little changes evolve into big ones, I don't think I could handle them. But thus far my mood has stayed pretty well up, most of the day, thanks to all the treatment I've had and am still getting. A special thanks to the miracle drug, lithium.

I just took my evening dose, 600 mg. In the morning I take another 300 mg.

I like who I am and where I'm at in my life – emotionally, academically, socially. I have a lot to be grateful for. But mainly I intend to focus on the positive aspects.

It can get very quiet and lonely here at this residence, but I can always be with my mom and her partner. My mom has emphasized that I'm always welcome to visit and stay overnight.

August 31, 1993

I'm totally useless. All I do is cause problems for people. God, I've made my mom's life hell and I've been such a burden on my friends and other relatives. It's a catch-22; there's no solution. I hurt people no matter what I do.

I want to stay in my apartment forever and do nothing. Door locked, phone unplugged. Talk to nobody. Pretend I don't exist. Depression for the rest of my fucking life??? No thank you. I don't want a life. But if I end it, I hurt my family and friends. If I keep on going, I hurt my family and friends. I hate myself. God, I hate myself. I wish I never existed to begin with. Why is this happening? God, I was doing so well. I was all better. Normal. Now I'm crying like a baby, moping around, hiding from people, eyeing my prescription bottles. There would be enough there, I think: 60 lithium, 50 desipramine, 12 chloral hydrate, and some over-the-counter stuff like Tylenol.

I must not do this.

How can I be suicidal AGAIN? I'm through that. Through. Over. Gone. No more. Fuck, I hate my body and my mind and my fucking weak spirit.

My psychiatrist at the hospital said to me yesterday at our appointment, that since my pre-menstrual time was approaching, I should increase my dosage of desipramine from 150mg to 200 or 300mg until my period starts, because the last two months when I was pre-menstrual, I became especially depressed. In July, I escaped from the psychiatric hospital and attempted suicide by an overdose of heroin; in August, I took off from another hospital to get heroin (without success) in a strange state of mind.

Now I'm down again. No, this isn't supposed to happen.

Please stop. Please stop. I must not do this.

It came so fast, about an hour ago, while I was studying for my psych exam. Kind of suddenly I started crying and thinking about how pointless everything is and how I'm a useless piece of shit and how I take, take, take and don't give.

In the last few months I've made my dad's life even harder than it was before, by telling the family about what he did to me years ago. In the last six months, I turned my mom's life into a mess and caused her so much pain and grief that I'm afraid she'll never get over it.

I just took a break to take two more desipramine, bringing today's dosage to 300mg. I also took a pee and got a can of pudding from my fridge to eat. These are my accomplishments of the hour.

I didn't work all summer, except for that one week in the Biology Department. I earned basically no money. I received no scholarships this year (for the first time). Not only did I make no money, I spent everything in my account in the space of two months this summer. I'm living on a student loan now. I don't think I'll ever be responsible enough to manage.

* * * * *

"Suicide is a permanent solution to a temporary problem," they say. The thing is, it doesn't feel like a temporary problem to me. I'm afraid I'm going to be affected by this disorder for the rest of my life; I'm afraid I'll be depressed most of the time and spend much less time in a normal state.

I'm tired. The extra desipramine has made me drowsy, I think. Or it could be pre-menstrual syndrome. My heart won't quit racing, either.

Other than that and some depression, I'm feeling terrific. Ha, ha, blah, blah, blah.

* * * * *

I hate myself.

I'm disgusted with the kind of person I am. I can't or won't control my suicidal thoughts. They keep entering my mind. I should be able to stop myself from thinking this. In some doctors' minds, I am chronically suicidal and manipulative. I'm never going back to the University Hospital's Emergency Room.

I'm going to butter a piece of bread, gourmet cook that I am. And I'll go to bed early tonight. What happens now? What do I do? Everything's falling apart and it's only been fully together for a couple of weeks. If this is the result of pre-menstrual syndrome's effect on hormone levels and metabolism, then it won't last for too many days. I wish it would go away now. The desipramine increase should help.

September 5, 1993

Thank you to whomever or whatever has control over my moods, whether it's outside forces, or the drugs I'm taking, or myself, or a combination. The feeling is so incredibly wonderful that it's difficult to write – it's like I just want to sit and feel it, not do anything at all. It has been so long, two or three years, since I've felt anything like this. I used to have waves of pure pleasure and contentment wash over me when I was younger, often while I was reading a good novel. Then as the depression set in, the moments of pure pleasure came less and less until they just stopped coming. The calm and contentment I feel now is more thorough and enduring than my pleasurable moments earlier in my life. The feeling, mood, state of mind is actually going to last for a while now! In the last couple of years, whenever I felt a bit less depressed and a little happier, this relief would be broken frequently by sudden, uncontrollable waves of despair and misery, usually lasting a short time but very disruptive. I could regain the happy mood again, but I learned to never trust the good feelings; they would never last and there was nothing I could do about that.

Now that's changed – I'm actually beginning to believe that my present mood is my very own; it will not suddenly leave me; it will stay a part of me. It is me.

Tuesday was a very bad day, but every day since has been good, to my relief. This is almost unbelievable. I'm going to survive!

By the way, this good feeling I've been describing is quite different from my "up" or mildly manic states, where I feel ecstatic, super-confident, and practically omnipotent. That buzzing, energetic feeling is a different sort of "good" than what I feel now. What I'm experiencing now is not pathological or dangerous. It's like I've finally found myself. I know all this sounds corny, but I can't help that. I know who I am now and how I was always supposed to feel, and I like this feeling; I like myself. The despairing, hopeless, painful feelings of the past are no longer how I identify myself, so I no longer have to hate myself. I'm not afraid of who I am; I am not a permanently depressed, pathetic wimp destined for suicide.

As much as I want to keep on enjoying myself, I do have to get to bed (tomorrow will be a busy day – it's the day before school starts). I don't have to worry about the mood vanishing overnight because I know it will be with me when I wake up. I have faith in it and in myself. I think this faith has nearly as much to do with the stability of my mood as the lithium and desipramine do. Somehow I've taken that step; I've learned to trust life.

September 7, 1993

Like with last Tuesday's dip, I didn't tell anyone (i.e. my mom or friends). I told my psychiatrist about last week when I saw her this morning for my appointment. I felt fine then; had no inkling my mood would plummet later. I just can't (or won't) tell my mom about bad times. I'm afraid of how she'll react. She asks me to be totally open with her, but I honestly doubt she would handle the truth very well.

Anyhow I'm on the upswing now and I'm hoping tomorrow's entirely good, without dips.

I'm scared; I admit it. Who or what controls these dips? Why can't I control my mood?

September 28, 1993

I'm feeling more confident than before, about my schoolwork, family issues, future. I have a way to go, though. Sometimes I go back to feeling like I can't possibly achieve anything – my marks this year will suck; my mom will get more, rather than less, worried about me and the whole goddamned world; I'll never make it into medical school, etc. etc.

But I've become good at telling myself that these are inaccurate, unfounded assumptions created by a neuro-chemical illness – the illness is being treated now, but the old thinking habits will occasionally return.

The point is that I am, by nature, a hard-working, enthusiastic, people-loving person. When I was depressed I was the opposite, but I'm myself again finally. I'll make it, through school, through family problems, through medicine, life, etc. Focus on fighting the discouragement that creeps up now and then.

October 21, 1993

It's really frustrating to keep forgetting things. I'm afraid my midterm marks aren't going to be great, because even though I study hard, I just can't recall enough of the material while test-writing. I hope this clears up fast.

Second problem is nightmares. Guess what – "they're baaaaack... " My dreams about being molested and raped by family members, dreams of blood and horror, shame, fear, loneliness – they're here again.

I thought I could put the incest issue to rest for a while longer, but it seems like I can't repress it. Last night was pretty bad – a dream centred around me murdering someone to prevent him/her from hurting and molesting a child. After the murder, my clothes were soaked with blood, and I removed them and tried to wash it out but I couldn't. So I buried them in the ground, and also buried the dead person. This dream was set in a rural environment similar to our land up the coast.

Another disturbing dream this week: My dad is sitting in my room (with me on the bed) and telling me stories about how he assaulted strangers by grabbing unsuspecting people as they were leaving a supermarket, putting a paper bag over their head, dragging them to a hidden place in a parking lot, and sexually assaulting them. He was laughing while he told me this. This is the first dream I've had of my dad actually molesting someone, I think (or maybe I dreamed that a few months ago but tried not to remember).

October 25, 1993

I just shot up a bit of heroin. I bought $30 worth at Main and Hastings tonight, and I've shot up two-thirds of it so far (small amounts at a time). It gives me just a slight rush each time, nothing scary.

This is the first time I've used since that day in July. I thought I would never think about heroin again, but I have. Resisted all urges until today. Shit, I hate myself.

I've been seeing an addiction specialist every two weeks. I think I will start going to Narcotics Anonymous meetings. It's obvious I can't resist the urge on my own anymore. The specialist has been wonderful; she's easy to talk to, and helpful and very empathetic. The fact that I used heroin for the first time in order to die, and not because it was a mood-altering drug, interests her. My inherent addictive potential (alcoholism in the family and lots of it) has gotten me into a mess that should never have happened. I have to work on controlling impulses now, and I have to start feeling comfortable and not humiliated when speaking about this drug problem that seems to be lurking around all the time. The specialist tells me that speaking to others – her, a close friend, and other recovered/recovering addicts is absolutely essential.

November 9, 1993

Before I start moaning and groaning, I want to say that the last couple of months have been great, on the whole. I haven't felt this good and stable for so long a period in years. I'm energetic and active, outgoing and motivated, and happy, too. I'm working with GOSA, the Global Outreach Students' Association, on their local committee. We're interviewing managerial staff at hotels and residences in the Downtown Eastside* to assess the level of awareness of infectious diseases, specifically HIV, hepatitis, TB, scabies and lice. From that information we'll decide on the type and format of an educational project, in conjunction with the Downtown Health Clinic (Vancouver Health Department). I've met some terrific people in GOSA – motivated, intense, intelligent, really nice people, mainly medical students, nursing students and the like. The project downtown is something I feel very strongly about. I'm glad to be part of it.

Next week I have an interview at the Autism Society of B.C. I'm hoping to volunteer; they have a "buddy" program where they pair volunteers with autistic children and youths. For a long time I've been interested in the disorder and thirsty for knowledge concerning its cause and nature. Now I can see the disorder manifested and more

---

* This is the area of Vancouver where she grew up - Ed.

importantly, meet and build a friendship with another person who happens to have autism.

Good – I mean fantastic – news about that summer research job I mentioned a while ago. I arranged an interview with one of the supervising researchers who had submitted project descriptions to the Dean's Office for students to see. I had my interview at St. Paul's Hospital last Friday. I expected nothing to come of it – after all my recent marks weren't hot; I'm just an undergrad, and medical students would be competing for these jobs, too. But the interview went terrifically. The head researcher was very easy to talk with and was just great about showing me the lab (actually labs, collectively called the Pulmonary Lab, in the research wing of the hospital), and introduced me to everybody (25 people – I can't possibly remember all those names). He said that he and his "associates" (technicians) were impressed with my C.V. "So would you be interested in the project?" he asked me. I couldn't believe he was offering me the job! Wow, what a great day that was! I was so happy, so confident. This job will be fascinating, challenging, and related to my areas of study. And with this on my resume and the head researcher as one of my reference letter-writers for medical applications, I've got a better shot at medicine. He even said that a paper will probably come out of the project (which, by the way, is on the RSV virus and how it might lead to asthma in children) and that "a published paper can do a lot for your medical school application." I'll say.

So with all this great stuff and more, why have I felt shitty the last few days? I even slept in and missed classes today. I wish I could get out of this pit and go back to my exciting, safe, comfortable life that I've been building during the last couple of months. I know I will eventually feel back to normal. But right now, life sucks. I talked to the addiction specialist the day after I used heroin last month and she convinced me to go to a Narcotics Anonymous meeting. So I did go, that very night. I'm going to my second meeting tomorrow night. It does help to hear others talk about conflicts and about how they're dealing or trying to deal with their addiction.

The nightmares stopped a while ago but started again two nights ago after Ron (he lives down the hall from me here in residence) and I made out and tried to have intercourse. I was enjoying it in a way, but also hating it and wanting it to be over. We couldn't go all the way because full penetration was impossible – it hurt me too much and it seemed just too tight in there to be physically possible – the vaginismus and vaginal dyspareunia, in technical terms. Well, the dreams of rape and molestation came back. I took a sleeping pill before bed as the psychiatrist had suggested, to try and block REM sleep. Didn't work so I took two last night. Slept twelve fucking hours. Dreams were vague but unpleasant.

I hate the feeling I have right now. Little voices are saying to me, "about 20 Gravol tablets will put you in a nice snoozy oblivious state of mind" and "heroin... heroin... heroin... just a pinch will make everything feel okay..."

Actually seeing that written down makes me realize how ridiculous those temptations sound. I do want to numb myself, but not in a way that is dangerous or addictive.

I know. I'll make some coffee. A lot. Let's see if I can stimulate myself into oblivion. Caffeine is the only drug I can think of that is safe to use regularly and in large quantities.

November 13, 1993

I think my apathy last week was a result of too much free time all of a sudden, what with Remembrance Day, plus a lab was cancelled leaving another day free from lectures/labs. I'm feeling more energized now, but still a little melancholy, interestingly. I should make it clear, however, that these small downs and ups are tiny, tiny, tiny compared to my previous swings. This is especially apparent from my mood chart which I've been updating every couple of weeks. It feels great to know that I'm finished with the tough stuff at least for a while. My mood is not going to interfere with my life like it has over the last couple of years.

"For the child who runs away from home, preferring to take her chances on the street, who carves up her arms with an X-acto knife, who boozes it up and pops handfuls of pills, and fucks four guys in a row from the tavern up the street, has been created: She did not spontaneously become this person on her own."

Myrna Kostash

Chapter Seven

Age Twenty-One

December 16, 1993
Age 21

I am so enraged at the people with power, usually male, who get away with anything; and at the justice system that turns a blind eye while other people suffer.

I wonder what to expect will happen next month at the sexual assault hearing involving that male nurse. Even without my full medical records documenting my dissociative experiences, post-traumatic stress disorder and my brush with prostitution – which gives the defence plenty of material to come up with reasons I might not be telling the truth – even without all my previous allegations of my grandfather, father, and the rape of last November, they could pretty easily acquit him with the "reasonable doubt" criterion. It's my word against his, and my word will not count for anything.

I will get to speak, at least. I will be able to tell the truth about his attempt to seduce me and his subsequent rape of me after failing at the seduction. The truth. No one in the courtroom has to believe me, and many probably won't. But being believed is a lot harder to achieve than I used to think.

My dad still strongly denies that he abused me. I got a letter from my half-brother saying he wanted to help however he could; he wanted to be my big brother. He couldn't make the choice of whose story to believe, but he feels for how I've suffered, and he says his relationship with our father has been strained for the last five years. My father makes it hard not to believe him, my half-brother says.

I can imagine; he's a natural arguer. It's good to know that my half-brother is supportive of me anyway. But it still boggles my mind how most of that family is trying to ignore the issue. Grandma practically admitted to me in her letters that she is aware of what happened. But no one will hold my dad responsible for what he's done. It's me, not him, who's left the family circle.

December 24, 1993

I'm scared of what might be in store. No more depression. No more, please. I have so many plans and things to do in 1994 – finish fourth year, testify at the assault trial, travel to Europe with Jan and Vicky, work in the Pulmonary Research Lab at St. Paul's Hospital, start fifth year at university, submit my application to medical school. If depression keeps poking its head in and getting in my way, I don't think I can make it through the coming year successfully.

December 25, 1993
Christmas Day

Merry Christmas.

It's a beautiful cold, clear day. We're getting ready for Christmas dinner. There will be five of us. As my mom said yesterday, we have so much to be grateful for. I feel so stupid being depressed, when everything is bright. I should be enjoying these days. I keep making or just about making cynical, sarcastic, or gloomy comments. I'm trying to hold back and be silent. I'm such a big grouch. Sullen, cranky.

Oh, let this change. I'm so lazy. It's an effort to move; I feel so heavy. Thursday is a long way away. I wish it would hurry up and come so my new psychiatrist can suggest something, and I can feel like there's a possibility for change.

December 28, 1993

This depression is sliding along – down – predictably. The quiet, sullen but manageable depression I've been feeling is about to cross into the desperate zone as I go lower, from "this sucks, but c'est la vie" to "I can't fucking take this."

It's funny. I can actually feel pricks of hopelessness come every so often, and the feeling is so physical. It's in my chest and it's a tight pain, combined with anguish and desperation. It goes away quickly but I'm on the border of crossing into constant desperation. Negativity. Nothing is worth doing; nothing can be achieved or changed; the world is awful and getting worse.

I don't have to let this go any further – I can fight it, by talking to myself, talking to a friend, opening up to my psychiatrist, keeping myself as active as possible. On Thursday, I plan to visit grandma who will be turning 80 on that day. I'll also see my half-sister and her kids who will be visiting from Salt Spring Island. It's the first time I will have seen all of them since my confrontation with my dad last February. It will be stressful – feelings of anger and outrage and also love toward these people who have been wonderful and nurturing to me all my life, but who also ignored the incest that had occurred in the past and was occurring while I grew up.

"There's both pain and joy in life, Lara. You have to learn to live with it..." my aunt said to me a week or so ago when I called her to ask what the hell was going on: Why was a rumour circulating through family and friends that I'd retracted everything I'd said about my dad; that the abuse was just in my imagination. My aunt denied knowing anything about this rumour. My mom's source says, however, that he heard that I'd written a letter to grandma, retracting everything. The letter I did write to her, which was addressed to both my grandma and my aunt, said nothing of the sort. I have a photocopy of it. Anyhow, I didn't press her on it because she really did sound sincere. But her attitude toward the sexual abuse of children ("My dad helped to protect me from other forms of abuse by sexually harassing me," she said) and toward living life made me so angry. She said, "It's not that I don't believe you – I do believe you experienced something. But your dad is being honest when he says it didn't happen. I know when he is telling the truth."

I asked her why she can't believe me about this, when she would probably believe me if I had instead been raped by a stranger. I've never lied to her; I'd never given her any reason not to believe me. She replied in a most disgustingly condescending tone: "I can't believe you just because you're Lara. There are other people involved in this, too."

December 31, 1993

The half-hour appointments I have with my psychiatrist allow just enough time for questions about eating, sleeping, general mood, and how the week has gone. It's "checking in" and not really psychotherapy. I'm out of practise at opening up to a therapist or psychiatrist.

This journal/diary is back to being my principal confidant. Some of the processing of feelings, worries, events that I do in here could be done in her office, she suggested, and we could change it to an hour each week. Oh, God, not back to the frustrating going in circles I experienced at the out-patients' department with that therapist and then the group "therapy." But actually this psychiatrist is very nice, down to earth, and has a good sense of humour. So far I've really appreciated her comments and suggestions, e.g. regarding my testifying at the upcoming trial. In response to my pessimism ("He won't be convicted, no matter what I say"), she said that what she'd heard from other people was that just speaking out and knowing you had presented the truth could give you a feeling of rightness. And this week she brought up the point that in many ways, this trial may be a symbol to me, consciously or not, of my previous experiences. So that's something worth considering as the trial approaches and as I react to it (and the verdict) afterwards.

February 14, 1994

It's Valentine's Day, an appropriate day to finally get around to writing in here, because the main news I have is that I've been seeing someone for a few weeks, and it's working out really well! I've known Bob since September, but hadn't started thinking of him other than as a friend, and also as the brother of a classmate who is a roommate of my friend, Karen. Anyhow, all these connections have let us run into each other a lot. Then he and I tried an official date, had loads of fun, and decided to keep going in this direction.

I admit I still have my doubts about a relationship – whether it's wise of me to get into one right now; whether I can manage to trust a man yet. And what about sex?

Well, to work backwards: sex with him is great (no pain, and that's a first for me) and I'm feeling more and more comfortable trusting him and talking to him about my concerns and about what has happened to me in the last year or two. The one thing I haven't felt ready to tell him about is my dad. That can wait.

We spend a lot of time together even if we both have lots of studying to do. We at least go to the library together and take our coffee breaks together. We often eat dinner together, here at my place or over at his dorm cafeteria. Often we also spend the night together. I really enjoy being around him. I feel at ease and good about myself, and I love his optimism and sense of humour.

March 13, 1994

Why in the world would I want to shoot heroin in a dark alley, getting ready for my next trick? It would be cold and wet and lonely – but somehow I would be free. Or at least feel free. I haven't given in to these urges. For some reason the last week has been especially hard. I don't really know myself after all. I'm supposed to know that I'm at university and I'm going to be a doctor. Who the hell is that? I lost the hold I had on that part of me.

I can't love the Lara who studies hard and stays healthy and together. The proper daughter, girlfriend.

I hate the Lara who wants to get high and be oblivious to the world and to what's going on inside, the confusion and the pain and disgust. Sex for money; yeah, so what? My body's just flesh. I might as well eat it. If I sell it, I'm at least getting something for it, and I'm in control, and somebody enjoys me. I'm appreciated. This is crazy but I can't tease apart the tangled mess of thoughts and desires in order to understand these feelings and confront them. But hey, I have my psychiatrist to talk to. I honestly don't know if I can pull it apart, or pull it together.

I'm not insightful or intelligent enough to understand what is the right thing to do. What's right and what's wrong dissolved into each other when my grandfather and father showed me how good a girl I was to let them screw me. Fifteen years later I'm still screwed up.

> Lobotomy or
> heroin or
> sleeping pills
>
>> None of these is
>> available right now;
>
> May I offer you a glass of milk or
> a textbook?

I'm drowning in the city rain   in my tears
                in the semen of mankind

I'm going for a walk now   some fresh air and rain will
do me good.

March 28, 1994

Sunday night two weeks ago I went to Main and Hastings and walked around the alleys, eventually sleeping in a doorway. Surprisingly the urge to "hook" and buy heroin disappeared; all I wanted to do was be there. As the night proceeded I felt more and more disconnected and unreal, kind of a relief because it prevented me from feeling anything much. I was woken up from my half-sleep in a back alley doorway by a policeman shining his flashlight at me. He interrogated me (no doubt thinking I was a teen-aged runaway) but I couldn't answer his questions in any meaningful way – partly because I didn't want to give him my name and partly because I just couldn't organize my thoughts into sentences.

He threatened to cuff me if I didn't tell him my name and although he spoke in gentle, sympathetic tones, I was wary of saying anything at all. So I bolted away from him and his car. He ran after me and got a hold on my jacket but seeing that I was going to let the jacket slip off, he reached for a firmer hold on me and missed. I got free and ran as fast as I could down that foul-smelling lonely alley, startling some garbage-perusing rat on my way.

I heard the policeman stop his chase and speak into his radio.

The rest of the night I kept an eye out for police cars, but had no further trouble. I caught an early morning bus back to campus, feeling pretty dazed and disoriented.

The dissociated feeling continued through the day. At my session with my psychiatrist, I tried to explain in rather mixed up, halting words how I was feeling. She seemed to understand. Her comfortable presence was very reassuring.

Toward the end of our forty-minute session I talked her into giving me a prescription for some Ativan because trying to get to sleep was difficult since I kept hallucinating that a man had a hand around my neck and a hand over my mouth.

Of course I also wanted the Ativan to play with, recalling how pleasant it had made me feel when I'd had it in the hospital.

At home, I promptly took all 14 tablets and zonked out for a while. Then Bob came over, and he convinced me to go for a walk for some fresh air. I took my bottle of desipramine with me and apparently took 12 which Bob noticed later. He was furious.

Wednesday I straightened out and decided to face reality by phoning my dad and giving him a piece of my mind. I was sober and very calm and I told him I strongly recommended he get some counselling; that I could be telling him to just fuck off, but instead I was asking him to get help. Listening to his stupid excuses and complaining about his current girlfriend reminded me how unpleasant talking to my dad is. The conversation didn't last long. But I felt stronger and in control; I'd stood up for myself. The rest of the week went really well, to my surprise.

The day after that depression I had a memory of my father videotaping me doing something sexual. It was vague but very real. Today I talked about it with my psychiatrist.

April 8, 1994

Funny and sad, how my mom works so hard to try to help me, and the only way we seem to be able to communicate that desire to help each other is through phony cheeriness and lots of food. I don't let her help any other way. I push her away. Don't even think about offering to understand my emotional problems, to "help." Just keep away.

I have to protect myself from her and others; I can't let myself be seen as vulnerable or hurt. I can't need help from them. And so I desperately crave help from people not emotionally attached to me – my doctor, strangers, a crisis line volunteer. Those people whom I can't hurt, who know how to protect themselves. When I seek help, I inevitably hurt people. Is there a "hidden anger" in me after all?

The unpleasant truth is sinking in these days: no one but myself can make my life the way I want it to be. I have the power to control it. It's up to me. If I want to be lazy and not study for exams, then there's no one to blame but me for the lousy marks.

* * * * *

Damn it! Somebody tell me what I'm supposed to be doing!
Friday night
        hooking
        shooting up
        wet alley
        studying
        living
  Life
    Nothing's real or firm.
    Dissociation is an escape.
It feels soothing, even though you are still faintly aware
of horrors outside your dimension.
God must be dissociated to do his/her job.
Why oh   why does the world
      cry
I don't want to come back to myself.
I know where to go.

April 9, 1994

Ended up downtown last night – what a surprise. Wandered around Skid Row, slept in an alley, made my way back around 6:00 a.m.

195

It brought relief, like finding – momentarily – a missing piece of myself. It also made me cold and hungry and stiff and smelly. Coming back to my apartment on campus makes me realize, again, how lucky I am to have this life to come back to. Don't take it for granted.

I'm rather tired, having had about three hours sleep last night and about five hours each of the two nights before that. Quite a change from my twelve-hour naps.

Earlier today I slept for about twenty minutes, and dreamt I was back in my hospital room at the Psychiatric Assessment Unit at Vancouver General Hospital; the male nurse had just raped me and I had locked myself in the bathroom and was throwing things around, trying to break a mirror or anything sharp so I could inflict the pain I wanted him to experience on myself instead – the "safe", non-confrontational way of dealing with anger. Anyhow, I awoke gradually out of this dream to find myself standing over my bathroom sink with shards of broken mirror everywhere. Bob had woken up and was restraining me from behind, getting the glass out of my hands. There were only two very small cuts on my palms.

I kind of drifted in and out for another few minutes. With Bob's soothing I got back in touch with "reality" and calmed down.

April 10, 1994

Who am I kidding? I hate living; I hate myself for hating living. I want to die. Back to the old cycle. I think this is the real me.

I can't sleep for more than three or four hours at a time. Can't eat anything unless it's salad.

Can't or won't concentrate on studying. And guilt, guilt, guilt for hurting the people I should be hurting the least.

Am I grateful for their unending love and support? It seems not. I'm willing to leave them with my death.

Fucking piece of worthless shit.

I fucking hate this disgusting thing I've become. Or maybe I was born this way.

I'm not going to do it with heroin, although that would be the most surefire painless way. I don't want people to think I was a junkie.

Pills are an option. Of course it would make more sense to jump off the Lions Gate Bridge but I don't have the courage to face death with a crash of broken bones. I want to be eased into it; I want it easy and painless just like I wanted everything in life because I'm a fucking wimp. And now a quitter, too.

* * * * *

Here I am being a fucking idiot. With the fucking jerk in my mind. Just get out of there! Either the jerk goes or I go.

100 Gravol
48 extra strength Tylenol
15 regular Tylenol
30 desipramine 50 mg
20 lithium 300 mg
28 Ponstan

April 11, 1994

As I was coming out of the fog yesterday, I felt an incredibly powerful feeling and realized that I'd felt it many times in the past but had forgotten. It's a dissociative feeling of watching the world from a long way away from my body; everything appears bleak and empty; there's a deep sadness and absolute lack of hope. At the same time, though, I feel a sort of resignation to this way of existing. There's no way to escape, so I just have to bear it. There's such a strong sense of loneliness, too. I've cut myself off from everyone around me, so I am totally alone; it's as if I don't believe there are other people in the world. It's just me, in despair, but not fighting it anymore.

This is the strongest feeling I've ever had, and I think it's something I felt years ago, fairly frequently, when the abuse was taking place.

It's scary to feel that way, but the fear is a faint, distant one, because I know that I'm somewhere where nobody can hurt me. I've made myself safe; but in doing so I've separated myself from all other life, so that I'm utterly alone.

There's no way I can ever again doubt that the abuse really happened. Remembering that feeling makes it all come together and make sense. Now I know "where" I was when I was being molested and how I distanced myself from what was occurring. I can finally remember forgetting. I'm not yet totally aware of what I was striving to forget, but I can remember the forgetting and how I accomplished it.

April 16, 1994

God, I want to scream. The cold empty feeling just haunts me and it's so easy to believe what it's saying: there is no meaning to life; life in this universe was an arbitrary accident and there is no omnipotent life force, no god who could care about the lives that are really just a joke. A waste.

I bet some people would say I need a religion. But if there's any reason to be religious, shouldn't I feel it on my own, sense a greater force or meaning, and not have to be taught? If it's there, it should be obvious to everyone, every living thing. I'm not aware of any greater purpose. Sure it feels good to do good things for yourself and for other people, but all the good happening in this world can't seem to keep up to the bad. There are more people suffering than not. Even someone as fortunate and well-off as myself, living in a first world country at peace, obtaining a first-rate post-secondary education, "great" future potentially ahead – even I can't feel good and hopeful. Goddamn it. I'm so lucky and here I am complaining. I should be enjoying the life I am fortunate enough to have.

Reminding myself of all this doesn't shake off the feelings of doom, the image of a dusty abandoned wasteland that hangs in my head insistently. I have to change this feeling. Even just for a few hours. Hey, I'm being responsible enough not to end my life; I'm just going to fry my mind tonight with a hearty dose of Gravol and desipramine, a little lithium, Ponstan and Tylenol thrown in for effect.

April 17, 1994

I think maybe I've developed some tolerance to the combination of meds I took although I really didn't think that would be possible with non-addictive drugs. But why else would I not get as much effect this time, with the same amount of meds?

I need a shower badly. Too lazy, though. I slept downtown again, and the odour of urine and bleach is still clinging. No energy. My own fault.

April 18, 1994

Part of me wanted to confess to my psychiatrist that I want to commit suicide, and that's all I can think of. But I know better than to admit that. Being locked up would just make me more suicidal right now. So when she asked if I felt like hurting myself, I said that the idea of death was really nice because of how easy it would be, but I know I'm responsible for my actions and that I'm capable of making mature decisions. Hearing myself say that was startling for me.

* * * * *

I have an incredible urge to do heroin right now. Bob and I and some friends got rather drunk at the Gallery Lounge on campus. Bob and the guys are now out somewhere smoking dope. Bob wouldn't let me come. Fuck him. He's such a patronizing hypocrite. I want a good high, badly. Getting drunk is nice but it's like just whetting your appetite. I'm just going to use a little heroin. I'll buy $50 worth and split it into quarters. No chance of overdosing. Just a little buzz. Please.

* * * * *

I just talked to my mom on the phone for a good twenty minutes. Ooooh, do I feel guilty. "Hi, mom! Doing great! Yeah, exams are going great!" Meanwhile, planning the drug transaction. And what to bring? A bottle of water, tissue paper, tourniquet, damn. I'll have to buy a syringe because I threw mine away. Bob better be back soon 'cause I can't leave till he gets here. I have his knapsack with keys, etc.

Where should I hunt down a dealer? I can't remember what the ones I dealt with look like. I guess I'll hang around Main and Hastings until I see someone trustable.

I'm going to get high tonight!!! Yes – it's going to be fantastic. Just a little bit at a time, maybe a tiny shot a day, to get me through to the end of exams.

May 3, 1994

In twenty minutes, I leave for the airport to fly to London with Jan and Vicky. I'll be spending five weeks travelling around Europe! The excitement is gradually building.

Yes, I did use some heroin that night. It made my stomach upset so I threw the rest away. Of course, regretted succumbing to the cravings. Talked with my psychiatrist about it.

Exams went superbly, and I'm ready for a great summer.

Now for Europe!

June 12, 1994

Yesterday I got back from my travels around Europe. I had an amazing time. I'll write about it later. Right now I just need to write here to calm the anxiety and horrible feelings of fear, dread, depression and dissociation that swallowed me up when I arrived back home.

June 22, 1994

At my session with my psychiatrist on Monday, she told me that my mom had written her a letter shortly after I left for Europe, saying that my mom wanted to see her because she had some crucial information, and saying that it was okay to break confidences in these situations. Of course the psychiatrist could not contact my mom without my permission. At the session, we puzzled over this letter, and my psychiatrist restated that being my counsellor and not my mom's, she couldn't have any involvement with my mom (unless I say it's okay – which I wouldn't). I was really perplexed about the "crucial" information. My mom had scheduled a session for her and me at a family therapist on Tuesday.

So yesterday evening I found out what's going on here: Shortly after I left for Europe, a month-and-a-half ago, my mom went through my boxes of stuff stored at her place and found the diary. She read the months of March and April (I wonder if that's all). She said she did this because during the last term I was (according to her) looking pale, thin, tired and sick. She had asked me a couple of times if everything was going okay and that she was available if I wanted to talk. She also asked me once during those months about my interest in heroin. I told her I had no interest in heroin, that things were going well. Believing I was lying, she waited till I flew to London and then read the journal and decided from it that I have a serious drug problem (took heroin in April, and Gravol and desipramine occasionally to "fog out"), and that I'm suicidal.

At the family therapist's office I tried to explain to her that I tend to write at my worst moments, so what's written is not representative of my day-to-day existence. Yes, I thought about the idea of suicide in the last few months. I also wrote many times that I want to pull things together. I'm not going to do anything stupid; I'm going to take the challenging path and try to succeed and that I'm planning to have a great summer. My dips are short-lasting and easy to recover from, compared to last summer.

I just wished my mom had been more persistent when she was asking me about my health last term; if she was that worried she shouldn't have sounded so casual when asking me – it was like she was begging a positive answer, and when I gave it to her she accepted it. I had no idea she was so concerned and worried. She never made a point of saying I looked thin and pale, etc. etc. The funny thing is that my psychiatrist wasn't excessively concerned about me last term. She believes I have been getting progressively better since I started seeing her last September (and she's right). I don't know if hearing her say that would even reassure my mom. She's too paranoid to listen to reason.

I was so angry at her – just outraged and almost incredulous. That she would invade my privacy like that just kills me. I know she did it out of concern, but she should have exhausted all other options first to try to determine if I was really okay or if I did need help.

She now knows about my "pull" towards hooking, something nobody except my psychiatrist knows. I feel humiliated having her know.

July 3, 1994

Things have cooled down between my mom and me. We had a second session with the family therapist on Thursday. I so badly want to get on with my life and not concern myself with my mom's excessive concern. Work is going really well; I've moved into an apartment in the West End (a fifteen-minute walk from St. Paul's Hospital); I'm starting to study for the MCAT* in September; I'm trying to keep myself on the right track.

I had a few fantastic days last week – loads of energy and optimism. My mood on the whole has been very good. However, I haven't felt comfortable being physically intimate with Bob. I think he's getting impatient with me. The last couple of days I've been feeling jumpy, nervous and occasionally panicked and claustrophobic indoors. This and the sexual problems may have to do with the imminent Court hearing regarding the male nurse. I don't feel particularly worried about testifying, but maybe unconsciously I'm becoming tense as I anticipate it.

Oh, well. This too will pass.

---

* MCAT is an acronym for Medical College Admissions Test. It is international and covers a wide range of topics during a nine-hour exam. - Ed.

I like my apartment: It's a spacious one bedroom suite on the 11th floor close to Robson and Denman Streets. It's $700 a month which is twice what I can afford, but my mom's giving me $200 a month towards the rent. She wants me to be in a furnished suite that isn't gloomy.

* * * * *

So am I content? Yes. But I'm afraid there's still so much to deal with, and I'm feeling wimpy. If you happen to read this, mother, you won't understand why witnessing the lives of prostitutes and junkies and teen-aged runaways on Hastings Street gives me the courage to not give up. You see them as pathetic. I see them as courageous and stubborn, to still be alive after what they've lived through. Each day is tough but they make it (some of them do, at least). Do they wonder why the rest of the city seems oblivious to their situation? Why there are people making $80,000 a year who think the homeless and jobless are scum who deserve nothing better?

I want them to know we're not ignoring them – we realize the pain is there. There have to be more people who care enough to look hard at the Downtown Eastside and decide that these lives could be better. No one should have to sleep in a back alley with rats or search through a garbage bin for supper when there is the wealth and opulence of the West End only a few blocks away. Inequality is everywhere around us, and no one would say it's fair, but why does it exist??? Because as long as you're healthy and have enough money to live and eat comfortably, who cares about the guy down the street who is gradually dying of TB or AIDS and is addicted to chemicals and is unloved. Anyway he smells bad and looks weird and therefore must deserve his fate.

July 8, 1994

I wonder if I'll ever enjoy sex again. It's hard to imagine those feelings ever returning to my body, after thinking about this upcoming preliminary hearing.

The defence lawyer is going to try to make me look like a slut, a whore – and one with a mental disorder. I dread the inevitable questions regarding my (slim) experiences with prostitution. The Crown prosecutor has warned me that this will definitely be brought up, and his objections may be overruled so I must be ready to go into the "story."

202

The way the male nurse asked me to have intercourse with him and later to give him "a blow" – I felt like I was a prostitute whose services were being requested. It was so demeaning. So I told him that I'd had experiences in the past involving unethical sexual relations and that it was damaging. I was hoping to dissuade him from continuing his disgusting line of "conversation" with me, but it didn't change his mind, and now that submission of mine gives strength to his side of the story by letting everyone know something humiliating and demoralizing about me that they need not have found out about, if I'd kept my mouth shut that day in the hospital. My worst fears are not that my history will throw my credibility out the window (although this would be painful and angering) but that Bob and Jan (who both plan to come to the hearing) will come into the courtroom despite my insisting that they remain outside the room. I said I would be more nervous if I saw anyone in there I knew.

If my boyfriend and best girlfriend find out what a slut I've been, I don't think I'll be able to stand the humiliation. I'll feel like less than a real person. And if in court I'm asked why I tried prostitution, I'll just have to admit that no, it wasn't for the money – I wasn't penniless or wired on drugs – it was because I longed for a sense of power and control that was lacking in my life. Offering myself to men for a price gave me that feeling of worth and importance, and an exchange that was business-like and for me, unemotional. "Safe" sex. The power and worth, of course, are illusions. The defence attorney is going to ask how I could be so stupid or mixed-up not to realize that from the beginning. And how can I expect to be believed that the male nurse raped me when the court knows I was a whore, and whores always want it, right?

I'm fed up with being female. And frigid.

Anyhow, aside from the above stresses, things are going quite well for me. I love my job, I love feeling like I'm doing something worthwhile, and working in the same hospital that gave me my life back last year. And I love these hot summer nights. The realization is gradually sinking in that despite the challenges and difficulties ahead, I am ready to deal with them – with anything. I know how to fight, and with my mood solid as a rock, I can plough my way through whatever tough times I run into. It's hard to accept this because it gives me no excuse to give up, give in. If I am capable of surviving, I simply must survive. I cannot be a wimp.

Something I do still worry about is how I've been disconnecting or dissociating occasionally, sometimes during an anxiety attack, sometimes for no apparent reason. Last week I resorted to sleeping in a dark spot of an alley one night near Main and Hastings (days after I'd felt tempted to, but had resisted) because I didn't feel safe anywhere else. It probably had a lot to do with happening to see my dad ride by on his bicycle – that was jolting and I wasn't the same for the rest of the day.

July 10, 1994

Hot and windy, this glorious pained city groans around me through another summer. The sun makes me want to sleep forever, or at least until this heavy feeling leaves me. I recognize the feeling well from last summer and the one before – I guess every summer of my life.

It's an unsettling mixture of good and bad. There's no point fighting it; it's centuries older and far stronger than me. If it's going to swallow me up, I can withdraw so that my vulnerabilities are not exposed, and hold my breath for the plunge with the hope that I won't drown. I know I can survive this, and anything. I'm light years beyond the chaos and uncertainty of last summer.

This coming week, the worst sides of myself will be exposed, perhaps to Jan and Bob as well as to strangers. I guess the male nurse is thinking the same thing. Sometimes I wonder if our lives have not been too different. The difference would be that I try not to let my neuroses and perversions hurt other people.

* * * * *

Lie back and soak in the beauty of the day. This flitting pleasure is dangerous because it offers a tantalizing escape from the heaviness I'm carrying around with me, but it doesn't stay with me for more than a few seconds at a time. So I look for ways to keep it with me, even artificially. This is when I tended to take a handful of mild pharmaceuticals, wanting to be able to control these emotions. I write that in the past tense because I don't, won't do that anymore.

I can control myself. I have a strength I didn't recognize before. It's what kept me alive as a small child. I didn't lose it along the way. I have no excuse for not making use of it now.

* * * * *

204

I feel so alone. The image of a barren wasteland comes back occasionally. It hurts, but it's okay. There's a seagull soaring in the white-blue wind in the sky.

So this is what pains feels like, minus depression. The two together were unbearable, but pain alone isn't. Interesting how groggy it makes me feel. No, no, no. I will not fill myself with drugs. Absolutely not. Not an option. Think of the aftermath, the physical sensations – stiffness, nausea, tremors. It's not worth the little bit of oblivion it offers.

July 12, 1994

The court hearing begins tomorrow. I feel fairly well prepared, although I'm still afraid my mind will go blank. I'm almost looking forward to seeing the male nurse (he may or may not be in the courtroom) so that I can glare at him and tell him what a sad, disgusting person he is. If I can't say that to his face, hopefully I'll at least have the strength to think it and feel it: anger and hatred.

Now everyone will know exactly what you did to me.

Bob has arrived. He'll stay overnight.

July 15, 1994

The hearing was less overwhelming than I thought it would be and the cross-examination was less nit-picky than I feared it would be. My mind didn't go blank; indeed, I was almost too composed and objective-looking on the stand. I turned off the emotional side of me.

And I survived!

I recognized him immediately. I looked him in the eye a couple of times while testifying; his expression was unreadable, but perhaps there was some fear there, hidden partially by smug self-assuredness. Once I caught his glance while I was describing the assault and after a second, he couldn't maintain eye contact; he looked away, looked down at the table where he was sitting.

I'm glad this part is over. I wasn't very anxious before and during my testimony, which surprised me. I've hardly thought about it since, and I don't plan to until before the trial (in January or February, '95). I'll get a transcript of my testimony at my meeting with the Crown counsel before the trial. I wish I could get that earlier.

Oh, and the hearing took only one day, not two. I was the last witness called, and was questioned for thirty or forty minutes. Much less grueling than I anticipated. And I didn't miss too much work.

I forget if I mentioned that I got a sample packet of Ativan from my psychiatrist last Monday. I told her about my trouble getting to sleep and my fear of not sleeping at all the night before the hearing. We both agreed that one or two Ativan the nights before the hearing would be a good idea, and with a sample packet of only six tablets (3 mg), I felt unlikely to be tempted to take them all at once. And I kept my word to her – I took them as prescribed. Except that I took two after getting home from the hearing, as sort of a reward rather than for anxiety. But I didn't overdo it at any point – I've been taking my desipramine exactly as prescribed, too. I'm definitely on the right track.

July 22, 1994

Keeping things in perspective:

At this time last year, in mid- to late July, I was convinced that I had to die. I was trying to overdose on prescription drugs, alcohol and heroin; I no longer believed I could make myself "not depressed" – which was all I wanted, not happiness or anything that special – and it seemed that the faith I'd had in modern medicine and psychiatry was actually unfounded. I was inherently depressed and nothing could change me.

Today I went to St. Paul's Hospital, not as a patient, but as a student researcher. I arrived at 8:00 a.m. for a lecture on molecular immunology (part of the Pathology 521 course) and then I worked from 9:00 a.m. to 6:00 p.m. with a half-hour break. I finished a hybridizing reaction of a PCR product filter with a human rhinovirus radioactive probe, and then ran an electrophoresis gel and began a Southern Blot. Work is fascinating, exciting, exhausting, frustrating and never boring. All the deadlines are scaring me a bit, but I'm feeling confident:

Aug. 12	Presentation at St. Paul's Summer Student Research Day
Aug. 20	MCAT (Medical College Admissions Test) - nine hours
Aug. 21	GAFF scholarship application
Sept. 6	Submit project summary to Associate Dean of Medicine
Sept. 23	Submit abstract for university's Health Science Students' Forum (and possibly do an abstract for a Seattle conference in May)
Sept. 30	Bursary application
Oct. 13	Presentation at the university's Health Forum
Dec.	Exams

Jan.   Medical school application including autobiographical statement, transcript of marks and three letters of reference

These days I've been working eleven or twelve hours a day and trying to study as much as I can for the MCAT. Everything else is on hold. These two commitments are probably the most important career-related challenges I've faced to date. And I'm meeting them!

August 7, 1994

I'm tired all the time. Instead of bounding out of bed in the morning to go to the lab, it takes me literally hours to drag myself out of bed and into clothes. I'm wasting so much precious time, but I don't seem to care enough about this to force myself out of the depressed moping and into activity. I'm inclined to think it's not possible to force this. Maybe that's just an excuse for not trying.

The other familiar symptoms are here too – almost complete loss of appetite, desire to avoid people, headaches and crying for no reason.

It has felt like six very long days. But tomorrow is my regular appointment with my psychiatrist, so I'm hoping (irrationally) that within that hour, everything will be made right. On Thursday I decided to increase my dose of desipramine from 200 to 250 mg. I'm not sure what the doctor will think of my electing to raise it without waiting to consult her first. But I have been on 250 mg before without any problems (other than mild side effects like shaky hands and blurry vision occasionally. I haven't had any side effects at all these last few days, which is nice).

Part of the despair depression brings on is with regard to the fact that there really is no cure for this disorder. The treatments are good but they don't work all the time. There is nothing to reassure me that next month won't be the worst month of my life. It feels like being under the control of some dark, evil force.

September 8, 1994

I haven't written in a month, I guess because I have no time.

Bob's found out about my messing a bit with prostitution in the past. Did I explain that? I forget. It was when I took twenty desipramine for a high that turned bad and he was searching for my psychiatrist's number. Bob saw some notes I'd written on my cross-examination at the hearing. This was a couple of weeks ago, which would mean I haven't written about the desipramine either. No big deal. I only wanted a few hours of escape from reality, but I underestimated the drug's potency and got a couple of days in hospital (on a non-psych ward, so it could have been worse).

(The excessive desipramine put her into convulsions before she went to the hospital. She was kept in for a while because her heart appeared to be damaged by the overdose. - Ed.)

Things have been up and down. I'm accomplishing things. The presentation at St. Paul's last month went great. The MCAT went really well. I've applied for and think I have a good chance at a $750 scholarship from my credit union. I have all the application forms for medical schools (UBC, McGill, all Ontario universities) and will have to start getting them completed.

But life is chaotic. I moved back to campus last weekend in a flurry, and still haven't had time to fully unpack.

September 9, 1994

This is the crunch, the point of determination. It's now time to decide how much I'm willing to give to my studies and work, and what I'm prepared to face in the future. Yesterday I gave the impression that I was having a horrible time lately, what with so little sleep and so much to do all the time; chaos and disorder, etc. But that entry was misleading: There were a couple of awful days when I wondered how I could keep going at this pace, but a lot of the time I feel positive and optimistic about my situation, and excited about the future. I actually can survive on four hours of sleep and crazy schedules, something I thought I could never handle and thus would prevent me from surviving medical school. I'm alive and kicking! I must have a decent amount of energy to be doing all this and therefore it's unlikely I'm experiencing a clinical depression right now. The "crying and fretting" were probably due only to the stress and tension of each day, which I'm finding myself much better at handling as time goes on. I have potential; I can attempt to fulfill it, and feel grateful I have these opportunities. If I don't take the risk of trying to do what I would like myself to be doing, obviously I have no chance at all of looking forward to myself doing these things – continuing in school, hopefully medical school and perhaps, later, graduate school: Continuing in a happy, supportive relationship; maturing into a person who is aware of her weaknesses and strengths and is able to set goals realistically but without fear of failing.

I think I can do this, and that's enough for now. I can trust that someday I'll know I can do this. People grow and change. I've passed through difficult and self-destructive stages, and I don't have to go backwards. They'll be behind me forever.

October 20, 1994

Almost a month has gone by – I guess it's about time I wrote. If I thought July and August were busy, I knew nothing about busy. The last month was crazy. A good kind of crazy – hard work, long days, great people, and the occasional break to relax and reflect. Balancing lab work at St. Paul's Hospital with course work at university has been a chore – difficult to orchestrate. But so far so good. And a week ago, I gave my talk at the university's Health Science Forum about the project at St. Paul's and my results thus far. The talk went fine, although not as well as my talk at St. Paul's in August, and I was more nervous about it even though the audience was smaller than in August. What a relief to have that done with.

The project goes on, of course, in its lovely never-ending way. It branches out, creating new questions as current ones are being answered. The head researcher is excited about the possibility of cooperativity among respiratory viruses and how that might play a role in asthma: My project is showing a much higher rate of mixed infections in the sick kids whose nasopharyngeal swabs we're looking at than traditional medicine would say is possible. Now that this incredibly sensitive diagnostic tool is here (PCR), some old dogmas are going to be turned into myths.

October 21, 1994

My MCAT scores came in the mail today. My mom dropped them off a couple of hours ago. I've been waiting for this tense moment for two months. It was a terrific feeling to finally see them, and to see that the scores are higher than I'd ever hoped for, ranging from 86th to 99th percentile for the multiple-choice tests, and 75th to 88th percentile for the essays. I'm thrilled – I think my mom's even more thrilled than I am. The MCAT is only a small part of the application process to medical school, but these scores will certainly help a bit, and perhaps make up for my lower average of 77% in my third year.

Sometimes anything seems possible. Right now I feel like I can do anything, and be anything I set my mind to. And always, always, even if the challenges seem too great occasionally, life is always possible. I won't give up.

November 1, 1994

I got a shock today when I received my marks for two mid-term exams I wrote in October. I got a 93% and a 96%, which blew me away. I felt fantastic for about an hour, then indifference, and then scared. Do these scores mean I'm okay, I'm fine, everything's great? Do they mean I'll be successful in medicine? No, no, no. And what if I can't live up to these standards anymore, or consistently, and how can I do this well at school while I'm so apprehensive about my ability to become a physician? I can't believe how utterly meaningless grades are. I never realized until now to what extent grades actually reflect inner harmony and strength. They DO NOT reflect it at all. There is no correlation.

Zippo.

I'd much rather feel confident about myself as an individual interacting with other individuals and get 60% grades than perform at the opposite extremes the way I am now.

Maybe I'm just punishing myself. Why not be happy? School and work are going great. I'm putting effort into improving the other aspects of my life, but they seem to be harder to deal with. It's not like I'm not doing well, however. My mood hasn't been this stable since a few years ago, that is, in the first year at university when life seemed perfect. I've made big changes in the last couple of years, even in the last few months. There is no doubt about the fact that I am making progress. When depression hits, I am learning to fight it instead of passively surrendering in the victim's role I'm so accustomed to and comfortable with.

I actually feel that there is nothing I cannot survive. I may not achieve everything I want to, but I WILL survive.

November 14, 1994

It's been a full couple of weeks. The regular stressors (school, medical school applications, relationships) seem amplified now that I'm in a ten-week group therapy program for adult survivors of sexual abuse at the Vancouver Incest and Sexual Abuse Clinic. Old feelings are coming up; the temptation to engage in old harmful habits, the feeling of inner disgust and shame. The feelings are as strong as they were the last times, but this time I'm stronger. I'm actually amazed at how well I'm able to fight the urge to hate and harm myself.

I have a future at stake. My future means something to me. This sense of tomorrow being important and every day down the road as having potential has never been stronger for me.

I had a good talk with my psychiatrist today at my weekly session with her. Tomorrow evening is the fourth week of the sexual abuse group from 6:30 to about 9:15. I'll be discussing and listening with a group of eight other women about the impact of sexual abuse on us and our coping strategies. It gets pretty emotional sometimes.

It's exhausting but rewarding, too. The rewards of feeling supported, feeling stronger, and having a greater sense of my own self come gradually and usually after a lot of processing of each group session. The day after our sessions, I'm a basket case. By the weekend, I feel empowered somehow. I don't give in to my urges to space out artificially. I don't sabotage promising projects such as short-story writing and volunteer work with the Autistic Society. Instead I let myself focus on whatever I can handle at the moment, and come back to the project at hand as soon as I can. It seems to work. I'm working in several directions at once, and I'm keeping it all together. Wow!

Sometimes the feelings of desperation and hopelessness do come back, but instead of thinking I'm facing the end of the world, I give myself a break – a relaxing evening with Bob, a game of pinball, a walk in the rain – and then I feel better.

"... the pain of severe depression is quite unimaginable to those who have not suffered it, and it kills in many instances because its anguish can no longer be borne. The prevention of many suicides will continue to be hindered until there is a general awareness of the nature of this pain."

William Styron

Chapter Eight

Age Twenty-Two

December 9, 1994
Age 22

Two exams down, three to go. I feel like sabotaging my future and getting strung out on drugs for a while. No, of course I won't, mother. But giving in and giving up responsibility for my life would be so easy, simple, so much easier than studying and worrying that I'm not going to make it as a doctor or a researcher or even a person. I'm pretty sure I'd make a good junkie, though. A damn fine junkie whore. Something I could really excel at.

The prostitutes out tonight must be cold. It's nippy out there, close to freezing. But they'll do anything for another hit. If my life revolved around obtaining drugs and that was all I needed to be concerned about, I could be so much more focused. I'd put all my energy into that, my heart and soul, and probably eventually my life. I'm trying now to be devoted to too many things. I wish I had the stupidity to give up and turn to drugs as my only devotion.

Go away world. I need a break.

December 10, 1994

I know exactly what I'm doing. No playing innocent. I want the world to vanish. I don't care what happens. I can't possibly be happy again, so why even try. What a wimp, right? What a pathetic wimp.

December 12, 1994

I want to put my hand into the fiery pink of the sunset. It's so beautiful. But then, everything's fine, everything's tolerable, because I have Ativan. My psychiatrist gave me six tablets for the week to help deal with the cravings for heroin, desipramine, any drug at all. Ativan makes me feel comfy and cozy, all wrapped up in a warm blanket, someone murmuring, "Everything's going to be all right."

I intend to fight off cravings for heroin, etc. and even try fighting the depression. Part of me doesn't want to sabotage everything and destroy my future.

"My future doesn't matter so what difference does it make if I become a junkie?" I asked my psychiatrist.

She replied that it does matter to me, on one level, and it matters to her. So I could give in now, drop out before graduating, become a junkie and work the street. End of the road. This would take away the pressures of the real world – school, medicine, a profession, a family…

"Ten years later, you'd be dealing with all that," she said. She's right. Better to cope now, not put off the struggle.

Saturday night, before Bob and I went to a party, I took eleven desipramine (550 mg) and got drunk on three cocktails at the Gallery Lounge. This helped me get through the evening and even have sex when we got home. I felt great. That is, part of me did – the emotional part that wanted to feel safe and not threatened about anything else. My physical body was pissed off: I could feel my heart thumping fast and irregularly, my limbs were twitchy, and I was sweating buckets. I woke up with a hangover, which is very rare for me, and I didn't physically feel very good all day Sunday either. But I didn't use heroin!!! I resisted. I'm proud of myself. And now I have a little Ativan to "take the edge off things," as my psychiatrist puts it, so that should keep me from craving desipramine. (I would rather take desipramine than heroin, but desipramine isn't all that safe either, so with Ativan I've got the ultimate in safe, mood-altering drugs. The fact is that I'm going to take SOME-THING, so it's best that it's Ativan.)

January 16, 1995

I can't cry in the presence of my psychiatrist. I feel the same pain as usual, but tears don't come as they do when I'm alone. She thinks I don't cry much. Actually, I blubber quite a lot.

I had my weekly session with her a couple of hours ago. I opened up as I always try to do, and let my words and my honesty out, letting the process cleanse me. Talked about emotions, but only experienced them in a muted form. Frustration, self-hate, worry, apathy. She tries to turn my perspective around and show me my words in a different light, the "bright side" of things. "Things aren't so bad; you're really doing quite well. This last year-and-a-half has been relatively stable for you. You're stronger than you realize."

She is so gentle and reassuring; she is the nurturer I would have within me but don't because my hate has driven it into hiding. So I need an outside nurturer and guide, and somehow she has sensed that and provided it, never judging, criticizing or expressing disappointment in me. Even when I give in to the impulses as I did three nights ago when I drank too much and passed out, and woke up in the University Hospital emergency ward. (Bob brought me there when he couldn't get any response from me.) She still holds back the exasperation she must feel when I "act out" and harm myself and throw away restraint. She asks me how I feel about the incident. I tell her about my vow from a year-and-a-half ago that I would never step inside that emergency ward again, unless as a medical student. Having broken it, I feel as low as I've ever felt. I tell her that I feel low, as a person, hoping she understands what I mean. On the brighter side, I've resisted using heroin or desipramine, partly by writing out a list of pros and cons vs. dissociation as ways of coping. The cons of drugs are many, of course.

But I left a loophole in this list, as she pointed out: I did not mention alcohol. As if it's not a drug. I'll always leave loopholes, I said. Or I'll find them; invent them if necessary. But I was careful with this binge, in the sense that alcohol poisoning is less immediately dangerous than a heroin overdose. It was the best I could do; or rather, the least worst.

"The list" from the entry of January 10, 1995 - Ed.

It is tempting to use drugs occasionally or frequently because they appear to offer an easy way of existing; an oblivion in which you can create your own realities/fantasies and be detached from the realities of other people. This suggests a way of living and fulfills impulsive desires (Want to feel good/different? Here, have a fix); satisfies curiousity (I wonder what mixing this with this would do to me?); absolves responsibilities (I'm high and, therefore, I can't be expected to work, study, or have a relationship); distances one from others with its drug-induced haze or fog; and satisfies sensation-seeking.

But isn't this really just a substitute for dissociation (which, as my psychiatrist said, is breaking down for me)? Weighing the advantages of drugs vs. dissociation:

1) Drugs are foreign chemicals; therefore, they are potentially harmful or lethal, therefore, on the one hand, bad (dangerous); on the other hand, exciting (sensation-seeking)

Dissociation is safe; i.e. no risk of physical harm in and of itself

2) When on drugs, I'm no longer really myself: I'm a product of mind-altering substances. I might as well be dead

When dissociated, I remain myself, although fragmented

3) Drugs have long-reaching consequences – tolerances, addiction, health risks

Dissociating is (probably) not addictive or damaging in the long run (i.e. easier to stop dissociating than to stop drug use)

217

4) Druggies are not thought highly of socially, while those who dissociate are not blamed to the same degree (psychiatric label is less stigmatizing than "junkie")
5) Drugs are expensive
Dissociating is free

Pros of drugs:

1) Drugs give a feeling of instant control over mood, thought, overall well-being (especially if fixing)

Dissociation leaves me feeling out of control, confused, powerless sometimes

2) Drugs can do their job in any situation while

Dissociating doesn't always work; i.e. I can't predict when it will help in a situation; when it will not help or make things worse; and even if I will be able to dissociate at a given time

3) Using drugs gives the impression of medicating oneself while dissociating is difficult to define and account for medically or physiologically

4) Drug use, especially combinations of different drugs, can give unpredictable and thus exciting results while

Dissociating is usually rather boring at best, and terrifying at worst when I feel I'm losing my mind; therefore, it's more fun to experiment with drugs

5) I know more about what happens physiologically in the brain during drug use than about what happens in the mind/brain during dissociation. Dissociation in a sense is a stranger concept and thus more fearful. But it is a natural capability of the human mind

February 3, 1995

The last two weeks were quite good. I began to feel much better, enjoying school again, spending less time obsessing, dissociating, thinking about using drugs. My interview at the University of British Columbia's Medical College on January 27th went all right. I was so nervous beforehand, not surprising since this interview is quite an important part of my application. But I did a fairly good job at not letting the nervousness show too much, and being myself. It didn't go perfectly, but I'm satisfied. My next interview is on Monday, the 6th. The final one is February 20th.

So anyway, my mood was great and I was enjoying each day up until yesterday afternoon. I got a call from the Crown counsel for the sexual assault trial. She told me that there was some bad news: the defence has made an application to have my medical records released. The Crown counsel opposed the motion because my records shouldn't be relevant to the case. So the court will have to decide and if the records are to be released, which is likely, then the judge goes through them and blanks out irrelevant information and gives it to the defence.

This was a blow. I've been assuming that my records wouldn't be sought because I haven't heard anything until now. How can I handle all those people seeing my doctors' and my psychiatrists' notes, my private feelings, my self-abusive actions? There will be a jury, too. How humiliating. I hate the part of me that is written about in my medical records from that time. I want to forget about it. How am I going to be able to hear it all and answer questions in court, in front of all those people?

It's been just over twenty-four hours since the phone call. With all my worrying, I'm stretching it into days of misery. It's funny how the old feelings rush back as if they never left: the feeling of being alone in a wasteland, afraid, unprotected, and resigned to that existence; the feeling of disorientation with respect to place and time, as if I'm existing in many places and times simultaneously, a child alone, a summer day with my father at the beach, a night downtown trying to score some dope, the feeling of being high on chemicals of any kind.

There's always the same feeling at one point or another when I'm high: I'm lost; I'm on a journey going nowhere; I'm completely alone, and this is all my fault. It's a summer day with my father, and something is not right; there is something very wrong, but no one sees it. I'm in one of those cartoon drawings where it asks, "What's wrong with this picture?" and I'm screaming for someone to see what's going on so I can stop pretending that everything's okay, and stop splitting into an unhappy, desperate girl, and be a good-natured perfect little girl for the world to see. But I don't let them see. I split.

I feel so overwhelmed that I think I'm incapable of doing anything but sleeping and maybe reading a bit. Bob's gone on a ski trip for the weekend. I'm really going to miss him.

* * * * *

Why the hell am I applying to medical school? Even if I do get accepted, I'm not going to last in that stressful program. I keep thinking that practicing medicine is the only thing I'd be happy doing for the rest of my life, but the stupid thing is how can I be happy doing that? How can I be happy being stressed out, exhausted, under constant pressure, in a position with so much responsibility? How can I be happy, period? So I'm resigned to being unhappy. I know, this is equivalent to giving up before I've even tried.

February 4, 1995

I want to disappear. I really feel incapable of surviving. My insides are screaming. Oh, God, how am I going to make it? I have to go on. But on Monday is my second interview for medical school, then Tuesday I see the Crown attorney, then I have a midterm paper due Thursday and a midterm exam on Friday. The following Tuesday and Wednesday I have two more midterm exams. I think I'm going to fail. I can't concentrate. I think I'm losing my mind. Or is this a nervous breakdown?

Same difference.

I miss Bob so much. I wish I'd gone with him on his ski trip. I'd thought I should stay home so I could get lots of work done, but that was before I heard from the Crown counsel. There's no way I can get much done tonight. I can't even read a half-page of genetics notes without starting to cry again.

* * * * *

I coaxed myself into leafing through my medical school applications and notes to prepare for Monday's interview. I spent fifteen minutes talking to myself about my interest in medicine, my future intentions, my reasons for wanting to be a doctor, etc. etc. Rehearsing. I can probably put on a normal face for an hour on Monday. Stranger things have been done. I'm so good at lying after all these years. Well, I lasted fifteen minutes here with myself. I have to work this charade for an hour on Monday. I'll practise more tomorrow night.

* * * * *

Last night I took the bus down to the industrial area by the waterfront in the Downtown Eastside. I walked along the train tracks, a familiar place to me from the nightly walks I used to take. I love trains. I felt calm, which was nice. However, I also felt stupid and lonely. I wanted to be with someone, a friend, Bob, someone. Running away to the waterfront doesn't make the situation any better for me any more. Being alone is not safe now; it's painful.

I'm often very good at blocking emotions. But these last few days, they've been tearing me up, destroying my insides. I can't believe how much it hurts.

February 8, 1995

Update: The interview (one hour, fifteen minutes) went pretty well, and I was very relaxed. (I don't get nervous when I've decided I don't give a shit about anything.)

Meeting with Crown counsel was disappointing partly because she kept me waiting a total of forty minutes. She was late arriving, then had to talk to someone in the hallway as we were walking to her office – "Please excuse us for a minute," the other lady said, so I walked to the other end of the hall and waited – and then in her office, after explaining the medical records disclosure application to me for five minutes, she had a phone call which she spent twenty minutes on as I sat and tried not to listen to this confidential conversation about some guy convicted of a "repulsive crime" who was not going to get light sentencing because he was still not taking responsibility for his acts.

Anyhow, the main thing that was disappointing – actually excruciatingly annoying – was the news that the trial will likely be postponed until September or later. This is the second time there's been a postponement at practically the last minute. It's no coincidence. Crown says defence is stalling on purpose. For crying out loud, it's been two fucking years since the bastard raped me, and he still hasn't been tried in a court of law. How long will this drag on for??? I just want to get it over with and put behind me.

February 20, 1995

I went into my psychiatrist's office today feeling like a burn-out. I'd heard earlier that the trial will be going ahead as scheduled, with the medical records disclosure hearing being squeezed in on the 27th. My doctors (i.e. psychiatrists) I saw up until March 1993 are being subpoenaed to appear in court on the 27th with my medical records, when a decision will be made regarding disclosure. So that means there will be four doctors. God, I wish this wasn't happening.

My current psychiatrist has some records from February and March 1993 (discharge summaries and the psychological profile done at

University Hospital). She's offered to go through them with me. I wasn't keen on that – I don't want to be reminded of those shitty times – but I should know what's in my records in order to be prepared. So I think I will read them next Monday with her (coincidentally the 27th).

I now have a lawyer who will represent me at the hearing on the 27th. I guess I'll meet with him sometime this week. Oh, shit, I just realized that my psychiatrist may not have access to my records on the 27th because they may be taken into court by another psychiatrist. Or would he be bringing photocopies? Fuck, I can't organize anything. I just want to hide.

Ironically my medical school interview went really well this afternoon. In spite of my mood I seemed to be able to turn on the cheerful, articulate side of myself. This surprised me because I didn't think that side was still a part of me. I was terrified I was going to blow the interview, this final interview that is the last step in what's been a long application process. But I didn't blow it. So I still have a chance at medical school, albeit a small one considering only one in five applicants gets accepted. This is very weird because in my psychiatrist's office today I felt like I was falling apart; I've never been so doubtful as to my suitability to medicine.

Two hours later I'm describing myself to the interviewer at the College of Physicians and Surgeons as someone who wants a profession that is challenging and stimulating and that involves working with and helping people. Yes, I can be a doctor. Yeah, right. How do I manage to lie so convincingly?

February 27, 1995

I've felt a dramatic change over the last week – I went from feeling I was falling apart to feeling I've never been so together, strong, confident. Maybe it was the realization that it only felt like I was falling apart, but I was still whole and sane and functioning despite the feelings of inadequacy.

I'm strong, alive and kicking! HA! No matter how they try to discredit me on the witness stand on Wednesday, I am proud of myself for who I am right now.

At my session with my psychiatrist today, I went over some of my records from February and March 1993 – the medical records that have been subpoenaed. She had only some of them, but I thought it would be useful to read what I can so I'm prepared for a cross-examination on

Wednesday. Tomorrow it will decided if the records will be disclosed at all – hopefully they won't be.

I expected it to be difficult to read my records from that time period and it was. The way I was acting out then – suicide attempts, recklessness, overdoses, cutting myself, etc. – it makes me ashamed now. And surprised. Five years ago I would never have predicted a period of instability like that. I was a different person, practically. But now I'm back to my stable, normal way of existing. The Lara whose psychological profile was written up in several pages of medicalese back in February 1993 whose diagnoses then were Major Depressive Disorder, Post-Traumatic Stress Disorder, Substance Abuse Disorder with borderline personality traits – she was a stranger, a creation of my confusion and desperation then. This persona has been buried, or rather left behind in the psychiatric ward when I walked out of there, victorious. That personality is history. I wish the records could be destroyed, because I don't want any reminders of this history of mine.

March 4, 1995

I'm actually optimistic; I just can't stop crying. This has been the hardest week I've had – well, maybe not ever, but one of the top five of my hardest weeks ever.

Testifying was difficult, the cross-examination being much more grueling than at the preliminary hearing last July. But I was prepared. I've been watching all the proceedings and I feel like I'm living in that courtroom. I don't want to miss a minute of it, because I want to know exactly why the jury makes the decision it eventually makes. I sit there at the back, watching the witnesses answer the lawyers' questions, watching the judge at His Lordship's desk, watching the expressions on the faces of the jury, staring at the back of the accused's head in the prisoner's box. When I can't stand to look at anyone, I stare at the royal crest on the wall above the judge's head, and pray to God and to the justice system in Canada. I've decided to believe in both this week.

There have been ups and down – the Crown and my lawyer were successful at the disclosure hearing in preventing any of my medical records from being entered; the defence lawyer is very good at what she does, and has pointed out some inconsistencies in my statements to the police, as well as focusing relentlessly on the prostitution issue. (I dreaded this – the humiliation I feel while listening to her belittle me publicly is overwhelming.)

When the video of the male nurse's confession (that is, to "consensual" sex) to the police was played for the court, I started feeling much better. He is one twisted man, verging on psychopathic, and I think this is very apparent to the jury.

The problem remains that it is unclear (from a legal point of view) whether I consented to sex, because I just "allowed it" and cried while he raped me in my hospital room. If the Crown can apply one of the laws involving sexual relations with a person in the position of authority or caregiver, this will help. But from the arguments I've been listening to between the lawyers, the law is very vague regarding a situation like mine. Perhaps this case will set a precedent.

March 12, 1995

Last Wednesday night at 9:00 p.m. after sixteen hours of deliberation over two days, the jury announced their verdict: Not guilty.

Hearing it was crushing. It felt like they were telling me I had not been raped; I made a fuss over nothing; I wanted to have sex with a strange man while committed to a psychiatric unit because of suicidal and dissociative thoughts.

It still hurts to think of this verdict, although the Crown has assured me that the jury believed me; they did not like him at all. They sympathized with me and wanted to be able to convict him. The problem was the law.

I did not resist the assault (after declining, in our conversation about ethics) because I implicitly trusted he would not assault me; he was in a position of authority, and his breach of this trust was shocking and overwhelming to me so that I felt frozen. I managed to retreat into the bathroom and eventually to say "Stop it, stop, it hurts." But in the eyes of many people, including the judge, the defence lawyer, the accused and at least some of the jurors, I allowed the rape to occur.

For the sex to have been nonconsensual, the law says he must have "exercised his authority" (not enough evidence he exercised it, whatever that means) or been "reckless or willfully blind" by failing to take the necessary steps to ensure I was consenting. (Defence argued that he did take these steps and that I agreed to sex – in fact, said "Okay, where can we do it?")

The justice system does not work. The resolution I expected to feel at the end of this trial is missing.

March 17, 1995

Are you going to be a defeatist and just give up? she asks me. But I didn't give up, I made it through two years of shit. I'm still here. I can't change the verdict. Let it be.

Let the system get away with it again.

I want to be oblivious: want a sugar daddy.

Fuck   I'm angry.   Cry. Try music. No.

Cut.   take apart razor.   It's like I'm back
in the past.   The BPD in me taking over again.

Leaving marks, cuts and scratches.

I'm not thinking. I do it on wrists, too,
which means long sleeve shirts for a while.
No swimming.

Stupid   Stupid   I see it all in the bathroom mirror
my frown   my grip on the blade
and the splotches of blood in the sink
Sick.   "Self-mutilation for pleasure," as a student
in biopsych said in his speech on stress-induced
analgesia. The class shudders. Who are
these BPD people? How disgusting.
I feel like a piece of crap, a freak.
Go to bed at 1:00 a.m. The patterns on the carpet move,
        black patches crawling.

The darkness is alive. It seems like someone
else is in the room. My skin crawls. I get up
and eat more ice cream. Back to bed, bandages on.
Can't sleep.   Doze from 5 a.m. to 9 a.m.

Where am I?
I want to go home   Goshiba

March 21, 1995

Well, I'm disorganized. Assignments not complete, dishes unwashed, laundry everywhere (been wearing the same jeans for two weeks) and my head is fading in and out. My first final exam is in one week. Self-stimulation (scratching) and self-medication (alcohol last night; nothing else) keep me occupied and sane.

Today is Tuesday so yesterday was Monday so I had my appointment with my psychiatrist yesterday. But I can't remember anything we talked about. Oh, yeah, I mentioned my dream about serving an indefinite sentence in jail, and what a relief I felt to finally be in a place where I could simply exist and not be expected to do anything much, while being provided with food and shelter. Perfect.

If I killed that guy. But of course I'm not capable of killing anyone. Not me, an anti-violence believer. But what if my only choices are violence against him and violence against myself? I'd rather kill him. Is that healthy?

I want to return to Kawiakee. Failing that, some Ativan would be nice. Any sedative. I'm going to phone Student Health Psych Services tomorrow and ask for something. The combination of bitter anger, frustration, grief, tension and pessimism is just intolerable. Yeah, sure it will be better. Right. I don't believe in happy endings.

March 31, 1995

On the 27th I woke up from a nightmare and while in a dissociative state, used a razor blade to make a cut in my groin that would let all my blood drain away. The spurting blood (I nicked a small artery, not the femoral artery fortunately) jolted me back to my body after watching the shower drain fill with blood for a while. I could feel myself starting to lose consciousness and I got scared – I was going to die unless I called for help. So I got an ambulance and spent two nights in the hospital. The stitches come out on Monday or Tuesday.

I've been feeling overwhelmed over the last few weeks – yes, but not suicidal. I didn't expect to slash myself. I can't even imagine doing it. I remember watching myself as if watching another person cutting herself. The blood was revolting.

I saw my psychiatrist yesterday and something unexpected came out. I can't write about it here; I just can't risk anyone finding out, and either believing me or thinking I'm crazy. She says she doesn't think I'm crazy. She's heard this sort of thing before; she's worked with this before.

I'm afraid she's the only person I'll ever be able to talk to about this. I don't trust myself, trust my memories enough, to confront the perpetrator(s) and/or make a police report.

I don't know whether to believe myself. I almost wish I were crazy, so none of it would be true.

* * * * *

Life goes on. I'm studying for exams. In a week, I fly to Ontario for interviews at Queen's University and at Western University. I'm excited about that, and nervous.

April 4, 1995

I'm in a state that could lead to obsessing, crying, rage, remembering things too heinous to write about, cutting again to fulfill this incomprehensible need to punish myself, to repeat the past, to absolve myself of a crime I believed I committed (in part) at an age when I didn't understand I had a choice. I didn't know these things they told me ("We can get to you no matter where you are; we know what thoughts are in your head all the time") were lies.

I won't do anything I would regret. I'll simply study for my exams and push back that confused, desperate person in me deeper so that she can't interfere with my obligations this month.

Yesterday there were so many things I'd intended to talk about with my psychiatrist but couldn't when the time came. I wanted to tell her how afraid I was that "they" were going to get me, whoever "they" were. And that I must be twisted inside my mind to be imagining these things. How could they be real? How could any of that have happened?

All that blood.

I need to see blood

FUCK I WANT THIS TO END. BE OVER WITH. GO AWAY.

I want to live in the present. But I'm afraid I can't bury the past until I've faced it head on.

To help me sleep, she prescribed Restoril (a benzodiazapine like Ativan). Since I won't be seeing her for three weeks (I'll be in Ontario next Monday, and the following Monday is Easter) she prescribed me three weeks' worth of Restoril. First she asked me if I'd be comfortable with that amount. Yes, of course I'd be. I am. I want to stay clear-headed.

* * * * *

I didn't do anything unhealthy today. I managed not to cut, not OD, not stray from my desk, not run to the waterfront or the downtown alleys. If this is called progress, it feels shitty. I feel awful. If it weren't for my exams and interviews coming up, I think I'd give in and "act out" to deal with this feeling I have. Fuck, I don't even know how to describe this feeling. It's grey, not any distinct colour. It's intense, confusing.

227

Almost primal. Can't put a name to it. At the simplest level, I feel alone, afraid, unloved.

I know that's not rational – I have friends and my mom and her partner and my wonderful boyfriend. He is so supportive. I wish I could say he's all I need. But even his warm hugs and reassuring words don't change this feeling, and I can't tell him what's behind the pain. You know, this sort of feels like the very beginning back two-and-a-half years ago when I suspected abuse but was very unsure and could not bring myself to tell anyone. I eventually did tell.

This is different though. Incest is imaginable, and unfortunately not terribly uncommon. What I'm remembering now is not imaginable. Yeah, I've heard and read about isolated incidents, but they're rare and usually left unproven after investigation. Most people, I think, don't believe this sort of thing happens at all.

Next level of the feeling: despair, self-loathing. A part of me is missing. I've sent it away to where it will be safe. My soul?

* * * * *

I've done a fair amount of studying and now the TV is on for company and distraction. I chatted with my mom on the phone a couple of hours ago. That was nice.

Bob's helping his dad with some business; he'll be gone the night. I'll see him after my exam tomorrow. I miss him. And I know I'm a drag to be around when I'm preoccupied like I am now.

* * * * *

The next section of this entry is scripted in occasional handwriting, but primarily in her personal secret coded alphabet. It has been de-coded here - Ed.

I have to get it out…

I THINK I WITNESSED THE MURDER OF A GIRL AND I MAY HAVE BEEN A PARTICIPANT. I THINK THEY MADE ME DRINK HER BLOOD. THEY POURED BLOOD ON MY NAKED BODY AND THEY LICKED IT OFF. ALL THAT BLOOD. BLOOD WAS SPURTING FROM HER. I THINK THAT IS WHY I NEEDED TO CUT AN ARTERY LAST WEEK. To punish myself, to do to me what they did to her? Why was I spared?

228

IS THIS (I MEAN WAS THIS) RITUAL ABUSE? I'M NOT SURE EXACTLY
WHAT HAPPENED. IT COULD BE THEY ONLY HURT HER, NOT KILLED HER. DID
THEY MAKE IT LOOK LIKE SHE WAS DEAD? WAS THERE A VIDEO CAMERA?
WHO WAS SHE?

April 15, 1995

I got back from my visit to Ontario last Tuesday. When I arrived in
Kingston on the 7th (actually 1:30 a.m. on the 8th) I felt hideous. I was tired
and pessimistic and lonely, depressed. After six hours of sleep in a
dumpy hostel, I felt worse. I nearly cancelled the interviews and came
home right then. But later that day, when I arrived at the place of the
medical student who billeted me and spent some time talking to her
about Queen's medical program and talking to the other applicants she
was billeting, I started feeling better. Hearing about the curriculum at
Queen's excited me – it sounded excellent, and she was very positive and
enthusiastic about it.

By the following day, I felt terrific. The interview, by a panel of
three – a doctor, a medical student and a community member – went
pretty well. After that, applicants were given a bus tour of Kingston and
then an information session with the Assistant Dean and several medical
students. I enjoyed the whole experience. I flew to London that evening
and stayed at the Nurses' Residence for all sorts of students and tourists.
My interview the next day went utterly perfectly. Maybe I was feeling
especially relaxed and confident because this was my fifth and last
interview.

The interviewer was really nice and easy to talk with. Everything
just clicked there and then, and I knew at a deep level that I would be a
physician, and a good one. He said toward the end, that he would
recommend me to the committee. He didn't think I'd have any trouble
getting into Western University. Just prior to the interview, I had to write
a thirty-five minute essay on an ethical issue, and that went very well,
too.

I think my chances of getting accepted are, from best chance to
worst: Western, Queen's, UBC. My choice of medical schools is the
reverse, unfortunately.

My mood's been going to extremes – the exam I wrote, the day after
returning, went horribly. I had studied a lot, but at the exam, I couldn't
seem to concentrate and remember anything. As with my exam on the
5th, I had to fight back the tears. I felt like a total loser. My mark in this

course will probably be in the 70s. Pretty dismal. But I'm feeling great again now, and I think my last two exams (and the overdue linguistics paper) will go fine. It's happening – I'm really going through with it! I'm going to make it to medical school. I'm so happy.

June 2, 1995

It's been a long time since I've written. In the last month-and-a-half I went to Crete for two weeks with my mom (her grad gift to me) – it was awesome there – and I spent a day in Seattle at a conference, presenting my last summer's work at St. Paul's Hospital – exciting because it's my first publication (just the abstract is published). Too bad this happened after my medical school application and interviews.

*　*　*　*　*

No word from the medical schools yet. I will hear from Queen's in a matter of days. I feel like I've been waiting forever.

I'm living in student housing for the summer, across from Bob. Roommates are nice, and it's great to have so much space. Two summers ago I lived in this same housing. Bad summer. Being here is reminding me of those times. Having my aunt and cousin visiting at my mom's place (they came up from California for the graduation ceremonies) reminded me of the summer three years ago – they just happened to be visiting back then when I finally cracked and secretly started therapy.

Lara, be happy with your life now. You have so much going for you and lots to look forward to if you get into medicine. It would be logical to be happy right now.

But instead I've felt depressed off and on for the last month-and-a-half. My graduating average calculated from certain 3rd and 4th year courses is only 79% – a disappointment. But I was expecting that. What totally surprised me was my 5th year average, coincidentally also 79%. I did much worse on my April exams than I expected. One percentage point away from a first class average. It's bizarre that last year (my 4th year) I got 81% and was taking more difficult courses.

My personal life has been affecting my academic life, and I hate that. I should be able to ace exams whether I'm depressed or not.

June 5, 1995

I just opened the letter from Queen's University which just arrived. I was not accepted. Not even for the wait list. I feel like I've been stepped on and squished into the ground where I belong, like a crushed ant.

I am a nobody.

I'm going to bed now. I can't take this feeling of failure and the little voice in my head saying, "I told you so. You're a loser." Why did I ever think I'd amount to anything.

* * * * *

I'm waiting for the meds to take effect. At the moment, I feel a bit drowsy and clumsy. It's hard to focus on this page. I took very small amounts of Restoril, Tylenol, Gravol, desipramine and Ponstan. This will help me forget everything for a while. I know there's no chance of lethalness (I don't want to die).

My big mistake was thinking I could become a different person if I were a doctor. This wouldn't happen because I can't run away from myself, leaving it behind me as I enter medicine.

I am stuck with myself. I thought that as soon as I started medical school, I'd be a new person. Of course I'm just the same old Lara. This aspiring to be someone else, and be an important person who can make changes in public health care, this was a fantasy more than a goal. I've always known I would drop out of medical school or burn out during internship.

June 6, 1995

The 75 mg of Restoril did the trick yesterday, letting me sleep the day away. The other stuff I took I don't remember taking, and I don't remember writing that last entry. But what I wrote is very true. I have this silly idea that being accepted into medical school would change me; but of course I have to be responsible for any changes. They won't happen just like that.

June 7, 1995

What I need is a reassurance that life will always be bearable, and if I know that I have an option of making life more bearable occasionally (not regularly) via a mood-altering drug, I feel reassured.

Maybe it doesn't make sense that I think I could handle an illicit drug without getting addicted or overdosing when I know I can't pace myself with the every-day psychoactive drug alcohol. But naïvely or not, I want to trust myself with this.

Of course if I get into medical school, I'll forget all about this because I'll have good reason to avoid drugs (my job, my function in society, will depend on me being clear-headed). But if all three schools turn me down which is a real possibility, I think I may turn to an artificial way of coping. Because I will be, for the first time in my memory, just a person and not also a student. School has sheltered me and given my hours, days, years a structure which I've come to depend on. Without this outside structure (and discipline?) I believe I will, at least to begin with, feel lost and going nowhere. I'm terrified of living without guidelines (homework, exams, projects, degrees to obtain) because it will be like living without any meaning to anything. Why have my goals always been academic ones? Why can't I set goals for myself in other realms and feel comfortable striving for them?

Maybe I need approval from others, others in an authoritative position. If I am no longer part of an educational or other kind of institution, then there will be no one to tell me that I'm doing all right, and that I must keep pushing forward with life. Do I need a parent to be saying "Everything's going to be okay"?

June 12, 1995

The following entry is written in her own secret code, and is decoded here - Ed.

BLOOD
I WANT TO DRINK IT. WHY?

I WANT THE WARM TASTE IN MY MOUTH – THE OILY, METALLIC BITE WITH ITS LINGERING AFTERTASTE. BLOOD IS BEAUTIFUL AND FRIGHTENING, LIKE A GORGEOUS WOMAN WITH DEADLY POWERS. YOU WANT TO TOUCH HER, BUT HOLD BACK FOR FEAR OF DYING FROM HER POISON.

IF I KNEW HOW TO STITCH MYSELF UP, I WOULD CUT A VEIN AND WATCH THE BLOOD COME OUT AND FEEL IT ENTER MY MOUTH. IT COATS MY THROAT AS IT SLIDES DOWN.

I'M HUNGRY RIGHT NOW, BUT THE IDEA OF EATING MAKES ME FEEL SICK. THE THOUGHT OF BLOOD DOES NOT ELICIT A FEELING OF NAUSEA IN ME. I FEEL ALL MIXED UP INSIDE.

GOSHIBA, I WANT TO GO HOME

June 15, 1995

"The question I have is: Who are you? Who is Lara? And what do you want to be?"

My therapist asked this of me back in November of 1992. I don't think that I'm very much closer to an answer now. The feeling that I'm a stranger to myself makes me want to run away, literally run (or at least walk) for hours.

There's an idea – I'll go for a little walk around the campus.

And written in her secret code - Ed.

BUT WHAT I'D RATHER DO (OF COURSE I WON'T) IS HANG AROUND MAIN AND HASTINGS, FIX, AND LOSE MYSELF – FIGURATIVELY AND LITERALLY.

June 19, 1995

I felt more anxious and panicky than ever when I walked into Student Health Services today and into my psychiatrist's office for my appointment. I can't pinpoint the cause(s) of this anxiety, but it must have to do with my fear of delving into issues and finding out things I don't really want to know consciously. But on the other hand, I feel I need to know what happened back then, whatever it does to me mentally. I told her about the anxiety, and even asked her if there was another room we could meet in. I really would like to have our sessions out of doors, surrounded by greenery in the pretty enclosure behind the hospital. Of course we wouldn't have privacy there at the noon hour when people are eating their brown-bag lunches out in the open air.

I told her about my obsession and curiosity with BLOOD. I described the dream I had last night of witnessing the arrest of a woman for murder (a wrapped-up bloody body lay in the corner) and then of myself as a young child being interrogated by a policeman. This interrogation occurred in the children's library at my old elementary school, of all places. The policeman and some other people asked me questions about my involvement with the arrested woman. I had spent time with her and I was somehow connected to the murder. I told the policeman about a bunch of dolls she had given me, some of which were voodoo dolls with pins stuck in them. At one point during the questioning I began staring at a point on the carpet in an attempt to shut out everything around me, and then I curled up into a ball on the floor and put my fists over my eyes.

233

I heard someone say "She's gone." (Were they referring to me or the dead body?) And then I woke up to the alarm clock.

Questions that come to mind:

- who does the woman who was arrested represent?
- how was I connected to the "murder" from my perspective?
- why was the library the setting for the interrogation?

My psychiatrist had a very interesting idea about the library. I had explained to her that the library has a special place in my memory as being a friendly, comfortable place to spend lots of time as a child. A refuge even? Then she pointed out that my interrogation in the library, a safe place that suddenly becomes frightening, may have to do with my anxiety at coming to her office lately, a place I've normally thought of as safe.

She asked if I thought she's been pushing me. I reassured her that no, she's not pushing. She leaves the pushing up to me, and is always making sure I'm comfortable with how our sessions are going.

Aside from my anxiety about facing memories, my dread of entering Student Health Services – or any other clinical setting – may stem from my experiences two summers ago when I spent a lot of time in hospitals. Just like two years ago, I'm living in student housing and I'm not working (at least not yet – hopefully I'll find a summer job soon). The similarities stop there, but those are two big similarities. I can't let myself get stuck in the same state of mind I was in back in 1993, despite the reminders.

Bob had a different suggestion about my therapy anxiety. He reminded me that a few months ago (April) I'd told him that I wanted to stop therapy completely because I couldn't imagine myself as both a medical student and a psychiatric patient. The patient persona had to go, I figured. Now that I'm just days or weeks from finding out if I will be a medical student in September, perhaps this identity confusion is returning.

June 20, 1995

Guess what? I got a rejection letter from Western. They say my GPA from my last year was too low. I want to kill that interviewer who told me not to worry about my last year's grades, that I would get in despite them.

So that leaves me with just the University of British Columbia – where I want to go anyway. But will I get in? I doubt it. So for a year I will work at whatever job I can get and then I'll apply again to UBC and I'll also apply to the British Columbia Institute of Technology program in cytogenetic laboratory technology, a thirteen-month post-B.Sc. program which sounds interesting and allows you to make a starting salary of $43,000. Not bad.

It's not the end of the world. But it's a fucking big disappointment. I was so hopeful about Western. I'm going to write a letter to the interviewer to inform him that his information re admissions is incorrect. It doesn't matter that my interview with him went great and that he thinks I belong in medical school. It's my marks that count in the end, after all.

Funny, at Queen's, my marks were fine, but the interview and essays and references prevented me from getting in. At Western, the interview and essay went fine, but my marks prevented me from getting in. I'm just not good enough.

June 21, 1995

Job hunting is a real bitch this summer – Jan has spent over a month-and-a-half looking, and has also had no luck. Bob's sister, who just finished first year medicine, applied to sales jobs and got no reply. She's now a cheerleader for the Vancouver Voodoo Roller Hockey, which doesn't pay much considering the time she spends organizing and practising with the squad. Bob, with his B.Sc., had no luck applying to restaurants for waiting and line cooking jobs, so he's working for his dad instead. His dad hasn't paid him anything yet – in fact Bob had loaned him $100.

* * * * *

For at least a moment, I intend to forget about the hassles of medical school applications and instead just enjoy the deep blue colour of the sky, the warm wind coming through my window, and the beautiful music playing on my stereo. Today is the summer solstice, and I want to appreciate this longest day of the year and the entrance of summer.

Lara, if while you are in other less content states of mind in the future and you are not able to appreciate the beauty of life (if not my life, then at least the world around it!), then remember these words from your other self: I love life; it is a gift and that is why I want to be a healer. I can't allow myself to lose hope or to give up on life because I will never be sure what this precious gift has in store for me tomorrow or next month or year.

"Please don't kill yourself. Please wait for the clouding and unhappy state of mind to pass. Trust that it will pass." If I happen to be in a desperate state of mind in the future, I must remember to read the above words.

June 25, 1995

Last night, or rather between 8:00 and 10:00 a.m. this morning, I dreamed that I killed a man and I was trying to evade the police. I was in a large apartment building that had stores on the main floor (similar to my grandparents' old apartment building). I was on the balcony of one of the top floor suites and a man was there, too. He looked like a bum and smelled of alcohol. He was leaning over the balcony railing, close to passing out, when I pushed him off. He fell to the ground and was dead. I felt no remorse for having done this, but I didn't want to get caught. So I hid in various rooms and closets and bathrooms while making my way down to the main floor exit. When on the main floor, for some reason, I went into a clothing store and hid in a changing room. Peeking out, I noticed my grandmother was in the store. I was afraid she'd find me so when her back was turned, I ran out of the store and into a public bathroom. I locked myself in a stall. But someone had spotted me; I heard my mom and a man enter the bathroom. The man had a key to the stall and opened the door. I saw that he was a doctor, with a long white coat. My mom had tears in her eyes and that familiar look on her face that said, "Oh, Lara. What have you done now?"

I was determined not to get caught, especially by a doctor, so I ran out between them and somehow escaped out of the building. I walked around the streets until night time. I could feel something happening to myself – I was growing feathers. If I jumped, I could fly a few feet. They'd never catch me now! While I was practising flying, the rest of the world vanished and I was by myself. But then I felt a sharp prick in my arm. I opened my eyes and realized I was not flying: I was lying in a hospital bed and a nurse was putting an IV into my arm. I felt drugged and floating. I heard a few people talking nearby; one of them was a policeman and another seemed to be a lawyer. I heard them say, "It will be murder three or manslaughter at the very least."

I tried to get out of bed but the IV infiltrated and ripped my skin, so that a thick stream of blood came out of my arm. I was transfixed by the sight of the blood. Then the alarm clock went off and I woke up.

The following is written in very small handwriting on a separate page in her journal - Ed.

- guilt – dreams of jail and escape – blame an eight-year-old child?
- fantasies – killing, not of dad, of that male nurse. why guilt?
- killing him because I see him as more of a monster than a human being, while part of me loves my dad
- shivers thinking of him and the trial
- things I stared at in court – the coat of arms. the justice system will hold him accountable
- he got away with abusing me and maybe someone else
- murder is the ultimate crime, unforgivable to take another's life
- I feel responsible in part for going along with him – never standing up and saying stop doing this to me and to her
- I feel like a participant and angry at the people around me who didn't even look at what he was doing
- they let him get away with it, and I did, too
- and that male nurse got away with it. what's the point? how do you believe there is a right and wrong, if people are allowed to do wrong?

June 28, 1995

I just got back from a visit to the employment centre. I have a phone message saying that a letter arrived for me from the Dean of Medicine at UBC. This is it. I'm so afraid of phoning and hearing about the letter. The fact that it's arrived in June and not July is a bad sign. Rejections are sent off before offers. I think it's too early to expect an offer. Oh, God, what will I do if I'm rejected at UBC, too? I've asked for an appeal at Western's decision, but that's a long shot. The chances are very high that I will not be starting medical school in September. I'll just have to deal with that.

Fifteen minutes later: Well, surprise, surprise. UBC says no. "This year we had to reject many well qualified applicants because of the huge increase in the number of applicants." Very nice letter. And yes, there were 700 applicants this year for 120 seats, up from 600 last year. Cheer up. There are lots of people who got accepted on their second try.

But I can't help but feel incredibly disappointed. I wanted this so badly.

July 12, 1995

I'm angry now at a lot of people and situations whereas I was too afraid and mixed up to be angry three years ago. Now I feel a justifiable anger towards my father, and to some extent towards my aunt and grandma; I'm angry at that male nurse, and at the legal system for its blatant shortcomings; I'm angry at the couple of doctors (just a small minority of those I've seen) who told me to forget about the abuse and get into a relationship, and who said I'd had enough therapy when I was only at the beginning of my decline into hell (which I was partly responsible for). I'm angry at myself for needing to be hospitalized and for slowing down my progress by getting into heroin and pharmaceuticals.

I'm also pissed off at the admissions committees at the medical schools I applied to. And at my own lack of confidence in my abilities and strengths.

Feeling the anger is the only way I can leave these painful memories and personal disappointments behind me and move on, which is what I'm doing.

What would really help get me out of the slow-motion stagnation of the past two weeks would be a confrontation with my dad. I'd like to demand some answers from him regarding the other girl(s) involved and the other perpetrators. But if my dad won't even admit to molesting me, I don't think he would fill me in on what really happened with the other girl(s). But standing up to him and telling him I know the kind of person he is would be satisfying. Maybe I'll do that before summer is over.

July 24, 1995

Today with my psychiatrist, I spoke openly and honestly, telling her I know I'm a borderline and I don't see the point of more therapy – I'm not going to be cured of my self-destructive and impulsive urges. She noted that my personal relationships have not been of a borderline nature, aside from a few blips. It's true; generally I don't have the unstable, stormy relationships that typically go with Borderline Personality Disorder. I suggested I'm a "closet" borderline; that is, pretty good at masking it most of the time.

I said I needed to feel different, to fill the emptiness I feel inside – for example, try a new drug. I mentioned that I went downtown last night with money, wanting to get high and escape from myself, but ended up not buying anything (some common sense in me after all?).

"I see you going up to the edge of a black pit and looking in, and moving back; then going up to it again," she said. "What would it be like to be inside the pit?"

I answered that it would mean losing control and letting out anger, hurting others and myself.

"Since I've known you, you've done a good job of keeping in check those emotions to protect me and yourself. Today you've been more open with your feelings than I've ever seen you. How about, here in this office, you allow me to see you, the borderline? Put your toe into that black pit here, in this office, rather than jumping inside the pit when you're outside the office."

"But I don't know what I'd do," I said.

"Well, there are only three rules in here: You can't hurt yourself; you can't hurt me; and you can't trash the office."

I had to smile – I had just at that moment been fantasizing about trashing the office, thinking, "I hate these pink chairs, that overgrown plant, the stupid pictures on the wall."

"But what does that leave to do?" I said, half-jokingly.

"It leaves feelings, words, tears…"

I'd been close to crying several times during the hour, but my annoying self-control held me in check.

I feel I made more progress in that hour than I have in almost two years of therapy with her. And it was because I simply spoke my mind, not pausing frequently to rethink something or holding back words I felt were "inappropriate." Ironically, I was relaxed and uninhibited because I'd taken a Restoril in the morning, hoping it would help me in therapy. And it did. I didn't tell her that.

I'm very curious about L.S.D. But I'm not sure if it's sold around Main and Hastings where the more common drugs are sold. I'm afraid if I went down there and asked for a hit of acid that they'd laugh at me, or give me a blotter with nothing in it. I wouldn't know how to check it. I'm pretty gullible.

I want to go downtown again tonight and check out the situation, but I'm not going to get that chance again for a while. Bob went to sleep early last night at his place after a tiring day of scuba diving; I told him I was going to stay up late to type, so I'd sleep at my place. Normally we sleep together. That kind of opportunity comes rarely. He would have a fit if he knew I was downtown at night.*

---

* She made no further journal entry about her trip downtown - Ed.

I've been feeling an incredibly strong sense of deja vu lately. It's the long, sunny, idle days and the drifting senses of freedom and responsibility at odds with one another. And it's living in this student housing. And feeling somewhat useless, not being able to find a job. Actually, I have a job interview tomorrow, but it's for a job I know nothing about, at an alarm monitoring station. My B.Sc. would have no relevance to the job. But I want it anyway; I want to be over qualified so I know I can handle the job.

My sense of purpose is wavering, but I'm not feeling persistent depression. My mood varies from irritable, pessimistic, unhappy and lethargic; to buzzing, excited and sensation-seeking. I seem to be repeating the pattern I got stuck in two years ago.

Am I attracted to the potential for drama, excitement, crisis? There was some of that two years ago, I can't deny it. Most of the time I was feeling very low and depressed, but when my mood flipped up and my energy level improved for minutes, hours, or days at a time, I craved excitement. Which led to impulsive behaviour of the typically borderline nature. Getting into that downward spiral again, in which a forced and lengthy hospitalization (with electro-shock therapy) is necessary to get me back on track would be awful. Besides being difficult for me, it would be a further emotional drain on my mom and her partner, and on Bob.

And it would make future similar behaviour and depression more likely, I believe, in a sort of psychological kindling effect. The more pattern-like certain behaviour and mood becomes, the more unconscious and difficult to control they become, and the easier it may be to get repeatedly stuck in the pattern (my theory at least). So if I were to get into drugs and impulsive indulging, which would lead to worse and worse depressions in-between, I could be throwing away my future (not to mention the risk of death from accidental overdose). But maybe I want to throw away my future.

I'm currently pretty pessimistic about it anyway: I'm thinking the most I'll accomplish is going through the BCIT cytogenetics lab technology program and becoming a specialized diagnostic lab technician. I'm not expecting to be a doctor any more. So my dreams of getting a Ph.D. and/or an M.D. and doing research and contributing to other people's lives in a personal and unique way – forget it. Not going to happen. But so what. It's stressful to be a doctor. I'd probably do better, emotionally, as a lab technician. But there's a part of me that's saying, "It's medicine or nothing – I don't want a future if I can't accomplish my dream." So getting addicted to drugs and consequently losing Bob (at the very beginning of our relationship he said he couldn't get involved or stay involved with someone on drugs) and probably losing any capacity to hold down a job – that would be effectively obliterating my future; a very effective self-sabotage.

I've thought about using heroin and cocaine on many occasions over the last year, and the way I stop the ideas/cravings has been to put them off. "You can use heroin or cocaine if you don't get interviews at medical schools back east" and then, after getting the interviews, "Well, you can try drugs if you're rejected by Queen's." And after being rejected by Queen's but still having some hope and common sense: "Okay, wait until you hear from Western. Try coke only if Western turns you down, too." And then, "Just wait until the letter from UBC comes," and then, "Well, okay, you've been rejected by all three schools, but let's wait until you've tried to get a job. If you can't find a good job, then you'll be justified in seeking drugs to make things easier."

So I am capable of holding off the urges and cravings; the problem is whether I genuinely want to stay clean, whether I care about the rest of my life. I don't know right now.

* * * * *

It appears to have taken psychiatrists and psychologists, or rather the American Psychiatry Association, several decades to clue into the fact that up to 75% to 80% of Borderline Personality Disorder people were abused, especially sexually, as children. There's also a possible inherited risk, and an overlap with other categories in the DSM-III-R and the DSM-IV; e.g. Major Affective Disorder, Post-Traumatic Stress Disorder, and other personality disorders. Which means this is not a distinct, homogeneous category, but instead a heterogeneous one with multi-factorial etiology. Despite these current revelations of the mental health profession, Borderline Personality Disorder is still very difficult, time-consuming and costly to treat, and there is no definitive therapy or medications that will cure or even help the BPD person. We're the type of person to avoid therapy in the first place, or to accept it but not allow it to help – maybe because we're afraid of trusting a therapist; we're comfortable in the "sick role" and thus are afraid to terminate therapy and admit we're better, and/or we can't build up enough self-esteem and identity to benefit from practical therapy. Insight-oriented therapy often makes BPDs worse, probably because they've (we've) spent so long building defences and ways of coping such as self-mutilation, dissociation, substance abuse and denying past traumas that the idea of dealing with the trauma head on in therapy is unbearable.

So the general prognosis is dismal, except that about half (or more – I forget the numbers) of us "grow out" of the disorder by their 30s or 40s. They may still be dysfunctional in some ways, but through maturation have lost the complete combination of symptoms that labelled them borderline.

One passage in a book on borderlines that I read really struck a chord with me. Some of the literature on BPD I cannot relate to, but when I read this book, I instantly thought "they're talking about me." It was eerie, it was so accurate.

August 12, 1995

I want to kill my dad. I can do it – it's something I'm actually capable of. I'm useless with everything else – can't get a job, can't find an apartment. I think I'm having a nervous breakdown. I feel awful and guilty about my inability to cope. I should be stronger, but I want to just give up. I'm letting down Bob and my mom and friends. Especially Bob – he just got accepted into first year law at UBC. Why can't I be happy about things and supportive of him? I'm afraid of dragging him down into my confusion. I'm being totally self-centred. This is my breaking point. I'm a failure. What's left is to kill my dad. I need that resolution.

August 19, 1995

Who am I to decide when another person is to die? If I went through with it, I'd just be proving to my dad and everyone that I've become the monster he is. Funny, now that the urge to kill him has gone, I've been feeling like attacking myself instead. But when the anger was toward him, I felt no anger or destructive impulses toward myself. All or none; either he is totally bad or I am; no grey areas for either of us. I want to cut away this disgusting skin of mine and let my insides come out. Let out the frustration and hurt; watch it drip and ooze and spurt. Veins go cloudy blue and green in the light. My arm is from a foreign being; all it is, is flesh and bone. Not me, not my self, my person, my personality. Therefore it's not part of me. Nothing solid is part of my real self.

I want to bite through all the way. If I close my eyes will my body disappear?

I'm scared. I want to be told I won't be hurt. But who can make that promise? Only Goshiba, but I don't believe in him any more.

September 11, 1995

The disappointment in myself is so piercing that I feel I've already killed myself metaphorically with it; stomped on my spirit with frustration and disgust. I could do better than this; if I'm lucky I'll be going door-to-door doing enumeration for British Columbia Directories for minimum wage for a few weeks. I had an interview with a pharmaceutical company last week that I screwed up – couldn't remember how the Lowny Assag and ELISA test work, and the interviewer quizzing me was not impressed. Five years of fucking science courses and I haven't retained one iota of it. Where, oh, where has my little brain gone?

Had my session with my psychiatrist today. She was very supportive and empathetic as I complained of my depression and anxiety. I wish I could talk to her more than once a week, but really I should be talking to Bob who is always wonderfully supportive. I can't confide in only one person and expect miracles from her, as if an M.D. is equivalent to omnipotence. But talking my feelings over with Bob right now would be a little unfair to him as he's settling into his busy schedule at law school. I don't want to bring him down while he's enjoying the excitement of his second week. But I feel close to cracking. I don't see a reason to continue except to avoid hurting other people. I want to die but somehow without leaving the people I love with my own pain.

I cannot give up. I cannot say to hell with it; I'm blowing this joint. But I don't know how to face the despair ahead. I feel like I'm falling into that black pit in slow motion. I can make out my descent from the diminishing of real-world light as my self-world gets darker. Let it happen.

September 12, 1995

I feel like I'm at rock bottom. But of course, I'm not; there's a lot further to fall. I am trying to snap out of this, to muster some motivation, but it feels like I'm asking more from my brain than it can provide. Concentrating is difficult, thinking is stressful. I worked at that enumeration job for a whole twenty minutes today. I was a wreck. After my training is over I'm going to have to work seven hours a day, five days a week, in order to make enough money for rent and food alone. I'm going to try, but God, I'm scared.

I'm afraid I don't have the stamina – and this is such a simple, mindless job, the easiest job I could come across. Was it really the same Lara who did medical research last summer? She's gone and left this pathetic brainless shell in her place.

God, I'd forgotten how a solid depression feels, the kind that doesn't lift for even an hour. I feel so heavy. Just want to lie in bed and sulk and cry. I haven't felt this depressed since 1993. My psychiatrist suggested we try a different anti-depressant. She's also given me some Xanax (alprazolam) to try, an anti-anxiety benzodiazapine. I'm taking the lowest dosage (0.25 mg) just once or twice a day if I need it. At that level, its effects are very subtle, but I don't want to take a more usual dosage because I'd hate to become dependent on it.

September 15, 1995

I can see myself plainly now, and my situation. I realized a couple of minutes ago that the problem here is with me, not with my situation itself, alone. This new awareness has made me feel cold and empty; and looking at myself I see a pale translucent person who has been pretending to be solid and real. It's incredible how this feels, to have X-ray vision into oneself. All those walls I constructed in my head over the years are meaningless now. I see it all now. Two thoughts are beating at my skull: I hate what I see yet this is who I am, so it's take it or leave it.

The truth hurts, stabs.

I can't live this game any more, seeing only the superficial aspects of everything and ignoring what really exists and is going on.

It's all just a bubble, and I'm going to break it if I keep prodding it and looking for the reality in this world. Even love, which I thought was the strongest and purest thing that exists, even it falls apart. It means nothing. I love Bob more than anything and I know he loves me, and here I am nonetheless watching my reality fall apart, break down, watching myself break down. Is this a nervous breakdown? Seeing the truth behind the garbage means being given a psychiatric label, doesn't it? That's why the "patients" on the psychiatric wards I've been on seemed so much more real to me than the outside world. They see everything, not being able to put on blinkers like the normal people.

I've found the rocky bottom I always knew was there. Oh, God, I feel like a wimp. I think I'd better take a Xanax.

September 18, 1995

I've been wanting to write in here more frequently lately, because I need to get these feelings into words, but I put it off until I'm in a reasonably solid-minded state. I don't want to be writing gibberish. But then so what – who cares? This is my diary, I should be able to say whatever I want, however I want. But I don't want to sound like an idiot.

* * * * *

Things are getting complicated now. Aside from the moral and ethical issues around suicide and the pain it would cause others, ending my life right now would cause a mess in practical terms.

Bob would be stuck with full rent to pay (impossible on a student loan) so he'd have to move – just after moving and settling into our wonderful apartment, and sharing those special moments around moving in together. And he's very busy with law school, so for me to hurt him like that emotionally and put him into a financial mess and disrupt his schoolwork would be totally unfair and cruel. I can't do that.

And my mom, who has always been so concerned with my happiness and well-being, and has put so much effort into helping me out these last few years when my life got chaotic – how could I hurt her so much, her only child? She had to cope through her own mother's suicide, and to put her through losing her daughter as well would be utterly heartless of me – ungrateful, selfish, uncaring. I don't want to put her through more than I already have, with my previous attempts and hospitalizations and drug use. I could try to justify suicide by saying it would spare her from any further worry or disappointment in me, but that's pretty lame. She raised me as a single parent, and worked so hard to support us. She was always there for me when I asked for help or comfort or support, and all that time she herself was having to cope with her own problems of having grown up in a grossly dysfunctional family herself. I think she is a very strong person. But I don't know if even the strongest person could cope easily with the suicide of a daughter, or any family member, or a girlfriend. Damn it, I don't want to hurt these people who love me and who have been there for me. But as much as their love and support help, they can't cure a biological depression.

I need to end this because of what's going wrong inside my head. I'm so fucking frustrated with trying to control my moods and those fucking neurotransmitters with medications and therapy (three years of

245

both). Depression is going to rule my life forever if I stay alive. I read a statistic that 75% of people who have had one depressive episode will have another one; 90% who have had two episodes will have another one.

I can't live depressed. Yeah, I know many people do, without having to take their own lives. I'm not as strong as them, I guess, and more pessimistic. Right now I see a big black nothing when I think of my future. I don't want to work or go back to school; I don't want to have kids and be a housewife; I don't want a profession. I have no goals. Even back in 1993 when I felt at rock bottom, I still held the hope of one day going into medicine. Now I don't want to be a doctor and deal with all that stress and responsibility. The same goes for research. An industrial lab job would depress me and worry me – I hate working with radiation and dangerous chemicals.

So I see myself as a failure, and so wimpy Lara proves once again that she's really a quitter. Afraid to try, for fear of further failure.

Back to my responsibility as a daughter, girlfriend and friend: I should have enough moral strength to say to myself, forget it; you are not taking the easy way out because you would hurt other people to a greater extent than you would relieve your own hurt. It's not fair or right. So don't do it.

Well, when I rationalize, I'm clear on what's right and wrong. But when the depression and hopelessness cut into me at intervals during the day, I want so badly to die and leave this behind, and I feel torn apart by the fact that I do not have a choice. I must live. I can scream and cry all I want and beg Bob to let me go, but it all comes back to the simple fact that suicide is not acceptable in our society, and it would do more damage to other people than would be morally appropriate to inflict, no matter how shitty I feel. I'm stuck.

I've been very good these days about taking my meds exactly as prescribed. Now I'm switching to another anti-depressant, by the way, called Effexor but I'm beginning to feel the need to medicate myself into oblivion to avoid the depression (sleep is the only way I can seem to escape). Just with slightly higher doses than usual, so I don't have this continuous debate going on in my head about the reasons for and against suicide.

I can't let that debate coax me into thinking the pros outweigh the cons, so I want to avoid this agonizing, and the easiest way is by being sedated. As my psychiatrist has said, she doesn't condone my occasional overuse of sedatives, but if I'm going to over-medicate myself in some way, she'd rather I do it with small amounts of mild sedatives than with large amounts of desipramine or with heroin. I guess I use that logic myself to justify my self-sedation: at least I'm not on street drugs or harming or risking my life in any way.

I hope so badly that Effexor works for me. It will be at least two weeks before I'll feel the effects (standard with all anti-depressants), and that's difficult to face. Two more weeks of this???

September 19, 1995

I want to be carried away for a while, to sleep and take a rest from the arguments going on in my head. I want to feel like I'm floating away from everything, quickly and smoothly like the way the lullabies made me feel when my dad would sing me to sleep.

* * * * *

I'm sorry to be doing this. I know Bob will be disappointed in me, but I need a temporary escape. I'll be awake and back to the shitty real world in a few hours.

* * * * *

Well, I'm wide awake again. Good timing since Bob will be home from school any minute. The last five hours I slept soundly, no dreams; it was like the hours didn't exist – or rather, I didn't exist. Relief. I wish it could last forever. A coma might work. Then I'd be alive technically so I wouldn't have committed that awful sin, suicide, but my consciousness would not exist. But I don't know how to induce a coma.

September 20, 1995

When I used to look at the mountains and the ocean and the people walking along the beach with happy children, with the sky that perfect blue and the feeling of energy in the air, I would feel a sense of well-being because it seemed that there was a special meaning to everything, like we were all (the people and mountains and trees and sand) part of a grand design and therefore here for a purpose.

Last Friday when I felt that shift in my perception of everything, I realized that there is no grand design after all. We're here; everyone and

247

everything exists randomly and by chance; there is no reason or meaning to the existence of this planet.

I've been thinking lately about my childhood belief in another world, Kawiakee, whose god or spiritual leader was looking after me because I was really Ayesha from Kawiakee and would be returned to my home one day. I needed to believe in a god, if not for this world, then for another. This pretend-play and fantasy kept my spirits up and gave me hope, basically the hope that I would soon be leaving this world for another. Now this new awareness that there is no meaning to life has caused me to give up the fantasy that by dying, I would be returning to my true home. No, by dying I would simply cease to exist. There can be no afterlife if there is nothing special about life itself. We're just collections of chemicals; our minds and consciousness are the product of complex chemical interactions. We live, and then we die when the chemicals no longer interact properly. How can there be such a thing as a soul? I can't believe I ever thought there was. Religion is a game, a way of playing your life to maintain optimism and ward off fears of death, mortality.

September 24, 1995

End of the line.

I've made the selfish decision to end it all. I need peace from the useless scurrying of empty thoughts in my head, from the weight of depression, and from the images of a tiny body slumped in a shower turning the water red. I watched her die. I can't live with that any more. I'm preparing letters for my mom and her partner, for Bob, Jan, Vicky, my psychiatrist and maybe my lawyer. I would have liked to have seen the civil lawsuit with that male nurse through to its finish; to hear the judge say that he was wrong in what he did, but I can't wait the year-and-a-half that would take. But I think I can wait until after my mom's birthday and after her art exhibit opens next month. I don't want to ruin that for her.

The letters are harder to write than I thought they would be. I basically want them to know that no one could have stopped me; I was determined to carry this out, and certain I wanted to die. Blame lies with no one but me. While writing them I get a sick feeling in my stomach; the shame and guilt gnaw at me.

* * * * *

I read about a year ago that taking an overdose of two weeks' worth of desipramine is lethal. It didn't give the amount in milligrams, but two weeks of my regular dosage (14 x 200 mg) should be more than enough because my dosage is at the high end. I know from last August when I took 1000 mg to "blot out" that overdosing on desipramine is an unpleasant experience. I don't want to be conscious when the convulsions and cardiac arrhythmias come on, so I'll take 15 Xanax tablets and whatever Restoril I have left, before taking the desipramine. Coward that I am, I want as painless a death as possible.

September 27, 1995

On Monday evening, while Bob was still at university, I decided I needed to try every option before giving up. So I walked the three blocks to St. Paul's Hospital. I talked to their psychiatric nurse, then to the emergency ward physician who was very nice, then to the on-call psychiatrist. They recommended I spend the night there and then be transferred up to the psychiatric ward. So here I am, back on the same ward I was on in July and August of 1993 (but it's moved to a different section of the hospital). I have the same psychiatrist (once again) and we've decided electro-shock therapy would be the best thing to try.

So I'm giving things another two or three weeks. If the electro-shock therapy works – good (but I still don't like the idea of living a life in which I'm always dreading the return of depression). If electro-shock therapy doesn't work, I'll have tried everything and will feel more justified in going ahead with my plan.

My first ECT treatment is Friday.

I'm getting more noticeable desipramine withdrawal symptoms now – nausea and vomiting, headache, dizziness. It sucks. I'm still not sleeping well at night, despite the Ativan they give me. I'm tired of everything, as usual.

September 28, 1995

I was just given a Gravol injection for this damnable nausea, so I'm going to jot down the day's events before I get too groggy. I want to keep track of things on paper because the ECT is going to screw up my memory for a while.

Yesterday I met with the psychiatrist's associate and a psychiatric student for about a half-an-hour (would have been longer but I had to leave to puke). She took down the relevant information to fill in the gaps in my chart. She seemed nice. She wanted to know if I ever had felt manic; I said no, but described the episodes I had when my mood had been elevated above normal and I'd done regrettable things like invite a homeless person and a couple of his friends to stay at my place for a few days; and the time I rode around in strange men's cars to ask them their life histories.

I slept about two hours last night before being awakened by a nightmare (girl in a shower, bleeding). Tried to get back to sleep but had nausea and a stiff jaw and neck. Early this morning I finally fell asleep but was awakened twice by the sensation that my body was stiffening and I couldn't breathe. Today I tried napping with the help of Ativan, but had continuous nightmares about having seizures and about being fondled and groped by a man while lying paralyzed in my hospital bed. The seizure dreams are probably from worrying about the upcoming electro-shock therapy. Also, having many dreams is another symptom of desipramine withdrawal.

My mom's birthday is tomorrow. I'm going to call her now, before I start slurring.

* * * * *

Well, the Gravol grogginess has worn off, and I feel less depressed than I did earlier today when I was eyeing the tall building across the street from my room and fantasizing about jumping.

I hope I get no nightmares tonight. They were really scary today – the scariest thing being that I was always trying to scream but either couldn't make a real sound (but did scream in the dream) or couldn't make any sound at all. The nursing station is only a few feet away but I felt like it might as well have been miles away, since I couldn't call out and I couldn't wake up to walk to it.

Anyway, goodnight, and please, Lord, let tomorrow's electro-shock therapy be the beginning of a successful treatment for me.

The journal ends here.

On the evening of October 7, 1995, while on a weekend pass from the psychiatric ward, Lara was returned to the hospital, suffering from an overdose of medication. Resuscitation was attempted and failed.

A carefully worded letter was found addressed to her mother and her partner. There was another letter, written hastily on her journal note paper and torn out of the journal, addressed to her mother, Carole, and her partner, Al, and her boyfriend, Bob.

"(Suicide) is incomprehensible when it kills the young... certainly, no one has ever found a way to heal the hearts or settle the minds of those left behind in its dreadful wake."

Kay Redfield Jamison

AFTERWORD

So much is hindsight; a lot is speculation. My lay opinion on the anti-depressant called desipramine (tricyclic), upon which my daughter relied, has been formed more recently. According to the Textbook of Pharmacology edited by C.H. Smith and A.M. Ryenard, published by Philadelphia: Saunders, 1992:

"... the lethality of the tricyclic anti-depressant drugs is primarily the result of their effect on cardiac rhythmicity. In general, they are more toxic than the phenothiazine anti-psychotic drugs, and the frequency of toxicity is greater also because they are administered to a patient population that is at risk of suicide attempts; thus they should be dispensed with caution and in total quantities that are not likely to be lethal if taken all at once..." p.314

Obviously their toxicity makes them a risky drug prescribed in bulk to those who are suicidal. Moreover, it is common knowledge among health care providers that if patients want to obtain extra medications, they do so under a variety of guises.

Another issue, a side effect, is that this drug reduces libido, as do many anti-depressants. While this may have some beneficial effects on those who have been exceedingly promiscuous, for others who have struggled terribly with their sexuality and had difficulty establishing healthy relationships, could this loss of libido compound the very issues surrounding depression?

It is known that certain anti-depressants do not necessarily aid in regulating sleep patterns, which are always disturbed in depressive people. Because of side effects such as a racing heartbeat and a somewhat "hyper" effect, could they even be detrimental to sleep?

Another issue, less clear to me, is the research being done by medical practitioners who have worked at length with Borderline Personality Disorder patients. Some state that tricyclics should definitely not be prescribed to borderline patients – in fact some tricyclics may be detrimental to recovery. In the Journal of Personality Disorders, Vol 4, No. 2 (1990) Janice M. Cauwels explains that although widely used by depressed patients, amitriptyline might worsen many symptoms. She goes on to say that the drug has increased suicidality, paranoia, impulsivity, demandingness, assaultiveness, and distorted thinking. And she adds that another trycyclic, desipramine, has likewise been found to be ineffective in borderline patients or to make symptoms worse.

More recent evidence from British research indicates that the very popular S.S.R.I.s (selective seratonin re-uptake inhibitors), a newer class of anti-depressants, may, if taken by children, lead to an increase in suicidality. Some brands are simply not any more effective than sugar pills while some are indeed harmful. Virtually no pediatric trials have been done.

* * * * *

On other levels, I have not been idle. I have studied Bill C-15 of the Criminal Code in an effort to understand prosecution for child sexual abuse. I have filed a comprehensive report with the Sexual Offence Squad of the Vancouver Police Department with regard to the sexual offences committed over a period of years on this child.

On November 5, 2000, I wrote to the federal Minister of Justice asking about accountability regarding an alleged sexual offender and had no reply. Then I gave a copy of the same letter to my Member of Parliament who hand-delivered the letter to the Minister of Justice on March 12, 2001 in the House of Commons. On March 22, I received a very sympathetic letter from the federal Minister of Justice advising me to inform the Attorney General of B.C., which I did on April 6, 2001.

In an undated letter which I received on May 16, the Assistant Deputy Minister to the Attorney General of B.C. advised me (because of my jurisdiction) to contact the Sexual Offence Squad of the Vancouver Police Department. Which is where I started.

I have been in communication with the Department of Human Resources, giving information and many details concerning the abuse, because another relative in that family, a small child, was possibly next in line.

I have sought legal advice from a number of different avenues. I think that should another living child (now an adult) come forward disclosing abuse by the same person, and my daughter alleged there were other children involved, then the writings by my daughter can support that case considerably. As well, Craig Dennis and Valerie Howander of the law firm, Sudgen, McFee and Ross, gave hours and hours of time examining the details of her release from the hospital and sudden death.

I have written to Detective Fenimore of the Vancouver Police Department regarding the health care orderly (incorrectly identified as a male nurse) who raped my daughter in the psychiatric ward. As he was eventually acquitted of the charges, I asked that he be placed on ViCLAS (Canada's nation-wide Violent Crimes Linkage Analysis System). He has replied that it is done.

I have initiated a lengthy communication with the provincial Ombudsman's office which subsequently looked into the lack of a clear sexual harassment policy at the Vancouver General Hospital. A more comprehensive set of guidelines is now in place. A respected Vancouver civil lawyer, Megan Ellis, was preparing to go further into this with my daughter.

I have obtained all the medical records from the three major hospitals in Vancouver in which she was a patient on numerous occasions, either in psychiatric wards or in emergency wards.

On four occasions, I met with her long-term (1994-95) psychiatrist at Student Health Services at the University of British Columbia, going over the meticulous records of her weekly sessions with my daughter. In these records, the extent of the abuse in my daughter's childhood is detailed.

I have written to the B.C. College of Pharmacology, asking if they would stop permitting the dispensing of large quantities of toxic anti-depressants to depressive, suicidal persons. I have had a reply that it is an issue they have been discussing at Board meetings.

I have obtained all the records from the B.C. Coroner's Office, and subsequently also wrote a lengthy letter of enquiry to the then-current

Chief Coroner. The autopsy was not specific to what caused her death. I've had an even lengthier reply.

I have had brief meetings with the head psychiatrist at St. Paul's Hospital, their former family therapist, the Crown prosecutor of the sexual assault case in the B.C. Supreme Court, two investigating officers of the Vancouver Police Department, and with Vancouver's Women Against Violence Against Women (WAWAW) – well, the list goes on.

I have attended weekly sessions with Vancouver's suicide awareness agency, S.A.F.E.R., for almost five years as I attempted to sort out a huge collection of extremely complex feelings.

Carole Itter
2003

ACKNOWLEDGEMENTS

The publication of Lara's journals has been a collaboration with family and friends. Many thanks to Lara's aunt, Susan, for her generousity. My gratitude to her second cousin, Julie Mueller, for her keen ear, careful transcription to word processing, thoughtful suggestions and positive energy when I most needed it. Lara's close friend, Virginia Le, assisted in the transcription to word processing. Thanks to her partner, Robert Cuddeford, for his support and legal help; and to her friend, Jenny Chau, for her encouragement.

Lara's cousin, Sarah Itter; her third cousin, Annette LaPointe; and her great aunt and uncle, Maxine and Jim Kaiser, have been personal support to me. And as always, my partner, Al Neil. Rhoda Rosenfeld and Trudy Rubenfeld, thank you for your support.

Glenn Alteen at the grunt Gallery, Vancouver, exhibited my installation, "The Pink Room," which is a visual tribute to my daughter, as did Todd Davis at Open Space Gallery in Victoria. As well, I thank Elizabeth Fortes for the many years of wise and patient counsel. The literary and art community have been so understanding and helpful. A special credit to Megan Hunt for her fine graphic design of the cover; as my former student, she now inspires me.

Others who have read portions of the typescript and provided helpful comments are Lorraine Algera, Morgan Ashbridge, Joan Haggerty, Daphne Marlatt, Esther Rausenberg, Renee Rodin, Betsy Warland and Sandra Woolfrey.

QUOTATIONS

Quotations at chapter headings are credited as follows:

Chapter One: Reprinted by permission of the publisher from Daily Modernism: The Literary Diaries of Virginia Woolf, Antonia White, Elizabeth Smart and Anais Nin by Elizabeth Podnieks. Montreal: McGill Queen's University Press, 2000. p.7.

Chapter Two: Reprinted by permission of the author, Joy Kogawa, from The Rain Ascends. Toronto: Penguin Books Canada, 2003. p.12.

Chapter Three: Reprinted by permission of the author, Louise DeSalvo, from Virginia Woolf: The Impact of Childhood Sexual Abuse on Her Life and Work. Boston: Beacon Press, 1989. p.236-237.

Chapter Four: Reprinted by permission of the publisher from Women's Writing in Exile ed. Mary Lynn Broe and Angela Ingram. Chapel Hill, NC: The University of North Carolina Press, 1989. From essay My Art Belongs to Daddy by Mary Lynn Broe. p. 46.

Chapter Five: Reprinted by permission of the publisher from Betrayal Trauma: The Logic of Forgetting Childhood Abuse by Jennifer Freyd, p.62, Cambridge, Mass.: Harvard University Press. Copyright 1996 by Jennifer J. Freyd.

Chapter Six: Quotation reprinted by permission of former Canadian Foreign Affairs Minister, Lloyd Axworthy. Vancouver Sun, 27 Nov. 1999, final ed.: A22. [Original newspaper article covers a conference in Montreal on pedophile tourists exploiting children in regions desperate for tourist dollars.]

Chapter Seven: Reprinted by permission of the author, Myrna Kostash, from No Kidding. Toronto: McClelland and Stewart, 1987. p.132. Copyright Myrna Kostash.

Chapter Eight: Reprinted by permission of the publisher from Darkness Visible by William Styron. New York: Vintage and Anchor Books, Random House Inc., 1992. p. 33.

Afterword: Reprinted by permission of the publisher from Night Falls Fast: Understanding Suicide by Kay Redfield Jamison. New York: Alfred A. Knopf, Random House Inc., 1999. p.18-19.

ISBN 141201804-8